Huck Arate

7-21-15

THE HOMELESS JESUS IN THE GOSPEL OF MATTHEW

The Social World of Biblical Antiquity, Second Series, 10

Series Editor
James G. Crossley

Editorial Board
Robert B. Coote, David A. Fiensy, David M. Gunn,
Richard A. Horsley, Bruce J. Malina

THE HOMELESS JESUS IN THE GOSPEL OF MATTHEW

Robert J. Myles

SHEFFIELD PHOENIX PRESS

2014

Copyright © 2014 Sheffield Phoenix Press
Published by Sheffield Phoenix Press
Department of Biblical Studies, University of Sheffield
45 Victoria Street, Sheffield S3 7QB
www.sheffieldphoenix.com

A CIP catalogue record for this book
is available from the British Library

Typeset by the HK Scriptorium
Printed by Lightning Source

ISBN 978-1-909697-38-6

CONTENTS

ABBREVIATIONS

Biblical citations are taken from K. Elliger and W. Rudolph (eds.), *Biblia Hebraica Stuttgartensia* (Stuttgart: Deutsche Bibelgesellschaft, 1967); and B. Aland *et al.* (eds.), *The Greek New Testament* (Stuttgart: Deutsche Bibelgesellschaft, 4th edn, 1983). All English citations of the Bible are from the New Revised Standard Version unless specified otherwise.

Septuagint citations are taken from Joseph Ziegler (ed.), *Septuaginta Vetus Testamentum graecum*, vol. 16 (Göttingen: Vandenhoeck & Ruprecht, 1939); and the English translation is from Lancelot C.L. Brenton, *The Septuagint with Apocrypha: Greek and English* (Peabody, MA: Hendrickson Publishers, 1986).

Common Abbreviations

BAGD	W. Bauer, W.F. Arndt, F.W. Gingrich, and F.W. Danker, *A Greek-English Lexicon of the New Testament and Other Early Christian Literature* (Chicago: Chicago University Press, 3rd edn, 2001).
BAR	*Biblical Archaeology Review*
BCCW	Biblical Challenges in the Contemporary World
BCE	Before Common Era
BibInt	*Biblical Interpretation*
BJRL	*Bulletin of the John Rylands University Library of Manchester*
BR	*Bible Review*
BSR	*Bulletin for the Study of Religion*
BTB	*Biblical Theology Bulletin*
BZNW	Beihefte zur *Zeitschrift für die neutestamentliche Wissenschaft und die Kunde der älteren Kirche*
CBQ	*Catholic Biblical Quarterly*
CBR	*Currents in Biblical Research*
CE	Common Era
CRBS	*Currents in Research: Biblical Studies*
DSS	Dead Sea Scrolls
ETL	*Ephemerides theologicae lovanienses*
ETR	*Etudes théologiques et religieuses*

ExpTim	*Expository Times*
GBS	Guides to Biblical Scholarship
HALOT	L. Koehler, and W. Baumgartner, *The Hebrew and Aramaic Lexicon of the Old Testament.* (Leiden: Brill, 1994).
HBT	*Horizons in Biblical Theology*
HCBD	P.J. Achtemeier, *The Harper Collins Bible Dictionary* (San Francisco: HarperSanFrancisco, rev. edn, 1996)
HTR	*Harvard Theological Review*
HvTSt	*Hervormde teologiese studies*
ICC	International Critical Commentary
JBL	*Journal of Biblical Literature*
JETS	*Journal of the Evangelical Theological Society*
JR	*Journal of Religion*
JSHJ	*Journal for the Study of the Historical Jesus*
JSNT	*Journal for the Study of the New Testament*
JSNTSup	*Journal for the Study of the New Testament,* Supplement Series
JSOTSup	*Journal for the Study of the Old Testament,* Supplement Series
JTS	*Journal of Theological Studies*
JTSA	*Journal of Theology for Southern Africa*
KJV	King James Version
LNTS	The Library of New Testament Studies
LXX	Septuagint
MT	Masoretic Text
NCBC	New Cambridge Bible Commentary
Neot	*Neotestamentica*
NICNT	New International Commentary on the New Testament
NIV	New International Version
NovT	*Novum Testamentum*
NovTSup	*Novum Testamentum,* Supplements
NRSV	New Revised Standard Version
NT	New Testament
NTS	*New Testament Studies*
OT	Old Testament
RTR	*Reformed Theological Review*
SBJT	*Southern Baptist Journal of Theology*
SBL	Society of Biblical Literature
SNTSMS	Society for New Testament Studies Monograph Series
TBT	*The Bible Today*
TR	*Theological Review*
TS	*Theological Studies*
WBC	World Biblical Commentary

WUNT   Wissenschaftliche Untersuchungen zum Neuen Testament

Old Testament Pseudepigrapha

2 Bar.	*2 Baruch (Syriac Apocalypse)*
1 En.	*1 Enoch (Ethiopic Apocalypse)*
Pss. Sol.	*Psalms of Solomon*

Mishnaic and Rabbinic Literature

b.	*Babylonian*
Ber.	*Berakhot*
Gen. Rab.	*Genesis Rabbah*
m.	*Mishnah*
Naz.	*Nazir*
Qidd.	*Qiddushin*
Sanh.	*Sanhedrin*

Classical and Hellenistic Literature

Cicero
  Verr.   *In Verrem*
Dio Chrysostom
  Or.   *Orations*
Josephus
  Ant.   *Jewish Antiquities*
  War   *Jewish War*
  Life   *The Life*
Juvenal
  Sat.   *Satirae*
Philo
  Leg. Gai.   *Legatio ad Gaium (On the Embassy to Gaius)*
  Spec. Laws   *De specialibus legibus*
Pliny the Elder
  Nat.   *Naturalis historia*
Plutarch
  Ti. C. Gracch. *Tiberius et Caius Gracchus*
Tacitus
  Hist.   *Historiae*
Xenophon
  Cyr.   *Cyropaedia*

Early Christian Literature

(Arab.) Gos. Inf.	*Arabic Gospel of the Infancy*
Eusebius	
Dem. ev.	*Demonstratio evangelica*
John Chrysostom	
Hom. Mt.	*Homiliae in Matthaeum*
Origen	
Cels.	*Contra Celsum*
Prot. Jas.	*Protevangelium of James*
Ps.-Mt.	*Gospel of Pseudo-Matthew*

There is a great scene in the satirical thriller *American Psycho* (2000) in which the protagonist, Patrick Bateman, a stupidly rich investment banker portrayed by Christian Bale, encounters a homeless man and his dog down an alleyway. After offering the man charity, Bateman crouches down to address him sternly, 'Why don't you get a job?' he riposte. The homeless man responds, 'I lost my job'; to which Bateman retorts, 'Why? Are you drinking? Is that why you lost it?' Advising the homeless man that his problems stem from his 'negative attitude', which will only be solved if he gets his act together, Bateman's demeanour suddenly shifts from cold and condescending to an impassioned rage: 'Do you know how bad you smell?' Bateman jokes. He then opens his briefcase, pulls out a knife and repeatedly stabs the homeless man to death, before stomping on his dog and casually walking away.

If ever there was a personification of the sadistic violence of the 'free market', then Patrick Bateman is it. In between the routine narration of his daily life of business meetings, empty relationships, corporate lunches, designer business cards and copious amounts of high quality crack-cocaine, he engages in the spontaneous torture and murder of prostitutes and other minor irritants that cross his unfortunate path. The ideological statement is clear enough: violence and the capitalist system are inextricably and perversely linked. Yet this inconvenient fact must be repressed and obscured from our vision at all costs. Although we often struggle to see it, the homeless population, the underclass, the ghettoized and the permanently unemployed, all signify the unsavoury underside to the new wave of corporate dominance in the present-day political sphere.

The underlying premise of this book is a simple one: the production of homelessness cannot be interpreted in isolation from its wider economic, political and social context. The connection between Jesus and homelessness is accordingly explored through a vigilant re-reading of texts from the Gospel of Matthew by paying close attention to its systemic and objective (non-personal) creation. While a number of interpreters regard Jesus as essentially lacking home and hearth—increasingly estranged from his biological household as he pursues an itinerant mission—most depictions also *romanticize* homelessness in a way that downplays the destitution, desperation and reduced capacity for agency that would typically accompany such an experience. Guided by a reading framework informed by the Marxist critique of neoliberalism, including neoliberalism's complicity in the production of contemporary forms of homelessness, my reading of Matthew emphasizes the political and socio-economic underside of Jesus' homelessness and the ancient world as it is encoded within the Gospel text. What emerges is Jesus the expendable, the refuse of first-century Palestinian society, who, as a deviant outsider and perceived criminal threat, is eventually put to death on a Roman cross.

This book is based on my PhD thesis submitted to the University of Auckland in 2013. It is necessary, therefore, to begin by acknowledging the immense guidance and support of my supervisors, Elaine Wainwright of the School of Theology and Tracey McIntosh of the Department of Sociology. Thank you both for providing critical and stimulating feedback during every stage of the thesis's development. I also wish to acknowledge the institutional support of the University of Auckland itself, in particular, the generous provision of a doctoral scholarship.

The transformation of the thesis into a book was assisted by the critical and constructive feedback of George Aichele and Roland Boer who acted as external examiners for my PhD. I recall frantically reading through all several hundred pages of G.E.M. de Ste Croix's *The Class Struggles in Ancient Greece* in eager anticipation of my Oral Examination (otherwise known as the Viva Voce) so as to satiate the Marxist cravings of comrade Roland. Alas, somewhat disappointingly, the topic did not present itself in as much detail as I had anticipated. Needless to say, my tarrying with de Ste Croix's text has, of course, proved useful in my revision of certain parts of this book.

The influence of James Crossley of the University of Sheffield is no doubt reflected in this study's overriding concern with neoliberalism as an ideological undercurrent informing interpretive choices, deliberations and omissions in contemporary biblical scholarship. I spent time in Sheffield in 2011 as a Visiting Research Student in the Department of Biblical Studies just as James was putting the finishing touches on his book *Jesus in an Age of Neoliberalism*. Identifying neoliberalism as a (if not the) dominant ideological construction underpinning recent Jesus scholarship is a significant contribution to the field and has begun to open up new avenues for exploring how the Bible and biblical scholarship are complicit in, or potentially resistant to, a contemporary ideological horizon that has a wider breadth than simply aspects of identity and/or cultural politics.

I am deeply indebted to a number of other colleagues who have discussed critically with me the contents of this book, and some just for their jovial comradery. This includes, but is not limited to, Peter Bargh, Caroline Blyth, Emily Colgan, Katie Edwards, Deane Galbraith, Stephen Garner, James Harding, John Lyons, Debra MacDonald, Carlos Olivares, Christina

Petterson, Hugh Pyper, Abhishek Solomon and Nicholas Thompson. I have also received helpful feedback from the Bible and Critical Theory Seminar and various meetings of the Society of Biblical Literature. There was one other conference I presented a paper at and was uncharitably accused of eisegesis. Rather than rush to defend myself against the cardinal sin in biblical studies, however, I will let my readers decide my guilt for themselves. In many respects this study presents yet another example of how the supposedly indispensable distinction between eisegesis (reading into the text) and exegesis (reading out of the text) is both misleading and outdated.

I owe grateful thanks to the editors of journals in which I have published earlier versions of some of the material in this book. Parts of Chapter 2 appeared as 'Echoes of Displacement in Matthew's Genealogy of Jesus' in an issue of *Colloquium: The Australian and New Zealand Theological Review*. Chapter 4 is an appreciably revised and expanded form of an article that appeared as 'Probing the Homelessness of Jesus with Žižek's Sublime Object' in an issue of *The Bible and Critical Theory*. I am indebted to the reviewers of both articles, whose comments aided in honing the overall arguments. Thank you also to David Clines and Ailsa Parkin of Sheffield Phoenix Press for their editorial and professional assistance in getting this book into print.

I should, of course, especially acknowledge my immediate family, who have supported and encouraged me both during and after the PhD. Thanks go out for the loving support of my parents, Reginald and Sally Myles, and my brother, Andrew.

Robert J. Myles
November 2013

INTRODUCTION

It is the purpose of this present work to take up two related questions with regard to the Jesus of Matthew's Gospel. First, how have ideologies of homelessness in the world before the text shaped the reading and interpretation of Jesus? And, secondly, how might the text be re-read in a way that disrupts and advances beyond these dominant ideologies?

Although the image of a homeless Jesus appears frequently in both scholarly and popular interpretations of the Bible, most depictions seem compelled to 'romanticize' homelessness in a way that divorces it from the marginalizing reality and reduced capacity for agency that usually accompanies the experience. Jesus' homelessness is regarded as a positive trait of his characterization and the many ways in which homelessness is integrated into wider ideological–political discourses and trends are, somewhat conspicuously, downplayed or disregarded altogether.

This book employs socio-rhetorical criticism to re-read a selection of pericopes from the Gospel of Matthew that intersect the nexus between Jesus and homelessness. In doing so, it draws attention to the ways in which biblical interpretation is, often unknowingly, complicit in the construction of homelessness in contemporary political discourse and society. Given our shared ideological climate of postmodernism, otherwise known as the cultural logic of late (multinational) capitalism,[1] homelessness enjoys a special relationship to the power of the market, with its production intrinsically linked to economic and social policy. The contemporary 'post-political' concerns of cultural indeterminacy, individualism, the free market, deregulation and the privatization of welfare and other aspects of the state—built upon classical liberal ideals and collectively brought under the label of 'neoliberalism'—are as deeply rooted in New Testament (NT) scholarship as they are in constructions of homelessness in contemporary Western society.[2]

---

1. Fredric Jameson, *Postmodernism, or, The Cultural Logic of Late Capitalism* (London: Verso, 1991).

2. Crossley has recently brought the prevalence of neoliberal ideology to light in regard to historical Jesus scholarship. See James G. Crossley, *Jesus in an Age of Neoliberalism: Quests, Scholarship and Ideology* (BibleWorld; Sheffield: Equinox, 2012).

Since its advent during the Reagan and Thatcher governments of the United States and Britain, followed by its subsequent adoption by the left and quick exportation to the rest of the world, neoliberalism has now become an established ideological framework of the centre, in which governments of Western democratic nations perceive their role as concerned primarily with economic administration and management, in contrast to representing the class interests or ideological–political strategies of particular groups in society. According to David Harvey, neoliberalism has 'become hegemonic as a mode of discourse. It has pervasive effects on ways of thought to the point where it has become incorporated into the common-sense way many of us interpret, live in, and understand the world.'[3] Indeed, neoliberal discourse frames many discussions about agency, economics and individual morality as they pertain to Jesus, his disciples and their 'decision' to become homeless and/or separated from the household. This book will demonstrate how the connection between Jesus and homelessness is unsuspectingly entangled with these contemporary assumptions about the nature of homelessness and its relationship to wider society.

A thorough hermeneutical exploration of the connection between Jesus and homelessness achieves more than simply demonstrating an ideological basis to scholarship.[4] In addition we can advance our understanding of the pivotal role that Jesus' outsider status plays in rousing the conflict of the Gospel narrative that eventually leads to his death. While scholars traditionally focus on the teaching, healing and miracle-performing actions of Jesus, it is difficult to draw from this exactly how and why he ends up on the cross. In Matthew's Gospel, Jesus' antagonists surely do, at times, react negatively to him. But it is problematic to assert that his teaching and ministry are offensive or sectarian enough to alone warrant his execution.[5] There must be something more. This study argues that the surplus that gives rise to the offensiveness of Jesus, adding substance to his perceived dangerousness and delinquency, is entwined with his homelessness, or more precisely, his status as a displaced outsider.

To assist in these deconstructive and reconstructive objectives, the present work will engage with both biblical scholarship and a range of criti-

---

3. David Harvey, *A Brief History of Neoliberalism* (Oxford: Oxford University Press, 2005), p. 3.

4. In this book, 'hermeneutics' is understood in a general sense, signifying the art and process of interpretation. For an extensive discussion of various hermeneutical approaches to biblical literature, see Anthony C. Thiselton, *New Horizons in Hermeneutics* (Grand Rapids, MI: Zondervan, 1992).

5. This is not to deny the impact that Jesus' teaching and deeds of power have in offending the sensibilities of the power-brokers of society (e.g. Mt. 21.45-46), but these episodes are only part of the total picture. The production of deviancy is also entwined with Jesus' fatal rejection.

cal theories as they pertain to the ideological task at hand. Of particular importance is the work of Slavoj Žižek, whose theoretical insights provide a valuable platform from which to interrogate the ideological gap between Jesus and homelessness. According to Žižek, all successful ideologies refer to extrapolitical *sublime objects*: material objects elevated to positions of inexplicable importance. While these objects ultimately fail to reveal the full truth of their signification, this failure itself is seen as indirect testimony to the supreme quality of the object. Borrowing from the language of Jacques Lacan, Žižek suggests these things are 'Real', precisely insofar as they stand out from the reality of ordinary things and events.[6] This thesis will argue that the connection between Jesus and homelessness functions as a sublime object within biblical interpretation. Homelessness is idealized in Jesus in a way that encourages us to divert our attention away from the social and political questions that should really be plaguing us: namely, why do some people become homeless? And more pointedly, how is the wider socio-economic and ideological–political system complicit in the production and marginalization of the homeless population?

Žižek does not directly engage with the issue of homelessness at any length, however, and so a number of sociological and theological responses to homelessness are also employed as dialogue partners along the way. The biblical methodology utilized in the re-reading of texts is a configuration of socio-rhetorical criticism originally developed by Vernon K. Robbins. As will be argued, the Matthean text is richly encoded with rhetorical, intertextual, social and cultural features that potentially disrupt dominant ideologies of homelessness and displacement in the world before the text. The intention is not, however, to necessarily redeem or rehabilitate the text. Indeed, in some cases the text offers nothing worth redeeming. Rather, what emerges is a more judicious approach to the homelessness of Jesus that prioritizes the tension between biblical interpretation and the construction of social reality.

Homelessness and New Testament Scholarship

Major studies in the area of NT that deal explicitly with the categories of homelessness and displacement are virtually nonexistent. Nevertheless, the topic resurges every so often in different forms. An entry in the *Expository Times* from more than a century ago reveals a long-established diversity of opinion over the apparent homelessness of Jesus hinted at by Mt. 8.20, 'And Jesus said to him, "Foxes have holes, and birds of the air have nests; but

6. Slavoj Žižek, *The Sublime Object of Ideology* (London: Verso, 1989).

the Son of Man has nowhere to lay his head"'.[7] Does this saying describe Jesus' concrete experience of homelessness, a metaphorical experience of homelessness (whatever that means), or is it allegorical—pointing to Jesus' growing estrangement from first-century Judaism? All three of these positions are debated in the article, and at least the first two are still debated today (see further, Chapter 4).

More recently, John H. Elliott's book *A Home for the Homeless* employs social-scientific criticism as it was newly emerging in the 1970s and '80s to the NT letter of 1 Peter. Methodologically, Elliott seeks to expand conventional historical-critical exegesis by including models and categories from research in the social sciences to help reconstruct the social situation that occasioned the letter. The recipients of 1 Peter are addressed as 'aliens permanently residing in (*paroikia, paroikoi*) or strangers temporarily visiting or passing through (*parepidēmoi*) the four provinces of Asia Minor named in the salutation (1.1)'.[8] Elliott argues that the letter's rhetorical strategy is guided by this underlying social situation in its attempts to encourage and exhort 'believers struggling as suffering strangers in a strange land'.[9] Social-scientific criticism is useful for grappling with social and cultural forms as they are encoded within the world of a text, but has conventionally sidestepped a sustained engagement with its own ideological complications such as its entanglement with the assumptions of neoliberal ideology.[10] Elliott's study does, in fact, grapple with the ideology of the Petrine group,[11] but circumnavigates any discussion of ideology in the world before the text as it pertains to the construction of homelessness and displacement as a sociological category.

Within Gospel scholarship there are at least two noteworthy studies that intersect with the current topic. Michael H. Crosby's *House of Disciples* identifies the notion of 'house' and 'household' as a unifying theme in the Gospel of Matthew that establishes the identity and concerns of the early Christian churches.[12] Crosby develops an 'interactive hermeneutic' that attempts to do for the contemporary church what Matthew did for his own community, namely, illustrate the profound ethical implications of Jesus' teaching. Primarily employing redaction criticism, Crosby argues that the

---

7. John Robson, John Reid and Agnes Marwick, 'The Homelessness of Christ', *ExpTim* 8.5 (1897), pp. 221-26.

8. John H. Elliott, *A Home for the Homeless* (Eugene, OR: Wipf & Stock, 1990), p. 48.

9. Elliott, *Home*, p. xxiii.

10. See, for example, Crossley, *Neoliberalism*, pp. 169-84.

11. Elliott, *Home*, pp. 267-88.

12. Michael H. Crosby, *House of Disciples: Church, Economics, and Justice in Matthew* (Eugene, OR: Wipf & Stock, 1988).

key to understanding the context of Matthew's Gospel is the important social structure of the household in the first-century Greco-Roman world.[13] Made up of house churches, the early Christian community was effectively a household under the authority of the householder Jesus. In this context, Crosby reviews Matthew's perspectives on justice, the use of possessions, authority and the need for conversion of the heart if one is to live by the vision of faithful human life and the community of justice transmitted by Jesus. Crosby does not specifically engage with the question of Jesus' estrangement from normative kinship structures; however, he does speculate that within Matthew there is good reason to believe that Jesus had a house of his own (cf. Mt. 9.10, 28; 12.46; 13.1, 36; 17.25).[14]

Similarly, in *The Quest for Home*, Michael F. Trainor proposes a way of reading Mark's Gospel from the perspective of home and household.[15] He bases his reading on the assumption that all humans possess a deep need for authentic community and uses the domestic imagery of 'house' and 'household' in the ancient world as his primary reading lens. In doing so, he argues that in Mark the house becomes the architectural indicator for the disciples gathering in companionship with Jesus. The house is thus the place of intimacy and exists as an overarching structure for reading and organizing the Gospel.[16] Trainor's reading framework is directed by a selection of ancient Greek (Pythagoras, Plato, Aristotle) and Roman (Cicero, Ovid, Vespillo) philosophical and legal discourses around the family and household in operation during the time of Mark's composition. Unfortunately, however, there is no discussion of how contemporary philosophical and/or sociological voices have come to regard the issue, and so his reading tends to universalize the general sense of existential homelessness that has come to pervade not only the depthless, decentred and ungrounded conditions of postmodernity, but also the increasingly alienated and dispersive individualism of contemporary Western society.[17] Consequently, Trainor regularly employs hotly disputed terms such as 'home' and 'homelessness' without an adequate exploration of their contemporary ideological and/or discursive context.

13. For more on the household in Matthew, see Stuart L. Love, *Jesus and Marginal Women: The Gospel of Matthew in Social-Scientific Perspective* (Eugene, OR: Cascade, 2009), pp. 27-63; Stuart L. Love, 'The Household: A Major Social Component for Gender Analysis in the Gospel of Matthew', *BTB* 23.1 (1993), pp. 21-31.

14. Crosby, *House of Disciples*, 3.

15. Michael F. Trainor, *The Quest for Home: The Household in Mark's Community* (Collegeville, MN: Michael Glazier, 2001).

16. Trainer, *Quest for Home*, p. 6.

17. For more on these conditions and their implications, see Terry Eagleton, *The Illusions of Postmodernism* (Malden, MA: Blackwell, 1996); Jameson, *Postmodernism*.

While the studies of Elliott, Crosby and Trainor have succeeded in advancing our knowledge of the connection between households, justice and the early church, they still leave a number of unexplored avenues, particularly as new ideological ways of reading become more prominent and pertinent. Although Crosby's study focuses on the redefining of household structures within the Matthean community, for instance, he has little to say about how this might embody a counter-cultural ideology that conflicts with wider social and cultural norms. As a result, he does not discuss the consequences of estrangement from dominant models of household that might have been experienced by Jesus and/or the Matthean community. Conversely, Trainor pays little attention to the ideological conflicts of the world in front of the text that influence and limit interpretive possibilities. He instead centres on the experiences and ideologies of the ancient communities responsible for Mark's composition. A more integrated analysis requires critical awareness of both these spheres in order to avoid a one-dimensional reading.[18]

A final remark here is that none of these major studies has Jesus as their primary focus. This has meant especially in the case of Crosby and Trainor that crucial narrative events concerning the homelessness of Jesus are missed. Trainor, for instance, overlooks the relationship between the reasons for Jesus' execution and his apparent social uprooting. While his reading identifies 'a quest for home' through Mark, and culminates with the rejection and abandonment of Jesus by the disciples and God, Trainor misses the abnormality and indecency of a man without a conventional household that, combined with the contestation of public space, seems a plausible contributing factor to his execution by the ruling elites.

Elsewhere in the field of NT studies, the street homeless have been enlisted as test subjects for biblical scholars' anthropological experiments. A recent article by Susannah Cornwall and David Nixon employs the contextual Bible study method developed by Gerald West and John Riches to read the Bible with a group of homeless and vulnerably housed people at a soup kitchen in South-West England.[19] West has championed a liberationist approach to reading the Bible with so-called ordinary readers as distinct from trained biblical scholars in the academy.[20] Cornwall and Nixon's

18. As Gadamer would say, we approach the text with a historically effected consciousness (*wirkungsgeschichtliches Bewußtsein*) embedded in a particular history and culture. See Hans-Georg Gadamer, *Truth and Method* (trans. Joel Weinsheimer and Donald G. Marshall; London: Continuum, 2nd edn, 2004).

19. Susannah Cornwall and David Nixon, 'Readings from the Road: Contextual Bible Study with a Group of Homeless and Vulnerably-Housed People', *ExpTim* 123.1 (2011), pp. 12-19.

20. Gerald O. West, *The Academy of the Poor: Towards a Dialogical Reading of the Bible* (Interventions, 2; Sheffield: Sheffield Academic Press, 1999); Gerald O. West, ed. *Reading Other-wise: Socially Engaged Biblical Scholars Reading with their Local*

experiment, which consisted of a series of group discussions about biblical texts selected by the lead researcher (Lk. 4.1-24; 5.1-32; 7.36-50; 15.11-32), resulted in some novel interpretations, counter-interpretations, and insights into the world of their homeless subjects. The authors are honest to admit the limitations of their approach, however, such as the limited extent to which their findings might be universalized.[21] Further, the article does not provide much analysis of the construction of homelessness in contemporary discourse and society, its connection to the ideological–political and economic milieu of neoliberal capitalism, and crucially, the power dynamics between participants and observers.[22] While the contextual Bible study approach fosters some potentially interesting results, it is an inappropriate method for the current project, which is concerned primarily with the *wider ideological implications* of homelessness (in contrast to a reading site of homelessness) as it intersects with biblical interpretation and dominant social and political trends.[23]

Another area of NT studies that has occasionally made connections between Jesus and homelessness is that of historical Jesus research. This is because the so-called third quest for the historical Jesus has focused more upon understanding the social, political and cultural landscape of first-century Palestine, particularly Jesus' location in relation to Judaism and the Roman Empire. The work of Gerd Theissen, for example, applies social-scientific models to reconstruct the early Christian movement as comprising itinerant radicals and local sympathizers who modelled their lives after

---

Communities (Atlanta, GA: Society of Biblical Literature, 2007); cf. John Riches, 'Contextual Bible Study: Some Reflections', *ExpTim* 117.1 (2005), pp. 23-26.

21. Cornwall and Nixon, 'Readings', p. 12.

22. Some attempts are made to address the issue of power but they do not go far enough. The very setting of a 'soup kitchen', for example, is a paternalistic environment in which the street homeless are afforded individual charity in the form of an inequitable relationship. Another potential issue with the contextual Bible study approach is that oppressed groups will often rationalize their oppression using dominant ideologies that generally benefit the ruling classes. By claiming a collective identity, the 'homeless' might also re-inscribe their subordinate position in society. See Terry Eagleton, *Ideology: An Introduction* (London: Verso, 1991), p. 67; Gayatri Chakravorty Spivak, 'Can the Subaltern Speak?', in *Marxism and the Interpretation of Culture* (ed. Cary Nelson and Lawrence Grossberg; Urbana, IL: University of Illinois Press, 1988), pp. 271-314.

23. According to Žižek, 'one should reject the idea that the proper way to fight the demonization of the Other is to subjectivize him, to listen to his story, to understand how he perceives the situation'. Depicting the homeless population as 'real human beings', who struggle through life's daily challenges, can effectively neutralize their role in the greater ideological–political struggle by individualizing and privatizing their experience. See Slavoj Žižek, *First as Tragedy, Then as Farce* (London: Verso, 2009), p. 39.

Jesus. Theissen describes the wandering charismatic followers of Jesus as essentially homeless, lacking family (having abandoned or renounced family), lacking possessions and lacking protection. He writes:

> Giving up a fixed abode was an essential part of discipleship. Those who were called left hearth and home (Mark 1.16; 10.28ff.), followed Jesus, and like him became homeless. 'Foxes have holes, and birds of the air have nests; but the Son of man has nowhere to lay his head' (Matt. 8.20) is a saying which applied to them.[24]

The movement was made up of marginalized peasants and those of a 'marginal middle class' that reacted with a peculiar sensitivity to the upward and downward trends within society. In *The Shadow of the Galilean*, for example, Theissen uses a fictional narrative to paint a social world for the historical Jesus in which many peasants from the lower social strata are driven from their homes due to the systematic injustices of wealthy city dwellers and Roman oppression.[25]

A similar and fairly popularized line taken by notable scholars such as F. Gerald Downing, Burton Mack and John Dominic Crossan is the portrait of Jesus as a type of wandering Cynic philosopher.[26] Crossan argues that the Cynics (derived from the Greek word κυνάριον, meaning 'doglike') should be seen as examples of an introversionist approach to life that abandons the Greco-Roman world as irredeemably evil.[27] They spoke boldly and bluntly, travelled widely and used aphorisms and symbolic actions to present their arguments. Cynics adopted a deliberate independence from society and its

---

24. Gerd Theissen, *Sociology of Early Palestinian Christianity* (Philadelphia, PA: Fortress Press, 1978), p. 10; cf. Wolfgang Stegemann, 'Vagabond Radicalism in Early Christianity?: A Historical and Theological Discussion of a Thesis Proposed by Gerd Theissen', in *God of the Lowly: Socio-Historical Interpretations of the Bible* (ed. Willy Schottroff and Wolfgang Stegemann; Maryknoll, NY: Orbis Books, 1984), pp. 148-68.

25. Within the economic structures of a peasant society it was very likely for peasants to become indebted to wealthy landowners, especially if they struck a set of unfortunate circumstances such as a bad harvest. Theissen's fictional narrative includes typical examples of farmers and others who are forced to abandon their homes for fear of punishment over unpaid debt. See Gerd Theissen, *Der Schatten des Galiläers: Historische Jesusforschung in erzählender Form* (Munich: Christian Kaiser Verlag, 1986). Theissen's work has not been without criticism; see Richard A. Horsley, *Sociology and the Jesus Movement* (New York: Crossroad, 1989).

26. John Dominic Crossan, *The Historical Jesus: The Life of a Mediterranean Jewish Peasant* (San Francisco, CA: HarperSanFrancisco, 1991); F. Gerald Downing, *Cynics and Christian Origins* (Edinburgh: T. & T. Clark, 1992); F. Gerald Downing, 'Deeper Reflections on the Jewish Cynic Jesus', *JBL* 117 (1998), pp. 97-104; Burton L. Mack, *The Lost Gospel: The Book of Q and Christian Origins* (San Francisco, CA: HarperSanFrancisco, 1994).

27. Crossan, *Jesus*, pp. 72-88.

entangling alliances. This meant living simply, often in nature, and on occasions begging in order to survive.

It must be cautioned, however, that the Cynics' poverty was a chosen lifestyle, not one they were necessarily born into, as were peasants. In fact, most Cynics appear to have come from the educated elite and become 'cynical' about Greco-Roman society.[28] Stephen C. Barton sums up the contrast between the Cynics and the itinerancy of Jesus and his disciples as follows:

> [W]here the Cynics adopt a deliberate asceticism as an integral part of the wise man's revolt against culture and return to nature, the gospels speak more of involuntary deprivation and hardship in consequence of faithful missionary discipleship; and where the Cynics seek to reform the individual by a highly provocative onslaught on civilized conventions and popular opinion, there is in the gospels a positive summons to Israel and the nations to personal and social reform in preparation for the advent of God.[29]

Indeed, it is intriguing that even though a number of these historical studies highlight the intrusive imperial social structures and the collectivistic behaviour of the ancient world, Jesus' itinerancy is constructed as a self-directed choice.[30] As is further discussed in the next chapter, this trend is perhaps influenced by the majority of biblical scholars themselves experiencing a sufficient amount of individual mobility and agency within their respective social locations and cultures.[31] Moreover, the Cynic philosopher portrait of Jesus has been criticized for its tendency to over-Hellenize Jesus

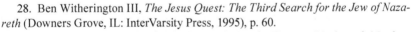

---

28. Ben Witherington III, *The Jesus Quest: The Third Search for the Jew of Nazareth* (Downers Grove, IL: InterVarsity Press, 1995), p. 60.

29. Stephen C. Barton, *Discipleship and Family Ties in Mark and Matthew* (SNTSMS, 80; Cambridge: Cambridge University Press, 1994), p. 52.

30. The discourse of displacement was widespread in Greco-Roman antiquity and led to the development of a number of themes or motifs integrally associated with its description, including the recollection of one's hometown, a wish for death, desertion, and linguistic and cultural isolation. See Jan Felix Gaertner, 'The Discourse of Displacement in Greco-Roman Antiquity', in *Writing Exile: The Discourse of Displacement in Greco-Roman Antiquity and Beyond* (ed. Jan Felix Gaertner; Leiden: Brill, 2007), p. 9. For recent overviews of the socio-economic context of first-century Palestine and Galilee, see especially Morten Hørning Jensen, 'Rural Galilee and Rapid Changes: An Investigation of the Socio-Economic Dynamics and Developments in Roman Galilee', *Biblica* 93.1 (2012), pp. 43-67; Douglas E. Oakman, 'The Shape of Power and Political-Economy in Herodian Galilee', in *Liberating Biblical Study* (ed. Laurel Dykstra and Ched Myers; Eugene, OR: Wipf & Stock, 2011), pp. 147-61.

31. Horsley makes a similar critique that Theissen's approach and methodological starting points have 'an "elective affinity" (Max Weber) with the social location and interests of most biblical scholars, who are middle class and liberals, but slipping somewhat in social status and on the defensive'. See Horsley, *Sociology*, p. 9.

and hence downplay his Jewishness.[32] This is particularly problematic for a reading of the Matthean Jesus with the Gospel's distinctive presentation of Jesus as the fulfilment of Jewish messianic expectations.

A useful and unique historical Jesus study is Halvor Moxnes's *Putting Jesus in his Place*, which utilizes the critical perspectives of sociology and anthropology to produce a reading of the historical Jesus that pays close attention to the roles of space and place.[33] He discusses how Jesus' movements from home place would have impacted his identity with regard to wider societal norms and expectations within the first-century context. The use of space and place—whether architectural, geographical or social—cannot be divorced from the concepts of home and homelessness that strongly indicate notions of rootedness or uprootedness in relation to significant places of meaning. Moxnes's study is, however, limited by the questions it asks; namely, what would it mean for Jesus and his contemporaries to *voluntarily* abandon integral social structures? Such framing tends to overlook the socio-economic forces that might *produce* estrangement from wider social and cultural norms, and can, moreover, potentially re-inscribe neo-liberal assumptions about the relative ease of social mobility in the world before the text.

A recent article by Robert L. Brawley goes against the trend of dominant scholarship by placing Jesus' saying about homelessness in Q 9.58 (Mt. 8.20) in the context of Roman imperial power as it was experienced in Galilee.[34] Brawley argues that homelessness is part of a broader picture that translates into loss of access to the resources of the land resulting from the promulgation of the Abrahamic covenant traditions. He attempts to reconstruct Jesus as an artisan who experienced downward mobility from landed peasantry by external social and political pressures and not by choice. In response to this, Jesus banded with the poor and dispossessed and demanded a restoration of the Abrahamic covenant, which included the ideal of equitable access to the resources of the land. While Brawley's article is commendable for its construction of homelessness as something produced within a wider socio-political context, it opens the door for a more robust investiga-

---

32. Markus Cromhout, 'J D Crossan's Construct of Jesus' "Jewishness": A Critical Assessment', *Acta patristica et byzantina* 17 (2006), pp. 155-78.

33. Halvor Moxnes, *Putting Jesus in his Place: A Radical Vision of Household and Kingdom* (Louisville, KY: Westminster John Knox, 2003). And more recently in Halvor Moxnes, 'Landscape and Spatiality: Placing Jesus', in *Understanding the Social World of the New Testament* (ed. Dietmar Neufeld and Richard E. DeMaris; New York: Routledge, 2010), pp. 90-106.

34. Robert L. Brawley, 'Homeless in Galilee', *HvTSt* 67.1 (2011): http://www.hts.org.za/index.php/HTS/article/view/863.

tion into the potential impact of our current ideological–political climate on biblical interpretation.

As has been observed, although the connection between Jesus and homelessness often surfaces within NT scholarship, a thorough investigation of its ideological and interpretive implications has yet to be undertaken. This provides the critical space for, and perhaps even necessitates, the current study.

Outline of Contents

Chapter 1 begins with a critical discussion of a number of important methodological assumptions, clarifications and considerations. This project is squarely situated within the current stream of ideological biblical criticism, not strictly a methodology in itself, but rather a hermeneutical stance that seeks to connect the task of biblical interpretation and scholarship to the diffusion and distribution of power within wider society. Competing ideological perspectives on the definitions and causes of homelessness and displacement in contemporary society are outlined and critiqued, before observing how such ideologies in the world before the text are, often unknowingly, complicit in shaping and limiting our interpretation of the biblical text. Finally, the various categories or 'textures' that make up Robbins's socio-rhetorical approach are introduced. After establishing how the inner texture, intertexture, social and cultural texture, and ideological texture are used to investigate the construction of homelessness within the text, I am ready to move into an interpretive analysis of the Matthean text itself.

Chapter 2, 'Displacement', brings together the ideological approach outlined in Chapter 1 with the beginnings of Matthew's Gospel and, in particular, the displacement of Jesus, Joseph and Mary during the flight-to-Egypt pericope in Mt. 2.13-23. The events of Jesus' infancy are foundational to his later life and ministry as they initiate a number of crucial themes that will be revisited as the Gospel narrative progresses. The genealogy in 1.1-17, for example, embeds Jesus in a cultural home that paradoxically gestures toward his future displacement. While conventional interpretations of the flight to Egypt focus on the intertextual allusions to Moses or to Christian apologetic notions of scriptural fulfilment, this chapter draws out the implications of the geographical and social uprooting that is experienced by both Jesus and his immediate family. The chapter also detects how this episode of forced displacement might contribute to the formation of a marginal self-identity, one that later comes into significant conflict with the normalized cultural and political institutions of society.

In Chapter 3, 'Reaction', I consider the beginnings of the Matthean Jesus' itinerant mission and the calling of his first disciples in 4.12-25. As suggested by its title, this chapter will argue that Jesus' ministry begins as a *reaction* against his wider ideological–political environment. Jesus' public activity succeeds that of his initiator, John the Baptist, who features as another homeless figure in the Gospel of Matthew. The beginnings of Jesus' mission and his calling of the first disciples to leave their livelihoods are often idealized as paradigmatic scenes. Aside from serving an obvious theological function, such interpretations also underscore the neoliberal discourse of the individual, free-roaming, moral agent, able to make isolated economic choices, while concurrently downplaying structural and systemic factors external to an individual that drive particular behaviours, reactions and outcomes. This chapter moves toward a critical re-reading of 4.12-25 that disrupts dominant ideologies of homelessness as they surface within this text and its interpretation.

Chapter 4, 'Destitution', centres on a significant and well-known lament of the Matthean Jesus, namely, that '[f]oxes have holes, and birds of the air have nests; but the Son of Man has nowhere to lay his head' (8.20). The surrounding verses in 8.18-22 are often thought to illustrate the cost of discipleship, and the pericope readily employs metaphors of animals and death to provide narrative amplification for the text's characterization of Jesus as an itinerant and marginal figure. The various textures neighbouring Jesus' lament of homelessness are explored to demonstrate how they supplement the destitution, desperation and offensiveness that typically accompany a homeless existence.

When Jesus returns to his hometown in 13.53-58, he is met with disdain and rejection. In Chapter 5, 'Rejection', I consider how this event is connected to his status as an expendable outsider. Having been uprooted from home place and normalized social space multiple times since his infancy, Jesus struggles to achieve recognition from the one place we might expect it the most, his hometown or πατρίς. Growing tensions within Jesus' wider kin group are used by the townsfolk as reasons to dishonour him. In drawing particular attention to how elements of setting within the text institutionalize differentiations of power, this chapter argues that Jesus' hometown rejection only further solidifies his exteriority from normalized society.

The narrative threads identified and expounded upon in previous chapters reach their climax in Chapter 6 with the arrest and execution of Jesus. Perpetual displacement and uprooting from home place have contributed to an outsider status for Jesus, and so he is deemed a criminal nuisance to the stability and security of everyday life. The chapter's title, 'Extermination', frames the guiding premise that undergirds the analysis of Jesus' arrest (26.47-56) and final moments on the cross (27.38-50), namely, that Jesus' homelessness and deviant behaviour are perceived by the jurisdictive apparatus of the reigning ideological–political order as a criminal threat that must be expunged, in order that society can return to its smooth, uninterrupted functioning.

Having introduced the objectives of this study, and plotted a course for navigation, I now move to a more thorough discussion of ideological biblical criticism and its application to the interpretive connection between Jesus and homelessness. This will provide a framework and justification for the methodological assumptions and interpretive strategy that will be employed in the subsequent reading of texts.

1

HOMELESSNESS AND IDEOLOGY

> His [Jesus'] chosen way of life is one of homelessness and insecurity (many homes, like Peter's, were open to him, but he had none of his own), and his disciples were called to share his style of life. This was a matter of choice, not of necessity, as Jesus' family was probably a comfortable, if not affluent, 'middle-class' one.   R.T. France[1]

> Another enduring perception about homelessness is that people actually choose to be homeless, whether from a desire to be free of societal restriction, as the hobo image suggests, or due to personal inability to measure up, as the alcoholic image suggests. The historical view that homelessness is a choice was heavily supported by the Reagan administration in the 1980s. In his exit interview with David Brinkley, Reagan professed that homeless people in Washington, D.C., sleep outdoors on heating grates by choice. Whether theorists romanticize (hobos) or demonize (alcoholics) the homeless, they are agreeing that homelessness is to some extent a choice.   Laura Stivers[2]

What happens if we place the dominant interpretations about Jesus' supposed homelessness in dialogue with the ideological politics of contemporary homelessness? Surprisingly, although a connection is often made between Jesus and homelessness in both popular discourse and NT scholarship, the question has evaded any sustained interest from biblical scholars. This study contends that particular ideologies about homelessness inform, whether explicitly or implicitly, the hermeneutical filters of dominant interpretations about Jesus. This, in turn, helps to construct social and spatial reality in particular ways that reinforce and reproduce such ideologies. In other words, the way we envisage and read Jesus' homelessness within the text affects the way we envisage and understand homelessness in the real world, and vice-versa.

---

1. R.T. France, *The Gospel according to Matthew: An Introduction and Commentary* (Leicester: InterVarsity, 1985), p. 160.

2. Laura Stivers, *Disrupting Homelessness: Alternative Christian Approaches* (Minneapolis, MN: Fortress Press, 2011), p. 50.

This chapter develops a new framework for reading the Jesus of Matthew's Gospel with regard to the issues of homelessness and displacement. It starts by describing the nature of the approach as ideological and committed to analysing the Bible in the light of contemporary issues that already shape its interpretation. After this, dominant and alternative discourses about homelessness are discussed in order to construct a more nuanced reading framework that can be brought into dialogue with both the Jesus of Matthew's Gospel and dominant interpretive trends within scholarship. The chapter concludes by outlining how socio-rhetorical criticism will be employed to produce an integrated analysis of the various textures of the text itself.

To begin, however, it is prudent to clarify which Jesus is being discussed in this study and what is meant by 'Matthew's Gospel' and/or the 'Matthean text'. While the common practice of scholarship is to view the Jesuses of the four Gospels as pointing to the same unique, historical Jesus, George Aichele, drawing on the theory of Gilles Deleuze, contends that what we actually get are four distinct Jesus simulacra.[3] The impetus to reduce these Jesuses to variant copies of a single historical model or archetypal identity reveals a deeply set theological interest, even if sometimes quite unconscious. If, however, we analyse each Jesus simulacrum independently, distinct meanings and reality effects begin to emerge. Aichele reasons that '[a] character, an event or even the entire world of a narrative is not the re-presentation or depiction of some prior concept or object, but rather it contributes to the creation of a [new] concept'.[4] Through its narrative denotation, each Gospel creates a referential illusion to a seemingly real person named Jesus. For the purposes of this study, the emphasis is placed on the Jesus simulacrum of Matthew's Gospel. This Jesus is traditionally understood by scholars as the proclamation of the Matthean community, appearing in its final written form in Koine Greek presumably sometime in the eighth decade of the first century CE.[5]

In terms of locating the community that produced the original text and among whom it was first circulated, various locations in both Syria and Palestine have held favour among scholars in recent decades. This study

---

3. George Aichele, *Simulating Jesus: Reality Effects in the Gospels* (BibleWorld; London: Equinox, 2011).

4. Aichele, *Simulating Jesus*, p. 34.

5. While the primary concern of this study is the nexus between Matthew's Jesus simulacrum and ideologies of homelessness and displacement, it is, of course, inevitable that different Jesuses and layers of the text will be discussed (including on occasion the historical kernel that is thought to lie beneath the story world created by the text) once in dialogue with scholarship that prioritizes the Matthean text's historical, canonical and theological functions.

assumes the location of Matthew's community is Antioch in the Roman province of Syria.[6] While the evidence for this location is disputed,[7] the generally held consensus for a location within a largely urban and Hellenized setting, containing a mixture of both poor and relatively wealthy households (suggested by the strong subtext of social justice within the Gospel), and a church undergoing a transition from a largely Jewish to mixed Jewish and Gentile Christian community, should suffice as a rough indication for what is hereafter referred to as the 'Matthean community'. Anthony J. Saldarini notes that while the story of Jesus and his disciples is not a strict allegory of the experience of the author and his group in the late first century, the story of Jesus and the disciples does in fact reflect the experience of Matthew's group and its social situation.[8] The relevance of some of these preliminary clarifications will become more obvious once comparisons between the social world of Jesus, the Matthean community and contemporary ideology are brought into more explicit dialogue.

Ideological Biblical Criticism

This study sits within the realm of ideological biblical criticism, not strictly a methodological approach per se, but rather a form of biblical criticism that seeks to uncover and promote rhetorical agendas within the three variables of biblical interpretation: the author, the text and the reader. As an umbrella term, ideological biblical criticism covers a wide range of approaches to the Bible and biblical studies in which readers are required to own their own commitments and agendas.[9] Within this book, ideology is positioned largely

6. See John P. Meier, 'Antioch', in *Antioch and Rome: New Testament Cradles of Catholic Christianity* (ed. Raymond E. Brown and John P. Meier; Mahwah, NJ: Paulist Press, 1983), pp. 12-86; Michelle Slee, *The Church in Antioch in the First Century: Communion and Conflict* (JSNTSup, 244; London: T. & T. Clark, 2003).

7. Gale, for example, suggests that the evidence could just as easily point to a location like Sepphoris. See Aaron Gale, *Redefining Ancient Borders: The Jewish Scribal Framework of Matthew's Gospel* (New York: T. & T. Clark, 2005).

8. Anthony J. Saldarini, *Matthew's Christian-Jewish Community* (Chicago: University of Chicago Press, 1994), p. 85. Saldarini argues that Matthew's community is a deviant group of Christian Jews who are part of the first-century Jewish community in the eastern Mediterranean. See also Amy-Jill Levine, *The Social and Ethnic Dimensions of Matthean Salvation History* (Lewiston, NY: Edwin Mellen, 1988); J. Andrew Overman, *Matthew's Gospel and Formative Judaism: The Social World of the Matthean Community* (Minneapolis, MN: Fortress Press, 1990); and the critical response of Douglas R.A. Hare, 'How Jewish Is the Gospel of Matthew?', *CBQ* 62 (2000), pp. 264-77.

9. For an overview, see Tina Pippin, 'Ideology, Ideological Criticism, and the Bible', *CRBS* 4 (1996), pp. 51-78; A.K.M. Adam, *What Is Postmodern Biblical Criticism?* (GBS; Minneapolis, MN: Fortress Press, 1995), pp. 49-53; Jonathan E. Dyck, 'A Map of Ideol-

within a Marxist framework.[10] The parameters of ideology, as such, deal with the means by which the social and political conditions of human life might be transformed through class struggle. This section outlines a working definition of ideology, discusses the hermeneutical shift to the reader and considers the public impact of private biblical scholarship before constructing a new space for ideological biblical criticism from which to probe the nexus between Jesus and homelessness.

Discourse and ideology, while hotly contested terms in contemporary scholarship, strike at the heart of the issues of both homelessness and biblical interpretation. This is because homelessness and biblical interpretation both emerge within a complex matrix of power dynamics and social interactions. Terry Eagleton observes that while there is no single adequate definition of ideology, its usage primarily makes reference not only to belief systems but also to questions of power. He argues that discourse (as an utterance of language) within a particular socio-economic context is always ideological. This is because discourse, understood in its Foucaultian form of signifying relations toward objects, subjects and other competing discourses, is always simultaneously complicit with power and the desire to control.[11]

In this study, ideology refers not necessarily to a 'false consciousness', but rather, as Eagleton describes it, to 'the ways in which what we say and believe connects with the power-structure and power-relations of the society we live in. . . . [T]hose modes of feeling, valuing, perceiving and believing which have some kind of relation to the maintenance and reproduction of social power'.[12] If we are to assume, in line with Slavoj Žižek, that the primary function of ideology is not to make theoretical statements or inter-

ogy for Biblical Critics', in *Rethinking Contexts, Rereading Texts: Contributions from the Social Sciences to Biblical Interpretation* (ed. M. Daniel Carroll R.; Sheffield: Sheffield Academic Press, 2000), pp. 108-28; David Jobling and Tina Pippin (eds.), *Ideological Criticism of Biblical Texts* (Semeia, 59; Atlanta, GA: Scholars Press, 1992); Armin Siedlecki, 'The Bible, David Jobling and Ideological Criticism', in *Voyages in Uncharted Waters: Essays on the Theory and Practice of Biblical Interpretation in Honor of David Jobling* (ed. Bergen Wesley J. and Armin Siedlecki; Sheffield: Sheffield Phoenix, 2006), pp. 80-86; Beverly J. Stratton, 'Ideology', in *Handbook of Postmodern Biblical Interpretation* (ed. A.K.M. Adam; St Louis, MO: Chalice, 2000), pp. 120-27.

10. For a critical survey of Marxist-oriented studies in biblical literature, see Roland Boer, 'Twenty-Five Years of Marxist Biblical Criticism', *CBR* 5.3 (2007), pp. 298-321. Note that in the present study, Marxist categories are not strictly employed as a heuristic lens; rather, modern biblical interpretation is conceived of as an ideological process linked to sustaining capitalist modes of production in the world before the text.

11. Eagleton, *Ideology*, pp. 1-5.

12. Terry Eagleton, *Literary Theory: An Introduction* (Minneapolis, MN: University of Minnesota Press, anniversary edn, 2008), p. 13; cf. Louis Althusser, 'Ideology and Ideological State Apparatuses (Notes towards an Investigation)', in *On Ideology* (London: Verso, 2008), pp. 1-60.

pretive judgments about political reality but rather to orient subjects' lived relations to and within this reality, then ideologies about homelessness are materialized within institutions and people's everyday practices and lives.[13] In other words, ideology is not simply an illusory representation of reality; it is rather social reality itself insofar as it is reproduced through this illusory representation. In this respect, ideology should not be essentialized to a discourse about presuppositions or bias. Rather, ideology is intrinsically concerned with the distribution of power and economic resources within materialized society. Again, Eagleton agrees:

> The claim that the whole of our thought moves within the frame of certain practical, 'primordial', pre-reflective interests is surely just. But the concept of ideology has traditionally meant a good deal more than this. It is not just out to affirm that ideas are inscribed by interests; it draws attention to the ways in which specific ideas help to legitimate unjust and unnecessary forms of political domination.[14]

Given that the Bible and its interpretation is subject to many spheres of institutional influence (whether from the church, the academy or popular culture), the connection between Jesus and homelessness, far from depicting the reality of this association, is part of the package of ideas that produces and reproduces the discursive formations that sustain and justify existing structural arrangements of political economy in a society.[15]

Shifting Hermeneutics
The paradigm shifts in the latter half of the twentieth century within the humanities in general and biblical studies in particular have given rise to a number of competing modes of discourse that have gradually uncovered the driving role of the reader in biblical interpretation. Fernando F. Segovia observes that, if viewed as a construct, the location of meaning within a text does not reside in the author or the world behind the text, but rather in the encounter or interchange between text and reader.[16] This shift raises ques-

13. Žižek, *Sublime Object*, pp. 15-16.
14. Eagleton, *Ideology*, pp. 181-82. Fredric Jameson describes ideology as a 'strategy of containment' that constrains thought to what is internally coherent in its own terms, while repressing the unthinkable which lies beyond its boundaries. See Fredric Jameson, *The Political Unconscious: Narrative as a Socially Symbolic Act* (London: Routledge, 1983), p. 53.
15. No individual or institution has sole ownership or control over the biblical text and its meaning. Rather, its interpretation and relevance is negotiated between competing power structures in society. As Althusser notes, however, institutions like the church teach '"know-how" . . . in forms which ensure *subjection to the ruling ideology*'. See Althusser, 'Ideology', p. 7.
16. Fernando F. Segovia, 'Cultural Studies and Contemporary Biblical Criticism: Ideological Criticism as Mode of Discourse', in *Reading from This Place: Social Loca-*

tions with regards to 'real, flesh-and-blood readers'.[17] How have the theoretical and methodological concerns of the discipline been influenced by the dominant demographics of its proponents (traditionally identified as Western male clerics)? What perspectives and agendas have been overlooked or excluded because of a bias in dominant social and geographical locations?

These shifts have resulted in the transition to a different ethics of biblical interpretation. A.K.M. Adam, for example, makes the distinction between what he labels 'integral' and 'differential' hermeneutics: essentially two competing paradigms for conceiving how interpretation operates in both popular and scholarly discourse. Integral hermeneutics (Adam's idiom for the traditional modernist framework of interpretation) takes it for granted that a text can have only one true meaning and that this meaning is imbued in the text itself by the original author. Within this framework ethical interpretation involves discerning the author's intentions at the time of the text's composition.[18] Differential hermeneutics, however, assumes that a text can have multiple layers of meaning that are not necessarily constrained by what the original author had in mind. This does not, as is often charged, indicate a plunge into interpretive relativism, but rather that the ethical obligations are moved from the author to the reader.[19] As such, if both perspectives are respected, critical interpreters ought to devise interpretations that are accountable not only to texts and authors but also to rival interpreters and audiences. While the practitioners of traditional approaches argue over whose interpretation is right or wrong, the ethical underpinnings of differential hermeneutics ask readers what sort of lives and interactions are engendered by our particular interpretative moves.

This change in ethical consciousness has generated an overwhelming number of reader-oriented studies to the point where the more popular (non-Marxist) ideological approaches have now become tolerated and in some cases institutionalized into the mainstream of the discipline.[20] Even so, ideological approaches still occupy a marginal fringe in relation to the immutable core of historical-critical scholarship, itself a product of

tion and Biblical Interpretation in Global Perspective (ed. Fernando F. Segovia and Mary Ann Tolbert; Minneapolis, MN: Augsburg Fortress Press, 1995), pp. 1-17.

17. Segovia, 'Cultural Studies', p. 8.

18. A.K.M. Adam, *Faithful Interpretation: Reading the Bible in a Postmodern World* (Minneapolis, MN: Fortress Press, 2006), pp. 82-88.

19. Adam, *Faithful Interpretation,* pp. 89-90.

20. Segovia suggests this with regards to postcolonial criticism, which emerged in the mid-1990s and is now firmly established within the discipline (indicated, for example, by the formation of regular sessions devoted to the approach at the annual conference of the Society of Biblical Literature). See Fernando F. Segovia, 'Postcolonial Criticism and the Gospel of Matthew', in *Methods for Matthew* (ed. Mark Allan Powell; Cambridge: Cambridge University Press, 2009), pp. 194-237.

nineteenth-century Enlightenment discourse.[21] The most familiar form of ideological biblical scholarship is feminist criticism, which takes the socio-political concerns of women to the text and to dominant methods of interpretation.[22] Similarly, postcolonial criticism has brought a new set of analytical tools that have been employed by a number of non-Western and Western critics.[23] Numerous other approaches have emerged, although are arguably even more on the periphery of the discipline.

In reacting to ideological (or what he labels 'advocacy') readings of the Bible, John Barton claims that attacks against the objectivity and positivistic characteristics of traditional historical-critical scholarship have been greatly over-exaggerated. He warns that

> objectivity is here being used as something of a straw man. Few biblical critics have ever claimed the degree of objectivity they are being accused of. What they have argued for is reasonable objectivity, that is, a refusal simply to read one's own ideas into the text or to have no sense of detachment from it even for the purposes of study.[24]

21. Some scholars have challenged the Enlightenment assumptions of historical criticism. Barton, for example, argues that the origins are not to be traced to the Enlightenment but rather to the Reformation. Either way, there are definite ideological underpinnings to the method that are often undisclosed or even ignored by its practitioners. See John Barton, 'Historical-Critical Approaches', in *The Cambridge Companion to Biblical Interpretation* (ed. John Barton; Cambridge: Cambridge University Press, 1998), p. 16. It has also been argued that both modern and postmodern biblical scholarship is a product of the Enlightenment, even when scholars imagine they are doing something quite different. See Stephen D. Moore and Yvonne Sherwood, *The Invention of the Biblical Scholar: A Critical Manifesto* (Minneapolis, MN: Fortress Press, 2011).

22. For an overview of feminist criticism's directions and influence within Matthean studies, see Elaine M. Wainwright, 'Feminist Criticism and the Gospel of Matthew', in *Methods for Matthew* (ed. Mark Allan Powell; Cambridge: Cambridge University Press, 2009), pp. 83-117; Janice Capel Anderson, 'Matthew: Gender and Reading', in *A Feminist Companion to Matthew* (ed. Amy-Jill Levine; Sheffield: Sheffield Academic Press, 2001), pp. 25-51.

23. Segovia, 'Postcolonial Criticism and the Gospel of Matthew', p. 194. Segovia suggests that Carter's work on Matthew and Roman imperialism is a Western example of postcolonial criticism that uses empire studies, although it is not openly perspectival and does not explicitly engage with postcolonial theory and/or discourse. See Warren Carter, *Matthew and the Margins: A Sociopolitical and Religious Reading* (Maryknoll, NY: Orbis Books, 2000); Warren Carter, *Matthew and Empire: Initial Explorations* (Harrisburg, PA: Trinity Press International, 2001); Warren Carter, 'The Gospel of Matthew', in *A Postcolonial Commentary on the New Testament Writings* (ed. Fernando F. Segovia and R.S. Sugirtharajah; London: T. & T. Clark, 2007), pp. 69-104.

24. John Barton, *The Nature of Biblical Criticism* (London: Westminster John Knox, 2007), p. 49.

While Barton admits that positivism does exist within the discipline, he suggests that historical criticism can be intellectually rigorous without being positivistic.[25]

It is difficult to share this kind of optimism, however, given the penetrating effect that the ideological underpinnings of various cultural contexts have had on supposedly detached scholarship. A quest for 'reasonable objectivity' has also enabled many practitioners to avoid critically engaging with the political and theological assumptions that undergird dominant methodological approaches. Take, for example, the influential three-volume ICC commentary on Matthew's Gospel by W.D. Davies and Dale C. Allison. Because of its careful and exhaustive exegesis, it has come to be regarded as a credible staple of Matthean studies. In the preface to the first volume, the authors claim their work continues in 'the tradition of disinterested and objective study in biblical criticism'.[26] As Žižek would surely remark, is not such a frank bracketing out of any ideological inquiry in fact an example of ideology at its purest? Indeed, their focus on predominantly historical and theological questions reflects their 'interestedness' in the authoritative function of the text (or the history encoded within it) for they both serve the church in their capacity as ordained Christian ministers. While their work is critical it also stays within the realms of Christian orthodoxy and would probably not offend its primary market: that of conservative Christian scholars and ministers in the United Kingdom and North America.[27] The 'objective' posturing of Davies and Allison's discourse, however, masks this partial nature of their research. As will become evident in the present study, many Matthean scholars couch their discussions of Jesus' apparent homelessness in the language of wider ideological trends without any apparent awareness. A more objective approach to biblical scholarship, then, might actually be achieved through a reasonable engagement with ideological criticism.

Biblical Interpretation and the Construction of Social Reality
Given the connection between homelessness and material conditions in the world before the text, a textual reading of the connection between Jesus and homelessness cannot be discussed in isolation from its ideological effects, including the ways in which biblical interpretation is complicit in the

---

25. Barton, *The Nature of Biblical Criticism*, pp. 49-51.

26. W.D. Davies and Dale C. Allison, *The Gospel according to Saint Matthew 1–7*, Vol. 1 (ICC; Edinburgh: T. & T. Clark, 1988), p. xi.

27. Crook has uncovered a theological agenda in Allison's more recent work on the resurrection: despite a careful commitment to proper historical enquiry, assumptions of *sui generis* religion subtly appear when discussing the limitations of historical criticism as it pertains to the resurrection. See Zeba Crook, 'On the Treatment of Miracles in New Testament Scholarship', *Studies in Religion* 40 (2011), pp. 471-72.

construction of social reality. Such a public and ethical underpinning to biblical interpretation is by no means a recent phenomenon. Ulrich Luz notes that during the Enlightenment, historical-critical exegesis itself had a strong emancipative character that it has subsequently lost. It not only displaced claims to the divine and eternal truths of the Bible by demonstrating the text's human origins, but it also showed how the so-called original meanings of biblical texts often contradicted ecclesiastical dogmas and norms. Both these features, according to Luz, helped to free the rational Enlightenment individual from the clutches of church authority.[28]

More recently, Hector Avalos has forcefully argued in *The End of Biblical Studies* that biblical studies as we know it must end. He declares that, from a secular standpoint, modern biblical scholarship has shown the irrelevance of the Bible, and so the continuation of biblical studies needlessly persists in upholding the Bible's relevance, significance and authority for contemporary society.[29] It is often objected to Avalos's arguments, however, that if biblical scholars were to remain silent, the text, far from losing its authority, would continue to be read by wider society in ways that sustain and perpetuate existing oppressive social relations.[30] Because many interpreters, including a dominant surge of literalist biblical fundamentalists, assert the public claims and values of biblical texts, biblical scholarship can no longer restrict its public to institutionalized religion or to the academy. What is required, then, is a transformation of the ethos of the discipline in which (ideological) claims regarding the ownership of the text and its meaning (including the institutional grip of scholarship) are critically assessed and addressed.

Given the cultural significance of the Bible within contemporary Western society, it seems pertinent to explore its interpretation in light of public issues that might bear influence on how the text is already interpreted, and how it might be re-interpreted with the aim of positive social transformation. Elisabeth Schüssler Fiorenza, for instance, argues that

> understood as a public-political discourse, biblical studies would be able
> . . . not just to investigate the literary and historical elements and contexts
> of a biblical text but also to critically reflect on what kind of role the Bible
> plays today in the social construction of reality and in the discursive for-

---

28. Ulrich Luz, *Matthew in History: Interpretation, Influence, and Effects* (Minneapolis, MN: Fortress Press, 1994), p. 11.

29. Hector Avalos, *The End of Biblical Studies* (Amherst, NY: Prometheus, 2007).

30. See, for instance, the defence of a public biblical studies in Elisabeth Schüssler Fiorenza, *Rhetoric and Ethic: The Politics of Biblical Studies* (Minneapolis, MN: Fortress Press, 1999), p. 29; cf. the response chapters to Avalos in Roland Boer (ed.), *Secularism and Biblical Studies* (BibleWorld; London: Equinox, 2010), pp. 101-38.

mations that determine individuals, religious communities, and society on the whole.[31]

With respect to the central concerns of this book, it would appear that biblical scholars are themselves entangled in the politics of contemporary homelessness. While lamenting the bourgeois behaviour of biblical scholars, for instance, Avalos remarks:

> Lest we think we are not a relatively elite and privileged class, consider a typical SBL Annual Meeting. In Philadelphia, most of us stayed, ate, and drank at the Hilton, Marriott, and other nice hotels. Meanwhile, homeless people were all around us. On occasion, I saw scholars nearly trample homeless people while rushing to yet another appointment or session, perhaps one on the supposed prophetic call to help the poor. We read papers to each other, but little of what we learn will feed the hungry or clothe the naked. Much of what we study is to fulfil our own curiosity and for our own enjoyment.[32]

Far from providing grounds to end the critical study of the Bible, however, Avalos's remarks lend themselves to a case for why biblical scholarship needs to interact more seriously with the study of ideology and wider ideological trends. If our scholarly pursuits are really driven by our enjoyment, then we ought to examine the ways in which our enjoyment structures ideological and political reality.

Opening a New Space for Ideological Biblical Criticism
Having observed the hermeneutical shift to the reader and determined the connection between biblical interpretation and the construction of social reality, it is time to return once more to the notion of ideology, and more specifically, its deployment within this book. In this section I open a new space from which to investigate the connection between Jesus and homelessness as it manifests itself in biblical interpretation.

Avalos's secular approach rests on the construction of a dichotomy between the 'false consciousness' of biblical studies and an ideology-free, secular criticism. Crudely put, this might be characterized as 'apologetics' versus 'evidence' or 'faith' versus 'science'. His advocacy for the end of biblical studies seems misguided, however, once we acknowledge that the modernist epistemology of positivism that undergirds Avalos's argument is itself a historical product that, as a totalizing discourse, constrains freedom of critical thought.

---

31. Schüssler Fiorenza, *Rhetoric and Ethic*, p. 11.
32. Hector Avalos, 'The Ideology of the Society of Biblical Literature and the Demise of an Academic Profession', *SBL Forum* (April 2006).

In an article exploring the 'Problem of Ideology in Biblical Studies', Randal Reed responds by suggesting that the work of Slavoj Žižek might open a new space for ideological biblical criticism, without having to try and find some (imagined) place outside of ideology.[33] Reed makes sense of Žižek's thought (which, to be fair, is far-ranging, eclectic and at times seemingly contradictory) as follows:

> Reality as we know it is not a totality, it is replete with gaps and holes. That lack of totalization is true even more so for ideology. There are in ideology also gaps and holes. Ideology often tries to pre-emptively fill these holes but they are always there. . . . The failure to properly symbolize the real means that there is always a remnant or supplement, which is part of the real that escapes ideology. Those pieces of the real that exist in ideology and yet elude it are then the places that create the possibility for ideological criticism.[34]

These gaps and holes, when exploited, reveal the contradictions inherent within all ideological systems. To anticipate the argument below, in the case of dominant interpretations of Jesus' homelessness, we get a seemingly 'romantic' or 'idyllic' form of homelessness without any of the negative side effects that typically accompany the experience. Homelessness is idealized in Jesus in a way that encourages us to divert our attention from the inherent contradictions contained within its wider ideological edifice. It is here that we encounter the Lacanian difference between reality and the Real: 'reality' is the social reality of actual people, in all their suffering and exploitation, while the 'Real' signifies the inexorable abstract construction of social reality.

In this sense, the connection between Jesus and homelessness functions as what Žižek, following Lacan, refers to as the *objet petit a*. As a leftover of our *jouissance*, the *objet petit a* is the cause of what Žižek labels the parallax gap. A parallax view is a change in one's observational position, allowing the same ontological object 'out there' to be seen from two distinct subjective stances. Within this conceptual framework, the *objet petit a* is 'that unfathomable X which forever eludes the symbolic grasp, and thus causes the multiplicity of symbolic perspectives'.[35] If Jesus is, for Christians and perhaps wider Western culture, the ultimate object of our theological desire, functioning in his salvific role as a mediator of our 'surplus enjoyment' (*plus de jouissance*), then his homelessness acts as a fantasmatic screen to shield us from the traumatic experience of homelessness proper and the apparent

33. Randall William Reed, 'The Problem of Ideology in Biblical Studies', *BSR* 40.4 (2011), pp. 17-23.

34. Reed, 'The Problem of Ideology', p. 23; cf. Žižek, *Sublime Object*.

35. Slavoj Žižek, *The Parallax View* (Short Circuits; Cambridge, MA: MIT Press, 2006), p. 21.

failure of our wider ideological–political system in which it emerges. In psychoanalytic theory, fantasy is not hallucinatory; rather it constitutes our desire and provides its coordinates. In other words, 'it provides a "schema" according to which certain positive objects in reality can function as objects of desire, filling in the empty places opened up by the formal symbolic structure'.[36] The fantasy provides a frame for anchoring our enjoyment (*jouissance*) in that which we are able to comprehend.

The romanticization of Jesus' homelessness thus features as a sublime object in biblical interpretation: a positive, material object elevated to the status of the impossible Thing. For Lacan, the Thing is, in language, what the blind spot is in our vision; it can be present in its very absence. Sublimation occurs when an ordinary object is raised to the dignity of the Thing.[37] Desperation and destitution are extracted from Jesus' homelessness in such a way that we end up with a representation of homelessness devoid of its central properties. This contradiction, however, sustains the fantasy around which the symbolic order is constructed.

Žižek describes the homeless population (along with the underclass, the ghettoized and the permanently unemployed) as a symptom of the late capitalist universal system: a reminder of the structural deficiencies that remain beneath the surface and negate the 'totalitarian logic of the proper capitalist utopia'.[38] Despite this, contemporary interpretations of Jesus' homelessness tend to perpetuate or re-inscribe existing dominant ideologies about the causes of homelessness in addition to a whole variety of assumptions about human nature, neoliberal capitalism and so on, that, in turn, become embedded in the spatial fabric of social reality. This disconnect between form and reality, or reality and the Real, gestures toward an exploitable ideological remnant. Far from being disinterested and objective, then, biblical scholars are themselves complicit in the politics of contemporary homelessness through their interpretive choices, omissions and deliberations, which are always ideologically situated.

This study argues that the sublimation of Jesus' homelessness functions as a gap within biblical interpretation. Its romanticization anchors our *jouissance* to dominant ideologies of homelessness in the world before the text by enabling the reader to organize his or her fantasy in a way that sustains the prevailing arrangements of power in society. Within this study, ideological criticism is employed as a means of *radical desublimation*; our hermeneutical gaze is focused on the crack that divorces Jesus' homelessness as a sublime object from the excess, excremental properties of homelessness

36. Slavoj Žižek, *The Plague of Fantasies* (London: Verso, 1997), p. 7.
37. Jacques Lacan, *The Ethics of Psychoanalysis, 1959–1960* (trans. Dennis Porter; London: Tavistock, 1992), p. 112.
38. Žižek, *Plague of Fantasies*, pp. 161-62.

encoded in the world of the text. In doing so, the structure of sublimation—and its fantasmatic support to the wider ideological–political edifice—collapses in on itself. Jesus the itinerant preacher becomes Jesus the displaced, the refuse of society, who is eventually disposed of on the cross at Golgotha. It is with these objectives in mind that I move to a more detailed discussion regarding ideologies of homelessness within contemporary Western society and culture. Following this, the implications of the construction of a homeless Jesus within the Matthean text can be further probed.

Contemporary Ideologies of Homelessness

Reflective judgments about the definition and causes of homelessness are embodied propositions that tell us as much about a subject's lived relation to political reality as about this reality itself. Whether we perceive Jesus as homeless and/or socially uprooted has a lot to do with the definitions of homelessness we employ. Does homelessness mean the same thing as houselessness, or does the term point to a more multidimensional concept? There is little agreement within recent scholarly literature as to how the concept of homelessness is best defined. It is more than just a theoretical problem because it also informs governmental and individual responses. Because definitions determine who counts as homeless, they are always in service to political and ideological agendas.[39]

This section constructs a synthesis of the varied contemporary perspectives regarding homelessness and maps an ideological position from which the current project will situate itself. As a reader primarily concerned with the connection between Jesus and homelessness as it manifests itself in Western, so-called developed nations, the perspectives that follow draw primarily on a tradition of literature on homelessness within advanced capitalist societies. Žižek's critique of ideology and neoliberalism, unfortunately, tends to universalize a (limited) Euro-Anglo-American perspective, inadvertently subsuming different contexts and categories of neoliberalism (such as gender, postcolonial, so-called Asian values, capitalism and so on) under a grander narrative.[40] Accordingly, the discussion that follows engages

---

39. Martha R. Burt, 'Homelessness, Definitions and Estimates of', in *Encyclopedia of Homelessness* (ed. David Levinson; London: Sage, 2004), pp. 233-38.

40. Neoliberalism is linked to the phenomenon known as globalization and has, accordingly, been exported around the world, including my own home country of New Zealand. According to Gray, the neoliberal experiment in New Zealand during the 1980s and 1990s was the most ambitious attempt at engineering the free market as a social institution anywhere in the twentieth century. He observes that '[a]mong many of the novel effects of neo-liberal policy in New Zealand has been the creation of an underclass in a country that did not have one before'. See John Gray, *False Dawn: The Delusions of Global Capitalism* (London: Granta, 1998), p. 39.

with some sociological and theological perspectives on homelessness from varying contexts, making room for distinctive peculiarities, before returning once again to Žižek's ideological critique, noting its importance for both current debates on homelessness, and, more crucially, the interpretive gap between Jesus and homelessness.

Defining Homelessness

To what experience or reality does homelessness actually refer? Any good definition of homelessness will, of course, start with a discussion of home. There has been a proliferation of literature on home across a number of disciplines that, generally speaking, construct it as a multidimensional concept. Home is variously described as conflated with or related to house, family, haven, self, gender and journeying.[41] A crucial distinction to be made at the outset, however, is that a house is not the same as a home. Within this study, 'house' refers to the physical structure in which a group of people usually reside, whereas 'home' refers to a more complex entity in which a person or group of people are connected to a particular place by a sense of relational social and spatial identity. The conflation of these terms is largely the result of an ideological process grounded in the emergence of capitalist modes of production and concepts of private property.[42]

While a house will often function as a home, it is possible to speak about home as place without the need for a physical structure, the house. In reckoning with the relationship between home and being, for example, Martin Heidegger reverses the common assumption that homemaking necessarily begins with a physical structure. Rather, he suggests that '[w]e do not dwell because we have built, but we build and have built because we dwell, that is,

41. Shelley Mallett, 'Understanding Home: A Critical Review of the Literature', *Sociological Review* 51.1 (2004), pp. 62-89.

42. It is argued in much of the 'home' literature that the seventeenth-century rise of the bourgeoisie led to a form of domestic morality aimed at safeguarding and privatizing familial property. Rykwert, for instance, suggests that an association of the previously distinct words 'house' and 'home' was solidified in English case law in the early seventeenth century. The terms are often conflated in contemporary popular discourse; for example, in the case of selling real estate and promoting home ownership. See Joseph Rykwert, 'House and Home', *Social Research* 58.1 (1991), pp. 51-62. Dupuis and Thorns suggest that governments of advanced capitalist countries such as New Zealand have actively promoted the conflation of house, home and family as part of a broader ideological agenda aimed at increasing economic efficiency by shifting the burden of responsibility for citizen's welfare away from the state and onto the home and nuclear family. See Ann Dupuis and David Thorns, 'Home, Home Ownership and the Search for Ontological Security', *Sociological Review* 46.1 (1998), pp. 24-47.

because we are *dwellers*'.[43] In other words, Heidegger thinks that our building activities—which consist of the founding and joining of both material
and/or imaginary spaces—are integrally associated with and arise out of our
innate capacity to dwell, to transform (meaningless) space into home place.

Accordingly, within the postmodern era, the notion of *identity* has become
more integral to understanding the concept of home. The practical theologi-
ans Steven Bouma-Prediger and Brian J. Walsh, for example, provide a phenomenology of home that incorporates the following eight elements:

1. Home is a space of permanence with a sense of enduring residence.
2. Home is a dwelling place, although it is not the same as a house.
3. Home is a storied place; homemaking transforms space into place.
4. Home is a resting place, an asylum of safety and security.
5. Home is a site of inclusion and hospitality. Within a home there are
   few strangers.
6. Home is a place of embodied inhabitation. There is a distinction
   between a temporary occupant and a permanent inhabitant.
7. Home is a place of orientation and familiarity.
8. Home is a place of affiliation and belonging in which one gains an
   identity. Home is a place of recognition and acceptance rather than
   disdain and rejection.[44]

Because the concept of home is complex and multidimensional, homelessness should also be regarded as complex and at its broadest level signalling the lack of any combination of the above phenomena. In this more
holistic framework, homelessness is not just the lack of a physical dwelling but a condition of exclusion and uprootedness from society. A broad
working definition that encapsulates these ideas is found in the following
description of home and homelessness by Bouma-Prediger and Walsh:

> To be 'home' is to experience some place as 'primal', as a place to which
> one has a profound sense of connection, identity, and even love. To be
> 'emplaced' is to have a point of orientation. Homelessness, then, is a mat-

43. Martin Heidegger, 'Building Dwelling Thinking', in *Poetry, Language,
Thought* (New York: Harper & Row, 1971), p. 148. On the problem of homelessness,
Heidegger writes toward the end of his essay: 'On all sides we hear talk about the housing shortage, and with good reason. . . . We try to fill the need by providing houses, by
promoting the building of houses, planning the whole architectural enterprise. However hard and bitter, however hampering and threatening the lack of houses remains,
the *real plight of dwelling* does not lie merely in a lack of houses. . . . The real dwelling
plight lies in this, that mortals ever search anew for the nature of dwelling, that they
must ever learn to dwell' (p. 161).

44. Steven Bouma-Prediger and Brian J. Walsh, *Beyond Homelessness: Christian
Faith in a Culture of Displacement* (Grand Rapids, MI: Eerdmans, 2008), pp. 56-66.

ter of profound and all-pervasive displacement. Homelessness is a matter of 'placelessness'.[45]

To be displaced from home usually brings about a number of unfavourable social and economic consequences. The common identification of homelessness with an extreme form of poverty, for example, underlines the close relationship between homelessness and economics. In terms of defining homelessness, however, this identification can become problematic if it focuses solely on those literally living on the streets (i.e. 'chronic homelessness'). In order to analyse homelessness as more than just what is visible, Chris Chamberlain and David Mackenzie propose a socially constructed definition based on the notion of minimum community standards. They contend that homelessness is a culturally relative concept that acquires meaning in relation to the housing conventions of a particular culture and argue that '[t]he defining of homelessness must involve the central task of identifying the community standards about the minimum level of housing that people have the right to expect in order to live according to the conventions and expectations of a particular culture'.[46] In other words, the norm of a particular culture or society in terms of adequate housing is used as a point of reference in order to determine any dissent from this norm.

Chamberlain and Mackenzie also construct a four-tiered model of homelessness that acknowledges the varying degrees and cycles in which homelessness is experienced. The model identifies three degrees of homelessness (primary, secondary and tertiary) with regard to the shared community cultural standards embodied in the current housing standards of so-called developed countries. Primary homelessness includes people without conventional accommodation; for instance, those living on the streets, in deserted buildings, improvised dwellings or in public spaces. Secondary homelessness includes people moving between various forms of temporary shelter, including staying with friends, in emergency accommodations, boarding houses or hostels. Tertiary homelessness includes people who live with minimal security of tenure, without their own amenities, and below the minimum standard as determined by the cultural norm. Finally, the marginally housed includes people living in housing or temporary situations that are close to the minimum standard.[47]
While homelessness cannot strictly be determined by whether one is

45. Bouma-Prediger and Walsh, *Beyond Homelessness,* p. 4.

46. Chris Chamberlain and David Mackenzie, 'Understanding Contemporary Homelessness: Issues of Definition and Meaning', *Australian Journal of Social Issues* 27.4 (1992), p. 290.

47. This schema, of course, cannot be used in a purely mechanistic way, and it makes room for cultural settings in which people do not have the minimum level of accommodation identified by the community standard (such as seminaries, gaols, halls

simply housed or not, the above model, if understood broadly to encompass the whole range of phenomena that usually accompany stable housing (for example, shelter, relationships and relative prosperity), carries significant weight in terms of one's social and spatial (dis)location. It also includes analysis of 'hidden homelessness' or 'invisible homelessness'; that is, to see homelessness as more than just those living on the streets, but as a much wider ranging social phenomenon. Furthermore, by constructing homelessness according to the 'normalized' expectations of a particular society, the model enables researchers to gauge how a significant spatial practice for contemporary society (domestic housing) can have a locative or dislocative effect. By breaking away from the norms of wider society, one is thrust into a marginal and deviant subject-position. Any conduct that is at odds with the practices of the normalized population is labelled as deviant, that is, the committing of 'behavior, thoughts, or attributes to which some people react negatively or would react negatively if they knew about it'.[48] Once identified, deviancy is often targeted as a justification to impose regulatory and discursive injunctions that have further exclusionary outcomes. Laura Stivers observes that '[c]onstructing a "diseased other" serves to define normality and stability; being housed or homeless serve as moral boundaries between who is respectable/clean or diseased/dirty'.[49]

Within this study, homelessness is understood as a multidimensional and multilayered concept that involves a marginalizing experience of dislocation, alienation and/or uprooting from home place.[50] It often expresses itself in tangible forms such as through displacement (to remove a subject from a stable place of orientation) or poverty (a lack of resources deemed necessary to maintain a reasonable standard of living in a particular cultural setting). Homelessness also manifests itself in varying levels of severity, from marginal vulnerability to chronic destitution. Because having a home is perceived as the norm, homelessness is often construed as deviant behaviour and deemed threatening to the smooth, uninterrupted functioning of social reality.

Causes of Homelessness

A distinction is often made in contemporary discussions of homelessness between *individualist* and *structuralist* causes of the phenomenon.

---

of residence), but nonetheless would not usually be regarded as homeless. See Chamberlain and Mackenzie, 'Understanding Contemporary Homelessness', pp. 291-94.

48. Paul Higgins and Mitch Mackinem, *Thinking about Deviance: A Realistic Perspective* (Lanham, MD: Rowman & Littlefield, 2nd edn, 2008), pp. 11-12.

49. Stivers, *Disrupting Homelessness*, p. 51.

50. For more on the marginalizing experience of homelessness, see Emily Meanwell, 'Experiencing Homelessness: A Review of Recent Literature', *Sociology Compass* 6.1 (2012), pp. 72-85.

These diverging myths and ideologies are actualized through institutional responses by government and social services and also shape the ways in which homelessness is constructed within wider society.

An Individualist Understanding. On the one hand, within the dominant individualist understanding an emphasis is put on an individual's decision to become homeless. Personal choice or individual failings are identified as determining factors that eventually lead to episodes of homelessness. Therefore, the blame, as it were, lies with the individuals affected. Those operating out of this ideology assume that homeless people simply require more discipline and training in the virtues of hard work, temperance and independence to influence different (or 'better') choices that will solve their lifestyle deficiencies.

An individualist understanding assumes that homelessness will be alleviated in wider society only if individuals change their behaviour and attitudes to fit with society's norms and expectations. As a result, people who become homeless are subjected to assimilation or criminalization efforts depending on how they are perceived by the dominant culture; those who are willing to be helped are deemed 'deserving' and are entitled to services that assist them in becoming reacquainted with normalized behaviour; those who are unwilling to cooperate and change their conduct are deemed 'undeserving' and subjected to laws that criminalize them.[51]

As part of this dominant narrative, then, an individualist understanding tends to downplay the homeless population's experiences of victimization by blaming them for their own so-called poor life choices. Their homelessness functions as a fantasmatic screen that further solidifies the reigning ideological–political order. Stivers, for instance, observes that

> Focusing on the moral failings of the victims of any social problem benefits those with power and privilege as it diverts attention from the inequitable institutions that are at the root of the problem. The way we justify repressive social policy that serves to buttress the status quo is to focus on the culture of the poor, that is, to show how poor people do not have middle-class values and then offer the paternalistic solution of teaching them to be 'upright citizens'.[52]

---

51. Stivers, *Disrupting Homelessness*, pp. 56-57. Most homeless services that work out of this ideology tend to focus on the 'problems' of the people they treat without challenging the economic, social and political exploitation they face in society. They teach 'life skills' to people with so-called underclass values and practices. As such, the approach poses no real threat to the established arrangements of social power in the community.

52. Stivers, *Disrupting Homelessness*, p. 15.

This understanding of homelessness has become thoroughly internalized into the modern Western epistemology: it not only grounds itself in common-sense, but feeds from and into the central concerns of neoliberal ideology that pertain to individualism, personal responsibility, and the privatization of welfare and other aspects of the state.[53] Crucially, it solidifies the belief that we all participate in society on a level playing field or with equal opportunity. Social class thus becomes a natural indicator of whether one has worked diligently and is intelligent enough to make the most of their opportunities. The plight of the homeless population becomes largely privatized and individualised; if they can be sufficiently disciplined in their economic and moral choices, then independence and normality should follow.

A Structuralist Understanding. On the other hand, a structuralist perspective holds that socio-economic factors such as the housing and labour markets which result from poor government policies predispose already 'at-risk' individuals to episodes of homelessness. In other words, homelessness is 'not a choice' but something that individuals are driven toward because of factors beyond their control. The causes are regarded as more complex, often involving a lack of empowerment or societal participation in addition to other cultural and social factors. Individuals are not equal in terms of the risk of becoming homeless; particular groups in society are more vulnerable than others and can be progressively disadvantaged over time. For example, a person with mental health problems is more likely to experience exclusion in free market socio-economic environments where there is inadequate low income housing and community support. Furthermore, the after-effects of colonization on an indigenous population can have a long-lasting impact over generations, resulting in a disproportionate overrepresentation of indigenous people in the homeless statistics.[54]

Bouma-Prediger and Walsh identify the following factors as contributing to the 'structural determinants' for the current crisis of Western socio-economic homelessness in the twenty-first century:

a. *Globalization*—Economic liberalization has led to a growing disparity between the rich and the poor in which economic growth is experienced predominantly by the wealthy and the poor are excluded from equal participation.

b. *Lack of affordable housing*—The supply of adequate housing that is affordable to the working poor, the unemployed and the sick does not often meet demand.

---

53. Harvey, *Neoliberalism*, p. 5.

54. See, for example, Chris Talbot, 'Social Exclusion and Homelessness: Everyone's Responsibility' (Adelaide: Uniting Care, Wesley, 2003), p. 15.

c. *Diminished social safety net*—The neoliberal political agenda believes the government should get itself out of providing social services, particularly housing, for those on the social and economic margins of society.[55]

If the responsibility for homelessness lies with wider society, as the structuralist understanding assumes, then public and governmental institutions ought to transform their systems and structures so that the more vulnerable are better protected from becoming homeless. For instance, this might include reforming the distribution of wealth and welfare. Institutions should be challenged to 'empower' the marginalized rather than exclude them, and to treat them as real people by restoring their lost dignity. A typical response from governmental or social agencies might involve the provision of low income housing and/or additional 'on the ground' social and mental health services.

While such measures go some way toward alleviating homelessness, they can cause resentment within the normalized population. This is because the structuralist understanding has become tainted by a reactionary counter-discourse against the welfare state, which is seen to foster dependency relationships between the state and a 'parasitic' underclass. Moreover, it is often objected that structural responses to homelessness can only go so far before they become too paternalistic and rob the homeless of their agency.[56] The most cutting criticism of a structuralist approach, however, concerns the limited impact it is ever likely to have at ending homelessness. While reforming inequitable systems and structures is a worthy enough pursuit, its net effect is to alleviate pockets of homelessness, while leaving the basic arrangements of power in society untouched.[57] Consensual and incremental reforms may work, possibly at a local level, but they do not address home-

---

55. Bouma-Prediger and Walsh, *Beyond Homelessness*, pp. 92-103.

56. See Susan Ruddick, *Young and Homeless in Hollywood: Mapping Social Identities* (New York: Routledge, 1996); Susan Ruddick, 'Heterotopias of the Homeless: Strategies and Tactics of Placemaking in Los Angeles', *Journal of Theory, Culture, and Politics* 3.3 (1990), pp. 184-201. See the response of: David Harvey, 'Social Justice, Postmodernism and the City', *International Journal of Urban and Regional Research* 16 (1992), pp. 588-601.

57. Writing on the housing crisis in Germany in the 1870s, Engels argues that the revolutionary politics of the proletariat cannot be achieved through a series of reforms because 'it is not that the solution to the housing question simultaneously solves the social question, but that only by the solution of the social question, that is, by the abolition of the capitalist mode of production, is the solution of the housing question made possible'. See Friedrich Engels, 'The Housing Question', in *Volksstaat* (reprinted by the Co-operative Publishing Society of Foreign Workers, 1872). Available online at http://www.marxists.org/archive/marx/works/1872/housing-question/index.htm.

lessness as a global phenomenon, linked to the ever-expanding, and sometimes rampantly destructive, capitalist basis of the global economy.

A Symptomatic Understanding. Having noted some of the inadequacies of the individualist and structuralist understandings of homelessness, it is prudent to chart an alternative ideological position from which this study can probe the nexus between Jesus and homelessness. For Žižek, the Hegelian logic of the 'negation of negation' (a self-referential double-negation) does not in fact mean the return to a positive identity through synthesis, but rather is achieved through a radicalization of the negative gesture. In other words, the antithetical component, which presupposes the formal dimensions of its thesis, must be radicalized in order to break free from the binding logics of the dominant ideology and demonstrate its deficiency as a totalizing ideology. The binary that upholds the dominant discourse, that homelessness is primarily the result of individual failure, requires the privileging of alternative narratives that not only counter it but positively break apart its dominance.[58]

It is, therefore, the contention of this study that the structuralist understanding of homelessness does not go far enough in negating the dominant discourse. In fact, by attempting to undermine the individualist understanding, it potentially re-inscribes the wider ideological–political constellation through its antithetical disposition. Rather than conceiving of homelessness as a lifestyle choice or a consequence of structural failure, this study radicalizes homelessness by suggesting that it functions positively as an 'excremental remainder' to the fundamental configuration of modes of production within advanced capitalist societies. It emerges not because of structural *failure* but because the basic arrangements of power within society are functioning smoothly and as expected.

As mentioned above, Žižek himself attributes contemporary homelessness to the smooth, uninterrupted functioning of the modern capitalist economic system. This excess, however, is rooted in the very ideological apparatus of the neoliberal-democratic system itself: by shifting the responsibility for citizens' welfare away from the state and toward the individual, neoliberal thinking solidifies itself as a supremely effective ideological formula. The presence of homelessness thus emerges as a *symptom* alerting us to the obscene underside of the reigning ideological–political order. In

---

58. Recent scholarship on homelessness has pointed out the misleading binary nature in which debates are framed, leading many to argue for a combined approach that takes note of both the structural components and the predisposition that certain 'at risk' individuals will have toward becoming homeless. See Paul Koegel, 'Causes of Homelessness: Overview', in *Encyclopedia of Homelessness* (ed. David Levinson; London: Sage, 2004), pp. 50-58.

Žižek's reading of Lacan, the symptom is a form of bodily communication that points to an underlying condition or disease. The symptom also functions as a mechanism whereby the subject unknowingly organizes his or her *jouissance* to the point at which the subject 'loves his symptom more than himself'.[59]

Conventional attempts to alleviate homelessness, whether operating out of individualist or structuralist understandings, merely prolong the life of the current ideological–political configuration, of which homelessness is an undesirable by-product. Therapeutic attention is turned away from reality and toward the fantasy of the Real, the dimension in which enjoyment is articulated. As a symptom of deeper afflictions, tending to the immediate needs of the homeless population is ultimately ineffectual and a distraction: 'as soon as we aim directly at them [the symptom], as soon as our activity is directly motivated by them, our procedure becomes self-defeating'.[60]

The proper 'solution' to homelessness is not to be found in a liberal shift of consciousness (e.g. by spreading the counter-discourse that homelessness is not a choice or that those affected are real people with feelings and so on), but through a seismic shift in the political economy. As we will see below, it is within this constellation of fraught ideologies that the nexus between Jesus and homelessness surfaces as an exploitable gap.

Jesus and Homelessness

Having determined a suitable definition of homelessness and considered its function within the wider ideological–political edifice of neoliberal capitalism, we now turn to its effects on biblical interpretation. How might the connection between Jesus and homelessness sustain the fantasmatic dimension that structures and upholds the reigning ideological–political order? Furthermore, how might we utilize this connection to disrupt dominant ideologies of homelessness as they appear in both biblical interpretation and the construction of social reality?

Ideology and Jesus' Homelessness
In his study of the historical Jesus, which pays close attention to the use of space and place, Halvor Moxnes cautions against reading Jesus through the lens of home and homelessness because of its loaded meaning for the Western, middle-class individual (or, perhaps more specifically, the ideology of the propertied, white, colonizing male). He writes:

59. Žižek, *Sublime Object*, pp. 71-92.
60. Žižek, *Sublime Object*, p. 91.

> Home place is associated with stability, safety, and support, often in con-
> trast to workplace or foreign places. Thus, home is associated with ideals,
> often filled with nostalgic emotions. Many will think that the ideas associ-
> ated with home are universal. Since they are so important to us, we auto-
> matically presuppose that they must have been the same for people in
> previous times and in different places as well.[61]

This conception of 'home' emerged during the rise of the bourgeoisie in the
eighteenth and nineteenth centuries, wherein the domestic sphere became
a place of refuge or haven away from the work and noise of everyday life.
Moxnes goes on to argue that these changes to the cultural presuppositions
of Western society have even had an impact on English translations of the
Bible. Over the centuries translators have increasingly rendered the Greek
word for house and household (οἶκος/οἰκία) as 'home'. This influences the
reception of the text by giving the impression that οἶκος/οἰκία refers to a
secluded private area, in line with modern bourgeois attitudes, instead of the
more public space of first-century Palestine. As Moxnes puts it, '[i]n many
instances this gives a "homey" feeling—it reflects a modern, stereotypical
use of 'home' even when it is not appropriate'.[62]

While contemporary experiences of home and its function for social
growth and cohesion are different from the experiences of those who lived
in the first century, this does not prevent contemporary insights from illu-
minating particular themes and/or textures within the text. Not only has the
precedent been set by the proliferation of ideological biblical scholarship
that brings concerns, clearly fuelled by contemporary agendas and modes
of thinking, to the rhetorical interpretation of the text, but historical-critical
scholarship has itself been 'outed' as an ideological product of the Euro-
pean Enlightenment. In fact, the '[e]xplicit use of modern . . . categories on
ancient material creates awareness that history is always reconstruction, and
it also makes it possible to identify differences between modern and ancient
societies'.[63] Such a position does not infer the impossibility of historical
reconstruction, but rather suggests that we cannot help but read the text as
moderns using modern categories and modes of thinking.

It is also evident that the ideological categories discussed above have,
to a large extent, shaped the ways in which the connection between Jesus
and homelessness has been interpreted within contemporary scholarship.
Because the majority of biblical scholars are bred and trained within the
dominant neoliberal capitalist culture (including the neoliberalization of

---

61. Moxnes, *Putting Jesus in his Place*, p. 25.
62. Moxnes, *Putting Jesus in his Place*, p. 26.
63. Denise Kimber Buell *et al.*, 'Cultural Complexity and Intersectionality in the
Study of the Jesus Movement', *BibInt* 18.4-5 (2010), p. 310.

higher education itself),[64] there is a dialogical relationship between dominant ideologies of homelessness and the interpretation of the connection between Jesus and homelessness. In fact, the homelessness of Jesus is predominantly framed as a lifestyle choice and consequence of his God-ordained mission, rather than a consequence of, or retreat from, inhospitable social, economic and political conditions. Could not Jesus' homelessness also be regarded as a symptom? Not, of course, as a direct result of capitalism, but rather as a by-product of the ideological–political and socio-economic edifice of first-century Palestine and Galilee.

On the rare occasion when scholars do explicitly consider the possibility of homelessness with respect to Matthew's Jesus simulacrum, the ideological points discussed above will almost inevitably shape their answer. In his commentary on Matthew, John Nolland, for example, insists that Jesus cannot possibly be homeless because he has a house in Capernaum (a detail unique to the Matthean text: e.g. 9.10, 28; 12.46; 13.1, 36; 17.25) and because Jesus and the disciples are expected to be provided with temporary lodging during their travels (10.12-14).[65] By equating *homelessness* with *houselessness*, however, Nolland uncritically conflates the concepts of 'house' and 'home', which, as indicated above, assumes the emergence of capitalist modes of production and concepts of private property (see further, Chapter 4).

Equally problematic are interpretations that uncritically romanticize (and in some cases spiritualize) the connection between Jesus and homelessness. The reasoning, usually implied, is that Jesus *chooses* to lead an itinerant life as part of his religious vocation. Gerd Theissen's characterization of Jesus as a wandering charismatic, for example, has been incredibly effective at promulgating a *voluntary* conception of homelessness in both historical-Jesus and Gospel studies.[66] While commenting on the mission discourse in Matthew 10, Luz, for instance, writes that

> Palestinian Christianity originated as a movement of itinerant radicalism. Its roots go back to Jesus; the disciples he called to follow him and to witness to the imminent kingdom of God as he did shared his style of life and were poor and homeless. They gave up their jobs and their family for the time they were together with Jesus. After their master's death many of them continued this way of life.[67]

64. See Joyce E. Canaan and Wesley Shumar (eds.), *Structure and Agency in the Neoliberal University* (New York: Routledge, 2008).

65. John Nolland, *The Gospel of Matthew: A Commentary on the Greek Text* (Grand Rapids, MI: Eerdmans, 2005), p. 366; cf. Crosby, *House of Disciples*, p. 3.

66. Theissen, *Sociology*; cf. Crossan, *Jesus*.

67. Luz, *Matthew in History*, p. 44; cf. Freyne, who asks '[w]hat of Jesus' more permanent followers of Galilean origin? The fact that a whole body of sayings has been transmitted in his name advocating attitudes of homelessness, separation from

This way of framing Christian origins feeds from the dominant discourse that homelessness results from choices made arbitrarily by an individual. Absent from this summary is any discussion of hostile political structures that may have contributed to these instances of itinerancy. It also re-narrates the common myth of the itinerant religious man who piously forgoes worldly possessions. The vocational framing tends to romanticize and thus obscure a number of textures within the Gospel that indicate, or might indicate, forced displacement.

As will be demonstrated in subsequent chapters, the spiritualization of Jesus' homelessness is an effective strategy of ideological containment. A more careful reading of the text would posit that Matthew's Jesus simulacrum is homeless because he is driven from normalized societal institutions, at times including shelter, as a result of external pressures and events. Jesus' homelessness emerges as a by-product to the smooth, uninterrupted functioning of the social, economic and political structures of first-century Palestine and Galilee as they are encoded within the Matthean text. Not only is this interpretive strategy more accountable to the politics of contemporary homelessness (the world before the text), but it also connects the Matthean Jesus to the political, social and economic struggles of his own context (the world behind the text that is encoded within the world of the text).

A New Framework for Reading Matthew's Jesus
As we have seen, the framework through which we interpret homelessness has tangible effects upon not only biblical interpretation but also the construction of social reality. A gesture of radical desublimation can be achieved through directly depicting what the homelessness of Jesus might actually look like; the reversal of the sublime object into abject: an abhorrent, excremental excess, without home or hearth. The current study approaches the Matthean text under the assumption that homelessness, understood as displacement or placelessness, is symptomatic of the arrangements of power in a society; it emerges as an excremental remainder to the smooth, uninterrupted functioning of the ideological–political order. This is the kernel or central defining category of the hermeneutic that will be brought into dialogue with specific episodes from Matthew's story of Jesus and the rhetoric

---

the family and poverty as the sure way to enter the kingdom he proclaimed and share in the glory of the coming Son of Man, is a clear indication that such a life-style was actually adopted by some at least of his followers and taken extremely seriously by them. Having its origins in Jesus' own attitudes this movement must have further developed after his death, as one can detect from the combination of his sayings with those of early Christian prophets within the same tradition.' See Sean Freyne, *Galilee: From Alexander the Great to Hadrian* (Wilmington, DE: Michael Glazier, 1980), p. 374.

of dominant Matthean scholarship.[68] The potent description of homelessness as undesirable waste matter (language borrowed from Žižek) assists
in disrupting the romanticization of Jesus' homelessness as it appears in
dominant interpretations of the text. In order to pursue this reading, the
definitions and categories of homelessness discussed above will be brought
into dialogue with a number of episodes from the Matthean text. How, for
example, does Jesus' characterization reflect agency, deviancy and/or displacement? How might settings and environments contribute to structural
challenges? And further, how is Jesus' behaviour construed with regard to
the norms of his own social context?

Such an approach draws to an extent upon existing social-scientific
approaches to the Gospel of Matthew that have already sought to catego-
rize the deviancy of Jesus within his Mediterranean social world. A limitation to existing social-scientific approaches, however, is that they rarely
give consideration to the ideological complications in the world before the
text. In their book *Calling Jesus Names*, Bruce J. Malina and Jerome H.
Neyrey employ cross-cultural, social-scientific models of 'deviancy' and
'prominence' on the Matthean Jesus.[69] The authors suggest that a deviant is
a person 'out of place' who is then labelled negatively by his contemporaries, whereas a prominent is a person perceived to be out of place to such an
extent as to be redefined (sublimated) in a new, positive way. They contend
that

> [t]he gospel of Matthew presents a retrospective interpretation of a person,
> Jesus of Nazareth, evaluated by those he called and/or helped as promi-
> nent, yet labelled by the gatekeepers of society as deviant. The gatekeepers
> won in their assessment; witness the acclamation of the Jerusalem crowds
> at the trial scene. Thus, 'Jesus the deviant' is duly shamed in public, sym-
> bolling the validity of elite judgment, elite interests and elite standing.
> Yet with his post-death appearances and even earlier, Jesus was perceived
> as prominent. Given the success of the Jerusalem elite in having Jesus
> labelled a deviant, it would be the task of those acclaiming his prominence
> to effect a transformation of the label.[70]

The gatekeepers Malina and Neyrey refer to here are the power brokers
of Jesus' society, not just the political and religious elite but members of the

---

68. This is not to suggest that the homelessness of Jesus is necessarily presented by
the implied author entirely through either a structural or individualist understanding.
Indeed there are a number of episodes that attribute significant agency to the Matthean
Jesus, but these need to be conceived of within the wider context of Jesus as a systematically and progressively marginalized subject.

69. Bruce J. Malina and Jerome H. Neyrey, *Calling Jesus Names: The Social Value
of Labels in Matthew* (Sonoma, CA: Polebridge Press, 1988).

70. Malina and Neyrey, *Calling Jesus Names,* p. 40.

normalized population who live according to the existing power arrangements in society.

This raises the question: if the text itself already engages in a process of
sublimation to romanticize Jesus' deviancy, how do we go about resisting
such moves? A hermeneutic of radical desublimation will attempt to focus
on the points at which both the text and social processes encoded within the
text break down. Purely descriptive models are useful as explanatory tools,
but it is only when these mechanistic categories fail that we encounter fissures in the wider ideological–political system. While a focus on the ancient
agrarian and imperial world of Matthew's Jesus simulacrum becomes the
highlighted social, political and economic context through which his apparent homelessness is explained, it is the ideological ruptures that occur in
both this encoded world and in our own context for reading that Jesus'
homelessness is to be interpreted.

Social Class. In terms of economic stratification or social class, for example, we run into a problem in that existing interpretations of Matthew's
Jesus simulacrum tend to assume, rather uncritically, that he enjoys relative economic security, given his identification as the son of a carpenter
in Mt. 13.55. In actual fact, as will be discussed in Chapter 5, it is unwar-
ranted to assume that Matthew's Jesus is working at all, given that this
very text brings his honour into disrepute by underscoring his failure to
fulfil familial economic obligations. Moreover, attributing financial security to Jesus makes little sense if we are also to regard him as essentially
homeless, an itinerant who resides largely outside the dominant kinship
structures of the ancient world in addition to the wider economic system.
Even if he was working prior to his public ministry, a comfortable leisured
existence could only be secured by the possession of land, of which Jesus
has none.

One major Marxist study on the history of class in the ancient world that
proves only partially helpful in determining the Matthean Jesus' social class
is G.E.M. de Ste Croix's *The Class Struggles in Ancient Greece* (which
actually covers a broad geographical and chronological period of the Greek-
speaking ancient world including the Roman era).[71] De Ste Croix draws
explicitly on Karl Marx's theory of class antagonism under capitalism to
develop a detailed breakdown of social class and the structural role of class
exploitation in the ancient Greco-Roman world. According to de Ste Croix,

---

71. G.E.M. de Ste Croix, *The Class Struggle in the Ancient Greek World* (Ithaca,
NY: Cornell University Press, 1981). See also the helpful summary in Roland Boer,
Criticism of Theology: On Marxism and Theology III (Historical Materialism, 27;
Leiden: Brill, 2011), pp. 103-58.

land and slaves were the principal means of production in antiquity, and direct forced labour, which enabled a small class of wealthy landowners to extract a weighty surplus, was the indispensable basis to the economic system.[72] De Ste Croix devotes considerable attention to the major class groups: landowners (or the propertied classes), retainers, peasants (including both farmers and artisans), freedmen, and finally slaves and/or unfree labourers. But what about those who do not work? An oversight to de Ste Croix's analysis is that he appears to assume 'full employment' in the ancient world, and so never adequately considers the discarded labour power resulting from the ruling classes' limited needs for employment. While he occasionally discusses instances of downward social mobility, such as through 'debt bondage', whereby a debtor sells himself into indentured servitude or even slavery, it appears that one cannot exist outside the dominant labour system itself, except in the case of death.

A category that de Ste Croix pays no attention to in his summary of Marx, but which ties the sociological process of deviancy to its base layer of economic inequality, is that of the *lumpenproletariat*. In traditional Marxist analysis, the *lumpenproletariat* refers to members of or below the working class who are not proletarians, that is, those who reside outside of the wage-labour system. Marx defined the *lumpenproletariat* as a group consisting of 'thieves and criminals of all kinds, living on the crumbs of society, people without a definite trade, vagabonds, *gens sans feu et sans aveu* [folk without hearth or home]'.[73] The *lumpenproletariat* own no means of production, do not work for wages, and are incapable of, or unwilling to engage in, regular wage labour in order to maintain themselves. In German, *Lumpen* signifies dirty old rags, scraps of cloth and so on, and is applied to rogues and deviant people. Marx intended this pejorative usage and viewed the *lumpenproletariat* with a moralizing and dismissive contempt. This is because, accord-

72. De Ste Croix notes that a slave-based mode of production did not apply exclusively in Hellenistic Syria through to Egypt. There it remained primarily a tributary system. See de Ste Croix, *Class Struggle*, pp. 227-28.

73. Karl Marx and Friedrich Engels, *Selected Works*, vol. 1 (Moscow: Progress Publishers, 1969), p. 219. Focusing on the criminality of the *lumpenproletariat,* Veltmeyer expands the definition to encompass 'people who are not regularly employed and, not owning property or other forms of income-producing wealth, are forced into lives of crime, parasitical dependence or other forms of social deviance. In this situation are a wide assortment of people—burglars, muggers, hustlers of all kinds, small time pimps, drug addicts, beggars, street prostitutes, alcoholics, tramps, low level dope dealers, main-streeters, hippies and others who have given up trying to find regular work. They reject productive labour and live off the system.' See Henry Veltmeyer, *The Canadian Class Structure* (Toronto: Garamond, 1986), p. 105.

ing to him, they possess little revolutionary potential given that they reside outside of the forces of production and have no class consciousness.[74]

Since Marx, the discussion of the *lumpenproletariat* has occasionally taken a less cynical stance. According to Frantz Fanon, for example, the *lumpenproletariat* possess a tremendous revolutionary potential because, while the productively employed working class is relatively privileged, the *lumpenproletariat* has nothing to lose. This feeds an innately destructive attitude toward the existing social order. Fanon cautions that unless organized by revolutionary forces, the *lumpenproletariat* can be easily misused by the exploiting classes.[75] This is observable within contemporary neoliberal politics in which sections of the *lumpenproletariat* (such as beneficiaries) are characterized as living off the labour of the mainstream working class; regarded as parasites, they are frequently targeted by reactionary politics.

The closest equivalent to the *lumpenproletariat* within the class structure of first-century Palestinian society is probably that of the *expendable* class, a classification conspicuously absent from de Ste Croix's detailed breakdown. The expendable class is an excessive excremental zero-value element, which, while formally part of the system, has no proper place within it. Gerhard E. Lenski suggests that within agrarian societies the expendable class consisted of up to 10 percent of the total population. Given that agrarian societies tended to produce more people than the dominant classes found it profitable to employ, they functioned as a surplus to the demands of labour. At the very bottom of the social hierarchy, they were also deemed to fall outside the purview of social responsibility.[76] According to Saldarini, the expendable class was for those whom society had no place or need. In a description that rings true of not only the modern homeless population but also the Matthean Jesus, he writes that expendables had been displaced for a variety of reasons, including 'population pressures or [because] they did

74. In one of his more polemical passages, Marx refers to the lumpen as 'the social scum, that passively rotting mass thrown off by the lowest layers of the old society'. See Marx and Engels, *Selected Works*, I, p. 118.

75. Frantz Fanon, *The Wretched of the Earth* (trans. Constance Farrington; London: Penguin, 1963). More recently, some scholars have identified the category of the *lumpenproletariat* as a potential political agent. See Nicholas Thoburn, 'Difference in Marx: The *Lumpenproletariat* and the Proletarian Unnamable', *Economy and Society* 31 (2002), pp. 434-60; Philippe Bourgois and Jeff Schonberg, *Righteous Dopefiend* (Berkeley, CA: University of California Press, 2009).

76. Gerhard E. Lenski, *Power and Privilege: A Theory of Social Stratification* (New York: McGraw-Hill, 1966), pp. 180-84. Lenski's work has had a significant impact on social-scientific criticism within Gospel scholarship. See Dennis C. Duling, 'Empire: Theories, Methods, Models', in *The Gospel of Matthew in its Roman Imperial Context* (ed. John Riches and David C. Sim; London: T. & T. Clark, 2005), pp. 49-74.

not fit into society. They tended to be landless and itinerant with no normal family life and a high death rate'.[77] As my re-reading of the Matthean text will show, although Jesus is initially associated with a family of artisans, he eventually descends the social ladder to occupy the socio-symbolic space of an expendable. A constitutive but excremental part of the surplus to the smooth functioning of the wider economic order, he is predictably disposed of on the cross at Golgotha.

Violence. A final ideological schematic that further radicalizes the structural determinants of homelessness can be found, once more, in the critical theory of Žižek. In his treatise on violence, Žižek distinguishes between two broad categories of violence in the world: first, *subjective* violence is the more overt form in which violence is performed by a clearly identifiable agent; second, *objective* violence, which includes both a 'symbolic' violence embodied in language and its forms and 'systemic' violence, or the consequences of the smooth functioning of our economic and political systems—the exploitation of individuals and groups inherent within the so-called 'normal' functioning of society.[78] In the case of the ancient agrarian world, the expendable class was the constitutive exception. Members functioned as both the displaced excess to the routine productive forces as well as the prime targets of exclusionary rhetoric and subjective manifestations of violence that kept the wider ideological–political constellation in order.

The prevalence of objective violence is especially downplayed within neoliberal ideology for it negates the central tenants of personal responsibility, equal opportunity, freedom of exchange and so on. So too, within contemporary biblical interpretation, the contribution of objective violence toward the production of Jesus' homelessness is often overlooked. By foregrounding the various layers of violence as they are embedded within the world of the text, however, the production of Jesus' highly vulnerable subject-position features as a significant component of his targeting and execution by the ruling classes. In other words, the surplus that gives rise to Jesus' offensiveness is entwined with his homelessness, or more precisely, his status as a displaced outsider. The overt violence of his crucifixion is merely a reflection of the covert violence of the wider economic, political and social system within which his character is thoroughly embedded.

With the ideological parameters of this project now established, it is important to address how these will be integrated into a careful reading of the Matthean text. The final section of this chapter introduces the strategies of socio-rhetorical criticism, after which I begin my re-reading of texts.

77. Anthony J. Saldarini, *Pharisees, Scribes and Sadducees in Palestinian Society* (Grand Rapids, MI: Eerdmans, 2nd edn, 2001), p. 44.
78. Slavoj Žižek, *Violence* (Big Ideas; London: Profile Books, 2008), pp. 1-2.

Socio-Rhetorical Criticism

The biblical methodology employed in this study is that of socio-rhetorical interpretation. First named by Vernon K. Robbins,[79] it has since become in its various manifestations a widely used interpretive analytics for the study of the NT.[80] It seeks to integrate a number of existing methodologies within the field of biblical studies by focusing on a selection of 'textures' in order to produce well-rounded and multidimensional readings of texts. According to Robbins, 'the hyphenated prefix "socio-" refers to the rich resources of modern anthropology and sociology' that socio-rhetorical criticism draws from in order to analyse class structures, social systems and power differentiations as they are encoded within the text, whereas the term 'rhetorical' refers to the analysis of language as it is constructed with the intent of persuasion. Robbins's more recent work has sought to incorporate six rhetorolects found in early Christian discourse, namely, prophetic, apocalyptic, wisdom, precreation, priestly and miracle.[81] Within the present study, however, the focus is placed on an exploration of the textures of texts, as outlined in his two guidebooks published during the mid-1990s.[82] In these works, Robbins divides the interpretive analytics into the following categories: inner texture, intertexture, social and cultural texture, ideological texture and sacred texture.

Ideological Texture
Within this book, socio-rhetorical criticism is configured to produce readings that disrupt dominant ideologies of homelessness in the interpretation

---

79. Vernon K. Robbins, *Jesus the Teacher: A Socio-Rhetorical Interpretation of Mark* (Minneapolis, MN: Fortress Press, 1984).

80. The term 'socio-rhetorical' has also been applied to a series of recent commentaries by Ben Witherington III. Watson notes that although Witherington's commentaries claim to be socio-rhetorical, 'they do not move beyond traditional historical-critical methods of interpretation with an emphasis in social history'. See Duane F. Watson, 'Why We Need Socio-Rhetorical Commentary and What It Might Look Like', in *Rhetorical Criticism and the Bible* (ed. Stanley E. Porter and Dennis L. Stamps; London: Sheffield Academic Press, 2002), p. 129. Similarly, there is not much in Keener's commentary on Matthew (in fact, a reissue of his 1999 historical-critical commentary) that might be considered to fit into the socio-rhetorical approach as it has been developed by Robbins; see Craig S. Keener, *The Gospel of Matthew: A Socio-Rhetorical Commentary* (Grand Rapids, MI: Eerdmans, 2009).

81. Vernon K. Robbins, *The Invention of Christian Discourse*, vol. 1 (Blandform Forum, UK: Deo, 2009).

82. Vernon K. Robbins, *Exploring the Texture of Texts: A Guide to Socio-Rhetorical Interpretation* (Valley Forge, PA: Trinity Press International, 1996); Vernon K. Robbins, *The Tapestry of Early Christian Discourse: Rhetoric, Society and Ideology* (London: Routledge, 1996).

of Matthew's Jesus simulacrum. This being the case, ideological texture is given priority and informs the interpretation of other textures. Because ideology generates every text and every interpretation, it is inseparable from the rhetorical and socio-cultural aspects of texts.[83] As Fredric Jameson argues, political analysis is not some supplementary method to literary criticism, but rather it features as the absolute horizon of all reading and its interpretation.[84] The interpretations that follow seek not an exhaustive exegesis of the text but rather to discover what meaning and meaning effects might emerge when the various pericopes are read through the ideological framework outlined above. This involves a strategic focus on textures that are best suited to the ideological–political considerations of each pericope. In bringing the ideological texture of the text into dialogue with the analysis of other textures, new meanings and meaning effects are able to materialize.

Exploration of ideological texture involves determining how the sublimation of Jesus' homelessness functions as a gap within biblical interpretation. As indicated above, the romanticization of Jesus' homelessness anchors our *jouissance* to dominant ideologies of homelessness in the world before the text by enabling the reader to organize his or her fantasy in a way that sustains the prevailing arrangements of power in society. Within this study, ideological criticism occurs as a gesture of radical desublimation; our hermeneutical gaze is focused on the crack that divorces Jesus' homelessness as a sublime object from the abject, excremental remainder of homelessness that is encoded in the world of the text. In doing so, the structure of sublimation—and its fantasmatic support to the wider ideological–political edifice—is potentially traversed.

Inner Texture

What Robbins calls the inner texture of a text concerns features such as the repetition of particular words, the narrative structure, alternation of speech and storytelling, argumentative and rhetorical textures, and the aesthetics of a text. The inner textual analysis in this study predominantly draws on the

---

83. See Elisabeth Schüssler Fiorenza, *The Power of the Word: Scripture and the Rhetoric of Empire* (Minneapolis, MN: Fortress Press, 2007), p. 21. For a response to Schüssler Fiorenza, see Vernon K. Robbins, 'The Rhetorical Full-Turn in Biblical Interpretation and its Relevance for Feminist Hermeneutics', in *Her Master's Tools? Feminist and Postcolonial Engagements of Historical-Critical Discourse* (ed. Caroline Vander Stichele and Todd Penner; Atlanta, GA: Society of Biblical Literature, 2005), pp. 109-28; Priscilla Geisterfer, 'Full Turns and Half Turns: Engaging the Dialogue/ Dance between Elisabeth Schüssler Fiorenza and Vernon Robbins', in *Her Master's Tools? Feminist and Postcolonial Engagements of Historical-Critical Discourse* (ed. Caroline Vander Stichele and Todd Penner; Atlanta, GA: Society of Biblical Literature, 2005), pp. 129-44.

84. Jameson, *Political Unconscious*.

tools of narrative criticism, which emerged in the 1980s primarily out of the engagement of scholars with non-biblical literary criticism and has since become a widely used methodology in its own right.[85]

Within narrative criticism a text is seen to involve an *implied author,* who is distinguished from the historical author of the text, an *implied reader,* who functions as the anticipated ideal reader, and the narrative itself, which employs the rhetorical device of the narrator to tell the story to a narra-tee.[86] Narrative critics determine how traditional narrative categories such as character, plot and setting, as constructed by the implied author within the narrative, are used discursively to enact or elicit a particular desired response from the implied reader.[87]

This study utilizes inner-textual analysis to determine how the connec-tion between Jesus and homelessness is narrated within the story world of the text, observing especially the narrative components that disrupt domi-nant ideologies of homelessness within the text and its interpretation. As the framework of our desire, fantasy is the primordial form of narrative. Draw-ing from psychoanalytic theory, Žižek observes that narrative emerges as a way of resolving some fundamental antagonism by re-arranging its terms into temporal succession. In other words, it is 'the very form of narrative which bears witness to some repressed antagonism'.[88] Narratives are not closed systems nor do they represent reality; rather, narrativization obfus-cates traumatic elements and textures. Breaks within the text are, in fact, more radical than mere narrative deployments, since they gesture toward the paradoxical arrangement of fantasy's transcendental schematic.

---

85. For use of narrative criticism within the NT, see Mark Allan Powell, *What Is Narrative Criticism?* (GBS; Minneapolis, MN: Augsburg Fortress Press, 1990); James L. Resseguie, *Narrative Criticism of the New Testament: An Introduction* (Grand Rap-ids, MI: Baker Academic, 2005). For its use in Matthew, see Janice Capel Anderson, *Matthew's Narrative Web: Over, and Over, and Over Again* (JSNTSup, 91; Sheffield: Sheffield Academic Press, 1994); Jack Dean Kingsbury, *Matthew as Story* (Philadel-phia, PA: Fortress Press, 2nd edn, 1988); Mark Allan Powell, 'Literary Approaches and the Gospel of Matthew', in *Methods for Matthew* (ed. Mark Allan Powell; Cambridge: Cambridge University Press, 2009), pp. 44-82.

86. Powell, *Narrative Criticism,* pp. 19-21.

87. Narrative criticism has tended to make the distinction between 'story' and 'discourse' in the construction of a text (in Matthew's Gospel, for instance, the story is the life of Jesus from his conception to his death and resurrection; the discourse of Matthew is the means whereby this story of Jesus' life is told). See, for instance, Kingsbury, *Matthew as Story,* p. 3. In the present study, however, discourse refers to the ideological–political effect of a particular linguistic construction both within the text and its interpretation. For a poststructuralist critique of the 'story' and 'discourse' binary, see The Bible and Culture Collective, *The Postmodern Bible* (New Haven, CT: Yale University Press, 1995), p. 112.

88. Žižek, *Plague of Fantasies,* pp. 11-12.

Engagement with inner texture, then, leads to an exploration of not only formal narrative elements but also disjunctions or gaps within the text. While the inner texture of the text lies within the configuration of words in the text itself, more meaning and reality effects can be explored through engagement with other aspects of the text's layered textures.

Social and Cultural Texture
Analysis of social and cultural texture involves the use of tools from the fields of cultural anthropology and sociology in order to understand various cultural phenomena in the world behind the text encoded in the world inside of the text. Social and cultural texture, as Robbins describes it, concerns the capacity of the text to support social reform, withdrawal, or opposition, and to evoke cultural perceptions of dominance, subordination, difference, or exclusion. The Context Group, an international collaboration of scholars, has pioneered this social-scientific approach to the study of the NT.[89] The approach has not been without criticism, however, in particular because it applies static generalized models onto polyphonic cultural settings.[90] Moreover, there are ideological complications behind the approach, especially with regard to the construction of Jewish identity and contemporary Palestinian-Israeli politics, which have been largely disavowed.[91] The following analysis is careful to nuance models as it investigates the social location of Jesus at various points in the Matthean narrative by discussing his relationship to dominant social structures and institutions of the first-century Mediterranean region, and more specifically in Palestine and Galilee.

Jesus' homelessness, if understood in terms of estrangement and displacement, can be assessed according to the central cultural and social institutions and political structures of Greco-Roman society. For example, the patriarchal family was regarded as the highlighted institution of concern within ancient Mediterranean social systems. It functioned as the basic social unit and acted as an organizing principle for all of life; it was there-

89. For a survey of social-scientific studies in the Gospel of Matthew, see Dennis C. Duling, *A Marginal Scribe: Studies in the Gospel of Matthew in a Social-Scientific Perspective* (Eugene, OR: Cascade, 2011), pp. 40-51. For a more general overview of prominent social-scientific topics, see Dietmar Neufeld and Richard E. DeMaris (eds.), *Understanding the Social World of the New Testament* (New York: Routledge, 2010).

90. Louise Joy Lawrence, *An Ethnography of the Gospel of Matthew* (WUNT, 2; Tübingen: Mohr Siebeck, 2003); cf. Zeba A. Crook, 'Structure versus Agency in Studies of the Biblical Social World: Engaging with Louise Lawrence', *JSNT* 29 (2007), pp. 251-75.

91. See especially Robert J. Myles and James G. Crossley, 'Biblical Scholarship, Jews and Israel: On Bruce Malina, Conspiracy Theories and Ideological Contradictions', *Bible and Interpretation* (2012), http://www.bibleinterp.com/opeds/myl368013. shtml.

fore the institution that became central to one's status and the derivative of all social meaning and position.[92] Similarly, the Greco-Roman household (οἶκος/οἰκία) was seen as an essential microcosm within the Roman Empire, under the emperor as the 'Father of the Fatherland' or head of the household, who exercised authority and protection in return for obedience and submissive devotion.[93] The Matthean Jesus comes into strong conflict with these and other institutions and so is progressively alienated from normalized society in much the same way as the contemporary homeless population become estranged from society.[94]

Another important area of social and cultural analysis concerns the process of marginalization, that is, the means by which a subject is distanced from the centre by external forces. Marginality continues to present a profitable way of approaching the Gospel of Matthew, given both the marginal characterization of Jesus and conventional constructions of the Matthean community.[95] For the purposes of this study, marginality refers to the peripheral, boundary-determining aspects of persons, social networks, communities and environments. Marginalization is the process by which people are peripheralized into deviancy on the basis of their identities, associations, experiences and environments. Hall, Stevens and Meleis propose the following list of seven properties that accompany the experience of marginalization:

1. *Intermediacy*—The boundaries that separate and protect within a social matrix.

---

92. Suzanne Dixon, *The Roman Family* (London: Johns Hopkins University Press, 1992), pp. 24-35.

93. Warren Carter, *The Roman Empire and the New Testament: An Essential Guide* (Nashville, TN: Abingdon Press, 2006), p. 32; Shelley Hales, *The Roman House and Social Identity* (Cambridge: Cambridge University Press, 2003).

94. Because biblical critics who employ the social sciences and cultural anthropology are not always forthcoming about the orientalist political relations that their scholarship produces, we ought to exercise caution when applying labels of negative connotation. See James G. Crossley, *Jesus in an Age of Terror: Scholarly Projects for a New American Century* (BibleWorld ; London: Equinox, 2008), pp. 110-28; Lawrence, *Ethnography*.

95. Carter argues that Matthew's Gospel legitimates a marginal identity and way of life for the community of disciples in Antioch. The Matthean community, he maintains, were on the edge of the dominant or normative cultural context and negotiated an ideological and social marginality in relation to the dominant structures and values of wider society. This included the Roman imperial system with its totalitarian ideological claims and sociological practices which were opposed to the community's theological, christological and eschatological narratives and practices. See Carter, *Margins*, p. 43; cf. Duling, *Marginal Scribe*; Paul Hertig, 'Geographical Marginality in the Matthean Journeys of Jesus', *SBL 1999 Seminar Papers* (Atlanta, GA: Society of Biblical Literature, 1999), pp. 472-89.

2. *Differentiation*—The stigmatization of identities at the periphery by those at the centre.
3. *Power*—The influence exerted by the centre of a community over the periphery with regard to access to resources, collective awareness and organization, and enforced conformity.
4. *Secrecy*—Networks that control personal information of a marginalized group for safety from the dominant group.
5. *Reflectiveness*—Marginalized persons live 'examined lives' out of necessity.
6. *Voice*—Marginalized persons and groups have ways of communicating that distinguish them from those at the centre, and therefore are silenced within the dominant stream of communication.
7. *Liminality*—Having unique experiences that have consequences for human development, maintenance of self-esteem, and health promotion and restoration.[96]

A number of these properties are evident in the characterization of the Matthean Jesus and further enhance our understanding of both the inner and social and cultural textures.

Intertexture
The intertexture of a text concerns a text's configuration of phenomena that lie outside the text. How are external sources, cultural references or historical events encoded within the text? The insights of post-structuralist philosophy enable interpreters to recognize that even language itself is contingent on agreed cultural systems of meaning that lie outside the text. As a result, 'how meaning is constructed depends not only on how one reads the social, cultural, and religious markers inscribed in the text but also on what kind of "intertexts," preconstructed "frames of meaning," common sense understandings, and "reading paradigms" one utilizes when interpreting linguistic markers and textualized symbols'.[97]

Robbins divides intertexture into four main categories. First, oral-scribal intertexture is when a text configures or reconfigures, either explicitly or without reference, language from other texts. This can occur through recitation, re-contextualization, or reconfiguration, and produces narrative ampli-

---

96. Joanne M. Hall, Patricia E. Stevens and Afaf Ibrahim Meleis, 'Marginalization: A Guiding Concept for Valuing Diversity in Nursing Knowledge Development', *Advances in Nursing Studies* 16.4 (1994), pp. 25-33; Joanne Hall, 'Marginalization Revisited: Critical, Postmodern, and Liberation Perspectives', *Advances in Nursing Studies* 22.2 (1999), pp. 23-41.
97. Schüssler Fiorenza, *Rhetoric and Ethic*, p. 92.

fication of a theme or argument.[98] Second, cultural intertexture refers to
'insider' knowledge that is learned through interaction or immersion with a
particular culture. It appears in word and concept patterns or configurations,
values, scripts, codes, systems and myths. Cultural intertexture appears in
a text through reference or allusion and echo.[99] Third, social intertexture
refers to social codes and institutions that are not culturally specific. They
include social roles (e.g. soldier, slave) or identities (Greek, Roman, Jew),
social institutions (empire, synagogue, household), social codes (honour,
hospitality), and social relationships (patron, kin, enemy).[100] Fourth, historical intertexture concerns events that have occurred at specific times in
specific locations that are encoded within the story world of the text. The
interpretation of these events requires knowledge of an event's social, cultural and ideological context.[101]

Sacred Texture
The final category of socio-rhetorical criticism is that of sacred texture.
According to Robbins, the sacred texture of a text emerges mostly from an
investigation into the other textures.[102] In the ancient Mediterranean, there
was no compartmentalization of politics, economics and religion. Indeed,
once we recognize that such distinctions are artificial, we can begin to
appreciate that social and political textures also have deeply symbolic and
theological meanings.

The concepts of home and homelessness themselves are more than social
and political in that they also embody particular spiritual and theological
dimensions, such as the desire for authentic human community. This desire,
in fact, is exploited as a fantasmatic component of the neoliberal ideological
constellation; dictating the appropriate social and economic arrangements
of power and individual behaviour. For example, structures of kinship, such
as the nuclear family, are naturalized as a means by which adults *must* work
to provide for their dependents. Exploration of the sacred texture of the text,
then, emerges dialectically through the underlying theological themes and
discourses within the text and its interpretation, in addition to the ideological categories outlined above.

Conclusions

In contemporary biblical interpretation, the connection between Jesus and
homelessness features as a sublime object, facilitating the re-inscription of

---

98. Robbins, *Exploring the Texture*, pp. 40-58.
99. Robbins, *Exploring the Texture*, pp. 58-62.
100. Robbins, *Exploring the Texture*, pp. 62-63.
101. Robbins, *Exploring the Texture*, pp. 63-68.
102. Robbins, *Exploring the Texture*, p. 130.

dominant ideologies of homelessness in the world before the text. This book attempts to traverse the fantasy that upholds and is supported by the romanticization of Jesus' homelessness by exposing its obscene underside within the various textures of the Matthean text. In this chapter I have outlined a critical framework and methodology for reading the Jesus simulacrum in the Gospel of Matthew. By bringing the Matthean text into dialogue with contemporary ideologies of homelessness and by identifying the intrinsic connection between biblical interpretation and the construction of social reality, we can expose the ways in which ideologies of homelessness have shaped our interpretive capacity as readers, as well as begin to explore alternative possibilities and ways of 'seeing' the homelessness of Jesus within the text.

The insights of ideological biblical criticism and the necessity for a more critical way of understanding the interpretive nexus between Jesus and homelessness has opened up the critical space for this study. Moreover, the lack of a thorough hermeneutical investigation into this connection provides the opportunity for a refreshed reading of the text, one that pays heed to the ideological construction of homelessness in contemporary society. By examining the text's ideological texture, inner texture, social and cultural texture, intertexture and sacred texture, we are able to produce interpretations that disrupt existing dominant ideologies of homelessness as they surface within the text and its interpretation. The task at hand, however, is not solely deconstructive; rather, a more nuanced interpretation of the Matthean Jesus emerges, one that is sensitive to the text, its author and the world in front of the reader.

With the appropriate reading framework now established and the socio-rhetorical approach introduced, the focus turns to a close reading of selected texts. The following chapters demonstrate how the homelessness of Matthew's Jesus simulacrum, as a sublime object in biblical interpretation, can potentially destabilize the logics behind the totalizing discourse of neoliberal capitalism.

2

DISPLACEMENT

refugee—noun   an individual seeking refuge or asylum; especially: an individual who has left his or her native country and is unwilling or unable to return to it because of persecution or fear of persecution (as because of race, religion, membership in a particular social group, or political opinion).[1]

Migrations do not just happen. There are causes making people leave their homelands as well as concomitant incentives contributing to it. In other words, there are pushing and pulling factors. Pragmatically, Herod's decision to kill all Bethlemite baby boys to get rid of Jesus is what forces 'the holy family' to escape to a host country looking for refuge.

Aquiles Ernesto Martinez[2]

From the perspective of homelessness and displacement, the most significant text within the infancy narratives and perhaps even the entire Gospel of Matthew is that of the flight to Egypt and return to Israel experienced by Joseph, Mary and their newborn son, Jesus (Mt. 2.13-23). That such an obvious narrative of socio-political displacement has been so overwhelmingly neglected by biblical scholars is nothing less than remarkable if not disturbing. This trend is not so difficult to understand, however, once we observe the predominant concerns of modern, bourgeois historical-critical scholarship, in addition to the infancy narratives' typical meaning for communities of faith.

In Christian piety, on the one hand, the individual stories in Matthew 1–2 have been mixed with the corresponding (and sometimes contradictory) material in Luke to form the 'Christmas story'. Such harmonizing attempts produce a different text, one that downplays the socio-political elements of

1. 'refugee', in *Merriam-Webster's Dictionary of Law* (Springfield, MA: Merriam-Webster, 1996), p. 414.
2. Aquiles Ernesto Martinez, 'Jesus, the Immigrant Child: A Diasporic Reading of Matthew 2:1-23', *Apuntes* 26.3 (2006), p. 90.

the narrative and accentuate its religious meaning for Christian believers.[3] On the other hand, the dominant concerns of historical-critical research are perhaps best represented by Raymond E. Brown's *The Birth of the Messiah*.[4] In this work, Brown studies in detail the historical-theological function of the birth and infancy of Jesus as it is portrayed in the Gospels of Matthew and Luke respectively. He contends that since scholars have long doubted the historicity of the infancy narratives, they should instead be regarded as vehicles for each evangelist's theology.[5] What we end up with, then, are narratives primarily valued for their 'spiritual' meaning; other textures, such as themes of persecution and displacement, gross manifestations of violence or intertextual allusions to Moses, are only important so long as they can enhance our spiritual edification of the text.

In his book *The Liberation of Christmas*, Richard A. Horsley, who brings a strong Marxist/liberationist hermeneutic to the infancy narratives, contends that the theology and purpose that scholars discover in Matthew's infancy narratives often reflect modern apologetic concerns more than the designs of the evangelist himself.[6] Dominant interpretations of Mt. 2.13-23, for instance, tend to focus on Matthew's use of the OT, whether through fulfilment citations or allusions to the figure of Moses and Israel's history as evidence for Jesus' messiahship. For example, R.T. France's commentary on this text is framed by the title 'A Demonstration That Jesus Is the Messiah: Five Scriptural Proofs'. He argues that the sole focus of this text is not the narrative, but rather 'a series of quite creative and sophisticated arguments to show how in the coming of Jesus a wide range of scriptural

---

3. Aichele argues that popular cultural adaptations of biblical texts often replace the meaning of the written text on which they are based; this is especially the case for functionally illiterate Christians. It could be argued that for many Christians the 'Christmas story' is now (implicitly) regarded as more canonical than the canonical texts themselves. For more on virtuality and the Bible, see Aichele, *Simulating Jesus*, pp. 18-23.

4. Raymond E. Brown, *The Birth of the Messiah: A Commentary on the Infancy Narratives in the Gospels of Matthew and Luke* (New York: Doubleday, 2nd edn, 1993).

5. See especially Brown's introduction in which he outlines three stages in the scholarly discussion of the infancy narratives: '(A) The perception that the infancy narratives differ significantly from the main body of gospel material; (B) The problem of historicity becomes more acute through the perception of the degree to which the two canonical infancy narratives differ from one another; (C) The historicity problem is somewhat relativized by the perception that the infancy narratives are primarily vehicles of the evangelist's theology and christology' (Brown, *Birth of the Messiah*, pp. 26-36).

6. Richard A. Horsley, *The Liberation of Christmas: The Infancy Narratives in Social Context* (New York: Crossroad, 1989), p. 6; for more on apolitical readings, see Ramon D. Echica, 'The Political Context of the Infancy Narratives and the Apolitical Devotion to the Santo Niño', *Hapag* 7.1 (2010), pp. 37-51.

materials finds its destined fulfilment'.[7] By suggesting that the intertextual components of the text feature primarily to bring out apologetic proof of Jesus' messiahship, however, France effectively downplays the social and political dimensions of the text. Such interpretations underemphasize the role that political hostility plays in marking out Jesus as a marginalized subject, arguably an equally important attribute of his identity as that of being the Messiah.[8] There is also a related tendency to romanticize the displacement of Joseph, Mary and Jesus by framing the flight to Egypt as a 'travel narrative' concerned first and foremost with exploring Jesus' geographical origins.[9] By extracting the harsh reality of displacement interpreters partake in the sublimation of Matthew's Jesus simulacrum, underscoring its function as a sublime object of ideology. In this respect, it acts as a fantasmatic barrier to the trauma associated with forced migration. The reader's gaze is averted from the spectre of mass infanticide and divine injustice that anticipates Jesus' displacement, and instead attempts to salvage theological capital in the text's surplus of meaning.

There are, as always, exceptions to the general rule. Popular interpretations, such as those found in Christian art, have occasionally explored the motifs of journeying and that of the refugee. Martin O'Kane observes that the flight to Egypt uniquely offers 'an image with which many have identified—those who have experienced exile or displacement literally, as well as those for whom the experience of exile or diaspora has been, or continues to be, an issue which they must confront in terms of their own personal or communal identity'.[10] Palestinian Christians have also sometimes identified with the text, given their experience of displacement and connection to the

---

7. R.T. France, *The Gospel of Matthew* (NICNT; Grand Rapids, MI: Eerdmans, 2007), p. 40.

8. An intriguing exception among Evangelical commentaries is that of Keener, who includes a few paragraphs under the subheading 'Yet Matthew Also Teaches That Jesus Was a Refugee'. Keener points out that although Jesus and his family survive the massacre by Herod, they survive as refugees, 'abandoning any livelihood Joseph may have developed in Bethlehem and undoubtedly traveling lightly'. See Keener, *Matthew*, pp. 108-109.

9. Hatina, for example, categorizes Matthew 2 as a 'travel narrative' that attempts to explain why Jesus, although born in Bethlehem, travels to Egypt and ends up 'settling' in Nazareth. See Thomas R. Hatina, 'From History to Myth and Back Again: The Historicizing Function of Scripture in Matthew 2', in *Biblical Interpretation in the Early Christian Gospels: The Gospel of Matthew* (ed. Thomas R. Hatina; London: T. & T. Clark, 2008), p. 98.

10. Martin O'Kane, 'The Flight into Egypt: Icon of Refuge for the H(a)unted', in *Borders, Boundaries and the Bible* (ed. Martin O'Kane; Sheffield: Sheffield Academic Press, 2002), p. 15.

geography of the story.[11] A recent contextual reading by Sharon Betworth focuses on the violence done toward children within the narrative.[12] Furthermore, a small handful of scholars have read the text through the lens of immigration and refugeeism.[13] While these readings stand in contrast to the dominant scholarly interpretation of this text, they are, in many respects, insufficient, given both their brevity and lack of any deliberate ideological scrutiny of the dominant discourse.

This chapter re-reads the flight to Egypt, paying attention to the discursive effects of dominant ideologies of homelessness as they shape biblical interpretation. It is only by traversing through the opposite of a romanticized, individualist conception of homelessness that a space outside of neoliberal ideology is able to formulate itself. After addressing the wider literary context of Matthew 1–2 through an examination of the Matthean genealogy, the re-reading of 2.13-23 begins with an analysis of the inner and social and cultural textures of the text, before moving to the text's strategic use of oral–scribal intertexture. What emerges is a heightened sense of the storytelling of the text in which the objective constraints placed upon Joseph, Mary and Jesus reveals their inability to act and move freely within the story world. The text highlights the structural barriers that displaced groups of people encounter through entrenched objective violence and its occasional (excess) manifestation as reactionary terror. Their displacement occurs as an excremental remainder to the political and economic instability of Herod's regime in addition to God's salvific injustice. Against this backdrop, the text also establishes Jesus' outsider identity. The intertexture of the text provides narrative amplification for these key themes. By disrupting the ideological fantasy of a unified, romantic travel narrative, the reader is able to encounter the traumatic reality of forced displacement that resonates within the various textures of the text.

11. Mitri Raheb, *I Am a Palestinian Christian* (trans. Ruth C.L. Gritsch; Minneapolis, MN: Fortress Press, 1995), pp. 106-107; see also Naim Stifan Ateek, *Justice and Only Justice: A Palestinian Theology of Liberation* (Maryknoll, NY: Orbis Books, 1989), pp. 74-94.

12. Sharon Betsworth, 'What Child Is This? A Contextual Feminist Literary Analysis of the Child in Matthew 2', in *Matthew* (ed. Nicole Wilkinson Duran and James Grimshaw; Texts@Context; Minneapolis, MN: Fortress Press, 2013), pp. 49-63.

13. Martinez, 'Jesus, the Immigrant Child', pp. 84-114; Thanh Van Nguyen, 'In Solidarity with the Strangers: The Flight into Egypt', *TBT* 45.4 (2007), pp. 219-24; Thomas H. Graves, 'A Story Ignored: An Exegesis of Matthew 2:13-23', *Faith and Mission* 5.1 (1987), pp. 66-76; Warren Carter, 'Matthew 1–2 and Roman Political Power', in *New Perspectives on the Nativity*, ed. Jeremy Corley (London: T. & T. Clark, 2009), pp. 77-90.

Setting the Scene

Before getting to Mt. 2.13-23, we must first understand its function within the literary context of Matthew 1–2. A number of commentators observe that the first two chapters in Matthew deal primarily with the identity of Jesus: who is this person, and where does he come from?[14] These beginning chapters frame the rest of the Matthean text by providing a detailed account of the protagonist's origins and articulating the Gospel's purpose. As will be observed below, the motifs of death, violence and displacement recur frequently during Jesus' infancy.[15] In his book on Matthew's passion narrative, Donald Senior observes that from the very beginning, 'Jesus' death looms before the reader. The atmosphere surrounding Jesus' birth is filled with threat as Herod stalks the newborn Messiah. Infants are slaughtered and the family of Jesus are forced to flee.'[16] By knowing something about Jesus' origins, the reader is enlightened as to his mission in later life, which, at its most basic level, is to 'save his people from their sins' (1.21).

The Genealogy (Matthew 1.1-17)

The Gospel of Matthew begins by introducing the ancestry of its Jesus simulacrum. In briefest outline, we have in the genealogy a history of origins that traces the line of God's promise first through the founding of Israel, then in the emergence of the royal line, and finally in the hopes carried beyond the collapse of the Babylonian Exile.[17]

Its discursive intent is to link Jesus to a wider context and larger narrative. On the rhetorical function of genealogies, Nolland writes that '[g]enealogies established individual identity; reflected, established, or legitimated social structures, status, and entitlements to office; functioned as modes of

---

14. Harrington, for instance, adopts the breakdown of the infancy narrative into the following: Matthew 1 focuses on 'who is Jesus?' and in Matthew 2 the emphasis shifts to a series of places, thus 'where'. See Daniel J. Harrington, *The Gospel of Matthew* (Sacra Pagina; Collegeville, MN: Liturgical Press, 2007), p. 46; cf. Douglas R.A. Hare, *Matthew* (Louisville, KY: Westminster John Knox, 2009), p. 5; Hatina, 'From History to Myth and Back Again', p. 98; John P. Meier, *Matthew* (Collegeville, MN: Liturgical Press, 1980), pp. 1-2.

15. For example, although not explored in this study, even the unusual 'miraculous' birth of Jesus has been interpreted through the lenses of honour killings and rape. See Matthew J. Marohl, *Joseph's Dilemma: 'Honor Killing' in the Birth Narrative of Matthew* (Eugene, OR: Cascade, 2008); Jane Schaberg, *The Illegitimacy of Jesus: A Feminist Theological Interpretation of the Infancy Narratives* (Sheffield: Sheffield Phoenix, anniversary edn, 2006).

16. Donald Senior, *The Passion of Jesus in the Gospel of Matthew* (Wilmington, DE: Michael Glazier, 1985), p. 17.

17. Parts of this section appear as Robert J. Myles, 'Echoes of Displacement in Matthew's Genealogy of Jesus', *Colloquium* 45.1 (2013), pp. 31-41.

praise or delineations of character or even as basis of exhortation'.[18] As well as honouring Jesus by placing him in a cultural and familial home, the genealogy's three-part structure—culminating in David, the exile, and Jesus—creates expectations that in Jesus we find a Messiah figure or agent of liberation. For Warren Carter, the opening verses of Matthew in the context of Roman imperial theology point to the basic issue of sovereignty; the text asserts that God's purposes, and not Rome's, are being worked out in human history. He writes:

> The genealogy demonstrates, among other things, that God supervises human history, that God's purposes especially run through Israel (not Rome), that God's purposes are not always faithfully embodied by humans but they are not thereby hindered (kings, exile), and that all sorts of humans (wicked and faithful, famous and obscure, firstborn and insignificant, male and female, Jew and Gentile) are caught up in these purposes.[19]

The rich intertexture within the genealogy provides a plethora of interpretive data and possibility. In recent decades, the reference to the four female figures (Tamar, Rahab, Ruth and the wife of Uriah) interwoven into the mostly patriarchal genealogy has commanded the attention of scholars. These four women are said to share (with Mary) a certain irregularity with respect to their social roles. Their inclusion ruptures the tradition of citing only male forebears and so offers a reading site of resistance against dominant male ideology.[20] A subtheme of displacement also apparent within

18. Nolland, *Matthew*, p. 70; cf. Marshall D. Johnson, *The Purpose of the Biblical Genealogies with Special Reference to the Setting of the Genealogies of Jesus* (SNTSMS, 8; Cambridge: Cambridge University Press, 1969), pp. 146-228; Johannes A. Loubser, 'Invoking the Ancestors: Some Socio-Rhetorical Aspects of the Genealogies in the Gospels of Matthew and Luke', *Neot* 39.1 (2005), pp. 127-40.

19. Carter, *Matthew and Empire*, p. 60.

20. See Elaine M. Wainwright, *Shall We Look for Another? A Feminist Rereading of the Matthean Jesus* (Maryknoll, NY: Orbis Books, 1998), pp. 53-66. Wainwright builds on the previous work of Anderson who views these four women as models that interpret and present Mary's female difference by celebrating female initiative, faith and reproductive power, but are also domesticated by patriarchal constraints. See Janice Capel Anderson, 'Mary's Difference: Gender and Patriarchy in the Birth Narratives', *JR* 67.2 (1987), pp. 183-202; cf. Janice Capel Anderson and Stephen D. Moore, 'Matthew and Masculinity', in *New Testament Masculinities* (ed. Stephen D. Moore and Janice Capel Anderson; Semeia Studies; Atlanta, GA: Society of Biblical Literature, 2003), pp. 72-76. Levine suggests these women represent 'people oppressed by the dominant political, religious, and social system'. Levine, *Social and Ethnic Dimensions*, p. 62. See also Schaberg's critical response to these various feminist positions and their detractors in Schaberg, *Illegitimacy*, pp. 236-44. For a recent non-feminist contribution from a 'gender sensitive perspective', see Peter-Ben Smit, 'Something about Mary? Remarks about the Five Women in the Matthean Genealogy', *NTS* 56 (2010), pp. 191-207.

the intertexture of the text has, however, been almost entirely ignored.[21] As demonstrated below, of the forty names mentioned in the genealogy at least fifteen can be connected to episodes of forced displacement, itinerancy and/ or homelessness. This, then, offers a reading site of desublimation against the romanticization of Jesus' homelessness as it is constructed in the world before the text.

The Gospel begins with the words Βίβλος γενέσεως Ἰησοῦ Χριστοῦ υἱοῦ Δαυὶδ υἱοῦ Ἀβραάμ ['The book of the genealogy/origin of Jesus the Christ, the son of David, the son of Abraham'] (1.1), indicating an emphasis on two characters central to the OT tradition. On the one hand, 'Son of David' signals the royal dimension of Jesus' ancestry and associates him with the legitimate rulers over Israel.[22] In the context of displacement, however, the reference to David evokes the story of his escape from King Saul (1 Sam. 19.1-24), foreshadowing Jesus' own flight from political hostility in Mt. 2.13-23. On the other hand, 'Son of Abraham' invokes the founding of the Israelite people in the calling of Abraham and the promises made to him (Gen. 12; 15; 17; cf. Exod. 3.15-16). Those descended from him are included in the people of God.

While David is primarily associated with his role as king of Israel, and not as a displaced refugee, echoes of displacement within the story of Abraham are perhaps more prominent. The emphasis on Abraham indicates that Jesus belongs to this group of people, and specifically to the Jewish line of descent.[23] The first narratives concerning Abraham in Genesis 12–13 focus on his constant geographical shifting due to the combination of divine injunctions and inhospitable socio-political conditions. Abram appears as a nomad who, upon receiving a call from Yahweh, journeys from his home-town Ur through to the land of Canaan. On the way he dwells in Haran (11.31), where Yahweh promises to make his descendants into a great nation (12.1-5). After entering Canaan, he stops in Shechem (12.6), and

---

21. One exception is the work of Eloff, who, building on N.T. Wright's idea that Israel saw itself as still in exile at the time of Jesus, argues that Matthew's stress on exile is an attempt to present Jesus as a resolution to the story of Israel. See Mervyn Eloff, 'Exile, Restoration and Matthew's Genealogy of Jesus Ὁ ΧΡΙΣΤΟΣ', *Neot* 38.1 (2004), pp. 75-87; N.T. Wright, *The New Testament and the People of God* (Minneapolis, MN: Fortress Press, 1992), pp. 385-86.

22. A social-scientific treatment of this royal legitimation of Jesus can be found in Duling, *Marginal Scribe*, pp. 91-119. See also Willitts's study on the political ramifications of the Matthean text's Davidic framework and the shepherd-king motif: Joel Willitts, *Matthew's Messianic Shepherd-King: In Search of 'The Lost Sheep of the House of Israel'* (BZNW, 147; Berlin: de Gruyter, 2007).

23. Huizenga argues that 'Son of Abraham' functions as a sacrificial christological category, presenting Jesus as the anti-type of Isaac. See Leroy Andrew Huizenga, 'Matt 1.1: "Son of Abraham" as a Christological Category', *HBT* 30.2 (2008), pp. 103-13.

then moves to Bethel (12.8). Following this, a famine prompts Abram to wander farther south (12.10). Finally, due to severe famine, he is displaced to Egypt. Shortly after arriving, however, he is pursued by Pharaoh's men and so journeys through the Negeb to Bethel (13.3) before settling again in the land of Canaan (13.13). Abraham's constant shifting foreshadows the itinerancy that will feature as a major component of Jesus' life and ministry.

While the emphasis of the genealogy is placed on David and Abraham, many other names evoke the memory of homelessness and forced displacement, often with a connection to Egypt, famine, the Exodus, or the Babylonian Exile. Their inclusion alludes to underlying antagonisms within the narrative, and ruptures the genealogy's discursive effect to embed Jesus within a cultural and familial home. Abraham's son Isaac (Mt. 1.2) was, like his father, subjected to a famine and forced to move to Gerar (Gen. 26.1-33). Yahweh commanded Isaac not to go to Egypt, rather he should 'settle in this land as an alien [παροίκει]' (26.3). As a result of severe famine in Canaan, Jacob (Mt. 1.2) migrated to Egypt at the time when his son was viceroy (Gen. 46.2-4). Aminadab (Mt. 1.4) was born of Aram during the Israelite exile in Egypt, and was the father of Nahshon, who was a prominent figure during the Exodus. Both Nahshon and his son Salmon were at least twenty years of age and so did not survive the forty-year sojourn in the wilderness before entering the Promised Land (Num. 26.64-65). Obed (Mt. 1.5) was part of an Israelite family from Bethlehem who were displaced to the nearby country of Moab because of famine (Ruth 1.1-5). From there, Ruth, a Moabite, was displaced back to Israel and had a son, also named Obed (4.21). During Saul's persecution of David, David asked the king of Moab for the protection of his parents and leaves Jesse (Mt. 1.6) and his mother with the king of Moab (1 Sam. 22.3-4). The Israelite king Uzziah (Mt. 1.9) became leprous and so 'lived in a separate house, for he was excluded from the house of the Lord' (2 Chron. 26.21).

The Matthean text makes special reference to Jechoniah and his sons (Salathiel) in relation to the deportation to Babylon (Mt. 1.11-12).[24] 2 Kings 24–25 describes Jechoniah as a king of Judah who was dethroned by the king of Babylon in the sixth century BCE and taken into captivity along with his entire household and three thousand prestigious Jews. The next name after Jechoniah's son Salathiel, Zerubbabel (Mt. 1.12-13), literally

---

24. Hood argues that the addition of 'and his brothers' to Judah and Jechoniah (1.2, 11) evokes Jesus' royal role. This is because Judah and Jechoniah are understood to have sacrificed themselves for their brothers in order to further the restoration of Israel, thus gesturing toward Jesus' future role as an agent of God's salvation. See Jason B. Hood, *The Messiah, his Brothers, and the Nations: Matthew 1.1-17* (LNTS, 441; London: T. & T. Clark, 2011).

means 'the offspring of Babylon'.[25] The phrase 'deportation to Babylon' is repeated four times in Mt. 1.1-17 and is used to divide between two of the three groups of generations; fourteen generations from Abraham to David, fourteen generations from David to the Exile, and fourteen generations from the Exile to the Christ. The text employs the Greek noun μετοικεσία to denote the 'deportation', echoing its LXX usage for the Babylonian captivity (2 Kgs 24.16; 1 Chron. 5.22; Ezek. 12.11) and literally meaning a 'transfer to another place of habitation'.[26] Nolland remarks that the term intends to call to mind all the suffering and sense of tragedy known from the OT accounts.[27] This includes a well-developed discourse of destruction interwoven through the OT tradition that recounts the shame, humiliation, uprooting and trauma associated with the exilic experience.[28] The emphasis on Babylon gestures toward the geographical and social displacement of Jesus and what will amount to an inferior political, legal and social status as an outsider within his local environment. As well as placing Jesus within the story of his ancestors, it evokes the destitution and desperation of displacement that interrupts attempts at its theological idealization.

The genealogy concludes with the introduction of the protagonist, Jesus, through his parents, Mary and Joseph. It reads, 'and Jacob the father of Joseph the husband of Mary, of whom Jesus was born, who is called the Messiah' (Mt. 1.16). As mentioned above, this verse is seen as the fifth and final gendered rupture in the genealogy of Jesus. Nolland observes that

> With Joseph comes a notable break in the pattern, 'A produced B'. The language created a detour around this pattern in a manner which would normally be considered a distinction without a difference. But this breaking of the pattern is striking and produces a puzzle for the reader until it is resolved in the narrative of vv. 18-25. Joseph seems to be being denied the normal role in procreation, but without explanation.[29]

While the discursive function of the genealogy is to ground Jesus in a stable home place, the final rupture displaces him from this lineage. The subtle characterization of Jesus as a bastard child problematizes any future claims to inheritance. The breakage in the text also foreshadows the breakage from home place that Jesus is about to experience in the flight to Egypt and signals the alienation from home place that Jesus will later encounter

---

25. 'זְרֻבָּבֶל', *HALOT*, I, p. 279.

26. 'μετοικεσία', *BAGD*, p. 643.

27. Nolland, *Matthew*, p. 84.

28. See further Anne-Mareike Wetter, 'Balancing the Scales: The Construction of the Exile as Countertradition in the Bible', in *From Babylon to Eternity: The Exile Remembered and Constructed in Text and Tradition* (ed. Bob Becking *et al.*; BibleWorld; London: Equinox, 2009), pp. 34-56.

29. Nolland, *Matthew*, p. 85.

during his itinerant ministry.[30] Such intimations underscore the abject conditions of homelessness; a tension is inaugurated between the desire for inclusion and familiarity with the stark reality of exclusion and displacement. In the next section, I explore how these echoes of displacement in Matthew's genealogy of Jesus are reified in the escape to Egypt and subsequent displacement to Nazareth.

The Flight to Egypt (Matthew 2.13-23)

The flight to Egypt follows in the wake of the extravagant gifting by the magi against the desires of Herod (2.1-12). These two stories are juxtaposed and form a dramatic contrast: while the magi worship Jesus, Herod the king of Israel threatens his life. The flight to Egypt also brings to an end the infancy narratives of Matthew 1–2, starting with the genealogy which, as we saw above, motions toward Jesus' impending displacement. After the stories of Jesus' unusual and miraculous birth, the protagonist and his parents are thrust into the desperate situation of having to seek asylum from their political overlords. A basic narrative of displacement exposes the objective nature of homelessness: it emerges not as a subjective, private experience but as something connected to external political realities.

Davies and Allison structure the pericope into the following divisions based on the three fulfilment citations:

A. Joseph is warned by an angel in a dream to flee to Egypt in order to keep Jesus safe from Herod + formula quotation (2.13-15)
B. Herod slaughters the infants + formula quotation (2.16-18)
C. After Herod's death, Joseph brings Jesus and Mary back from Egypt (2.19-23)
   1. A dream and the return to Israel (vv. 19-21)
   2. A dream and the move to Nazareth + formula quotation (vv. 22-23)[31]

One can also structure the text according to its four geographical movements: after fleeing from Bethlehem to Egypt, the narrative focuses on the Bethlehem massacre. The narrative then follows Joseph back from Egypt to Israel, and then finally to Nazareth in Galilee. Although similar to the

---

30. Some interpreters have recognized that Matthew's genealogy reveals much about the narrative that follows, although the underlying narrative of displacement has not featured in their assessments. See Dennis E. Nineham, 'The Genealogy in St. Matthew's Gospel and its Significance for the Study of the Gospels', *BJRL* 58.2 (1976), pp. 451-68; Herman C. Waetjen, 'The Genealogy as the Key to the Gospel according to Matthew', *JBL* 95 (1976), pp. 205-30.
31. Davies and Allison, *Matthew*, I, p. 257.

structuring above, a focus on the geographical movements of the central characters reveals the narrative of displacement that dominates the text. The close reading of 2.13-23 below is divided into these three scenes (2.13-15; 2.16-18; and 2.19-23) but is careful to distinguish between the two movements in the final scene.

The Initial Flight to Egypt

Within Matthew the protagonist's journey begins in Bethlehem. Unlike Lk. 2.1-7 there is no mention of a requirement to travel to Bethlehem from Nazareth for a census; rather, Bethlehem functions as Jesus' original home place (Mt. 2.1). Moreover, in v. 11 his immediate family are connected to a house and/or household (οἰκίαν) in Bethlehem, indicating a more established residency than Luke's account of Jesus' birth in a stable. Intriguingly, however, after the events of 2.13-23 Jesus will never again return to Bethlehem, and the region of Judea will be a place where he meets significant resistance, conflict and eventually death. Matthew 2.13-23 follows the gifting of the magi in 2.1-12. After indicating the magi's own retreat, Joseph himself is instructed in a dream by a 'messenger of the Lord' to flee into Egypt because Herod is about to attempt to destroy (ἀπολέσαι) the child (v. 13). Seeking safety for himself and his immediate family, Joseph obeys the command and flees (v. 14).[32]

Elements of historical intertexture encoded within 2.13-23, such as negative stereotypes of the Herods who were the long-time rulers of Palestine and adjacent areas, provide prospective ingredients for the text's desublimation. According to the *HCBD*, '[t]wo ancient traditions make him [Herod] either a descendant of a notable Jewish family with a lineage traceable to the Babylonian Exile or a slave in the temple of Apollo in the Philistine city of Ashkelon. Neither can be proved.'[33] The figure referred to in 2.13-23, Herod the Great, was appointed 'king of the Jews' by the Roman Senate and governed from 37 BCE until his death in 4 BCE. His title and long reign marks his unwavering loyalty to Rome. The first-century Jewish historian Josephus describes Herod as a 'half-Jew' [ἡμιιουδαίῳ] (*Ant.* 14.403-404). Although well known for his extensive building programs, Herod had a reputation for the harsh repression of any opposition. Horsley, for instance, accuses him of instituting what today would be called 'a police state, complete with loyalty oaths, surveillance, informers, secret police, imprisonment, torture, and

---

32. For more on the function of dreams in Matthew's infancy narrative, see Derek S. Dodson, *Reading Dreams: An Audience-Critical Approach to the Dreams in the Gospel of Matthew* (LNTS, 397; London: T. & T. Clark, 2009); Francois P. Viljoen, 'The Significance of Dreams and the Star in Matthew's Infancy Narrative', *HvTSt* 64.2 (2008), pp. 845-60.

33. 'Herod', *HCBD*, p. 416.

brutal retaliation against serious dissent'.[34] Josephus suggests that Herod imposed repressive laws going far beyond anything in the Torah:

> No meeting of people was permitted, nor were walking together or being together permitted, and all their movements were observed. Those who were caught were punished severely, and many were taken, either openly or secretly, to the fortress of Hyrcania and there put to death. Both in the city and on the open roads there were men who spied upon those who met together. . . . Those who obstinately refused to go along with his [new] practices he persecuted in all kinds of ways. As for the rest of the populace, he demanded that they submit to taking a loyalty oath, and he compelled them to make a sworn declaration that they would maintain a friendly attitude to his rule. Now most people yielded to his demand out of complaisance or fear, but those who showed some spirit and objected to compulsion he got rid of by every possible means (*Ant.* 15.336-69).

Jesus' displacement comes to life against this backdrop of Herodian tyranny, which is woven into the historical intertexture of the text. The Matthean community, likely containing a mixture of poor and wealthy households, would have knowledge of the repressive control of and external pressures on the lower social strata. Accordingly, the temporal setting '[i]n the time of King Herod . . .' [ἐν ἡμέραις Ἡρῴδου τοῦ βασιλέως . . .] (2.1) evokes for the reader the repressive regime and intensifies the political instability surrounding the narrative of displacement.

Elements of inner texture also alert the reader to the unsavoury experience of displacement as it is encoded within the text. This disrupts the romanticization of the flight to Egypt as a travel narrative or apologetic argument for Jesus' messiahship. As discussed below, the key verb ἀναχωρέω (to withdraw, depart) is repeated a number of times to highlight the evasive tactics of Joseph against the backdrop of Herodian hostility. Moreover, v. 13 describes the initial cause of their displacement: an angel gives the command to 'Get up/rise!' [ἐγερθείς] take the mother and child and 'flee' [φεῦγε] to Egypt *because* Herod is about to 'destroy' [ἀπολέσαι] the child. In Matthew, the verb φεύγω is often connected to apocalyptic notions of fleeing from persecution, such as in 10.23 and 24.16, and also occurs during the desertion of the disciples in 26.56. Herod's destructive intentions are encapsulated by the verb ἀπόλλυμι ('to destroy'), which is subsequently used to describe the hostile intentions of the Pharisees toward Jesus in 12.14.

---

34. Horsley, *Liberation of Christmas*, p. 47. In recent years some scholars have argued for a more sympathetic view of the historical Herod. See Byron R. McCane, 'Simply Irresistible: Augustus, Herod, and the Empire', *JBL* 127 (2008), pp. 725-35. For a response, see Judy Diehl, 'Anti-Imperial Rhetoric in the New Testament', *CBR* 10.1 (2011), pp. 15-17.

While repetition of God's instructions to Joseph highlights Joseph's trust in God and God's salvific provision for Jesus (the text first describes a dream that will prompt him to subsequently take action) it also emphasizes Joseph's passivity and lack of self-determination. Even when taking action, Joseph is still following orders; he expresses little, if any, agency except in obeying God and seeking refuge. Neither Mary nor Jesus possesses any capacity for agency within this text. In accordance with a subordinate gender position, Mary is silent and goes along with her husband. Jesus is likewise constructed as a flat character; he does not act or speak, and the attributes of dangerousness are externally projected onto him by Herod.[35] Luz points out that Jesus is nothing more than an 'object' in the text. The one who is directed by God to take action is Joseph, while Mary and the child are rendered silent and powerless.[36] This complexity surrounding the central characters' scope for agency causes an effect of desublimation in the text's ideological texture. Their displacement occurs not as a result of individual choice or moral failure but out of self-preservation and in response to external political realities.[37]

The lethal threat facing Joseph, Mary and Jesus in 2.13-23 is intensified by additional details of setting within the text's inner texture. Their initial flight occurs at night (νυκτός), a typological detail indicating the 'type of time' in which the action takes place. Within Matthew, night time usually symbolizes insecurity, desertion, death, and sometimes a loss or lack of faith: Jesus fasts 'for forty days and forty nights' in the desert and becomes famished (4.2); after his confrontation in the temple, Jesus goes out to Bethany, the periphery, 'for the night' (21.17); in his apocalyptic discourse, Jesus suggests that 'the night' is when thieves compromise the security of one's home (24.43); during the Last Supper Jesus points out that his disciples will become deserters 'this night' (26.31) and that Peter will deny him three times before the cock crows 'this very night' (26.34); and finally, after the resurrection, the priests and elders initiate a rumour that Jesus' disciples

---

35. Herod's actions resemble the symptoms of psychosis. He experiences a state in which the distinction between reality and the Real has been lost and which, since it leaves him unable to distinguish between hallucination and the perception of real objects, is tantamount to madness.

36. Ulrich Luz, *Matthew 1–7* (trans. James E. Crouch; Hermeneia; Minneapolis, MN: Fortress Press, 2007), p. 124.

37. The complexity of agency is frequently downplayed within neoliberal ideology which assumes that individuals (with the exception of minors) are free and equal in their exposure to risk. Responsibility for minors is projected onto parents through repressive, and sometimes punitive, measures, as part of the state ideological apparatus that binds subjects to the ruling ideology. See Althusser, 'Ideology', pp. 1-60. Boer uses this concept in his reading of the birth of Israel in Genesis. See Roland Boer, *Marxist Criticism of the Bible* (London: T. & T. Clark, 2003), pp. 14-41.

'came by night' to steal his body (28.13). Accordingly, Joseph's action to flee under the cover of darkness alerts the reader to the immediate danger of their journey; a trek through the Sinai desert involves risks of exposure, malnourishment and bandits. While travel at night is cooler and less water is consumed, it is still hazardous. The overnight drop in temperature in arid areas occurs rapidly, sometimes going below freezing, and presents a real danger for the ill-prepared, especially an infant who is more vulnerable to extreme environmental conditions.

Because the text provides minimal details about the actual movement to and stay within Egypt, interpreters project their own assumptions of what the experience of fleeing to Egypt might have been like. Davies and Allison note that the absence of details helped stimulate later apocryphal fantasy (e.g. Eusebius, *Dem. ev.* 6.20; *Ps.-Mt.* 18-25; *(Arab.) Gos. Inf.* 9-26).[38] Intriguingly, within conventional interpretations the harsh reality of displacement is regularly downplayed. Daniel Harrington, for instance, notes that Egypt, which came under Roman control in 30 BCE, was outside the jurisdiction of Herod and so remained relatively safe. He also writes that Egypt had been the traditional place of refuge for Jews both in the OT and in the Maccabean era.[39] As mentioned above, France frames the text almost exclusively in terms of prophecy fulfilment. He reasons that '[t]he point of mentioning the Egyptian visit at all, from the point of view of the fulfillment of Scripture, has been to prepare for Jesus' coming "out of Egypt"',[40] in accord with Matthew's citation of Hos. 11.1.

The experience of being forcefully displaced from one's home place, however, is often more debilitating than it is liberating. An exploitable gap emerges between the illusion of Egypt as a safe and stable destination, and the obverse, dismal reality of displacement that confronts Joseph, Mary and Jesus. In this instance of forced migration, the central characters endure a dangerous sojourn across the desert and presumably also experience instability once they reach their destination, for they become detached and isolated from their primary support structure, the household. While Egypt is occasionally a place of refuge within Israel's history, it is predominantly remembered as a 'house of bondage' (Exod. 20.2), evoking intertextually the enslavement and suffering of the Hebrew people.[41]

---

38. Davies and Allison, *Matthew*, I, p. 261.

39. Harrington, *Matthew*, p. 40.

40. France, *Matthew* (2007), p. 79; cf. Nolland, *Matthew*, p. 123.

41. Vermes points out that this very connection between Jesus and Egypt was seized upon by the rabbis and other early opponents of Christianity in their anti-Christian polemic. In the late second century, for instance, Origen's opponent Celsus ascribed Jesus' miracles to his supposed contact with Egyptian sorcerers: 'Because [Jesus] was poor, he hired himself out as a workman in Egypt, and there tried his hand

The Key Verb Ἀναχωρέω. As we have observed, the flight-to-Egypt pericope resists the romanticization of Jesus' homelessness by divulging a narrative of displacement. An element of inner texture that underscores the traumatic reality of forced migration is the repetition of the key verb ἀναχωρέω to denote the evasive tactics of Joseph, Mary and Jesus. Within 2.13-23 the verb ἀναχωρέω appears three times: first, to refer to the departure of the magi (v. 13); second, to signify the departure of Joseph to Egypt (v. 14); and third, to describe Joseph's departure from Judea to Galilee (v. 22). The verb has an interesting linguistic history. In later usage it became a technical term for monasticism (i.e. withdrawal from the world—hence 'anchorite'). Before that, it had been used to refer to withdrawal from public life, of withdrawal into oneself in contemplation, and, within Egypt, of withdrawal into the desert by peasants who were oppressed by taxation as a kind of strike-action.[42]

In the NT, ἀναχωρέω is distinctive of the Matthean text, which employs it ten times (2.12, 13, 14, 22; 4.12; 9.24; 12.15; 14.13; 15.21; 27.5), compared to just one appearance in Mark (3.7), one in John (6.15), and two in Acts (23.19; 26.31). *BAGD* states that ἀναχωρέω can denote a simple departure from a location, or express the action of withdrawing, retiring and/or taking refuge.[43] In Mt. 2.13-23 the NRSV renders ἀναχωρέω with the relatively impotent 'went', effectively downplaying the term's loaded socio-political overtones (a distinction should be made between ἀναχωρέω and the common verb ἔρχωμαι, the latter of which appears in v. 22 to signify Joseph's return to Israel). The strategic deployment of ἀναχωρέω within 2.13-23 suggests that a movement is undertaken *in response* to hostile external circumstances—in other words, it signifies forced displacement.

In an article discussing the use of ἀναχωρέω in Matthew's Gospel, Deirdre Good notes that the motif of 'withdrawal' is a feature of the Gospel that has been observed by scholars but rarely researched. Employing source criticism, she argues that the motif is part of a three-fold pattern of hostility/withdrawal/prophetic fulfilment and functions to advance the narrative by prompting Joseph or Jesus to go from one region to another. Good also suggests that Matthew's use of the verb is influenced by a prominent theme of the withdrawal of Wisdom in certain apocalyptic sources. She quotes the Ethiopic text *1 En.* 42 to observe a theme of Wisdom withdrawing from the earth:

---

at certain magical powers on which the Egyptians pride themselves; he returned full of conceit because of these powers, and on account of them gave himself the title of God' (Origen, *Cels.* 1.28). See Geza Vermes, *The Nativity: History and Legend* (London: Penguin, 2006), p. 126.

    42. J.C. Fenton, *Saint Matthew* (Middlesex: Penguin, 1963), p. 48.

    43. 'ἀναχωρέω', *BAGD*, p. 75.

Wisdom could not find a place in which she could dwell
But a place was found (for her) in the heavens.
Then Wisdom went out to dwell with the children of the people
But she found no dwelling place.
(So) Wisdom returned to her place
And she settled permanently among the angels.
Then Iniquity went out of her rooms
And found whom she did not expect.
And she went with them like rain in a desert,
Like dew on a thirsty land.[44]

Good claims that 'Wisdom did not stay on earth but returned to her divine abode having found no suitable dwelling on earth'.[45] She then suggests that because a wisdom influence has often been detected in Matthew's Gospel to the extent that one can now speak of Matthew's Wisdom Christology, the theme of Wisdom's withdrawal is the immediate background for Matthew's use of ἀναχωρέω; Matthew likely derives the motifs of hostility and withdrawal from a reading of several wisdom passages.

While thematic echoes to Wisdom's supposed 'withdrawal' appear in English translations, Good's assessment is likely precarious. First, the verse from *1 Enoch* is written in Ge'ez (or Ethiopic), with no corresponding Greek translation, and so Good fails to provide any demonstrable linguistic link between this text and the term ἀναχωρέω. The other sources she cites also lack any explicit relationship.[46] Second, Good's thematic association between Matthew's use of ἀναχωρέω and the withdrawal of Wisdom in apocalyptic texts enables her to effectively 'spiritualize' and thus depoliticize the forced displacement of Jesus in a convenient act of ideological sublimation. For example, Good contends that 'it is not *retreat from* hostility but rather *withdrawal for* the fulfilment of prophecy that demonstrates Matthew's intention in his creation of this pattern'.[47] Within the Matthean text, however, prophetic fulfilment does not lead necessarily to asceticism, but rather, it enhances the narrative of displacement (see below).

---

44. Deirdre Good, 'The Verb ἀναχωρέω in Matthew's Gospel', *NovT* 32.1 (1990), p. 8.

45. Good, 'ἀναχωρέω', p. 9.

46. Good claims the theme reoccurs in 2 Esd. 5.9 for which only the Latin text for the entire document is extant and reads: '*et abscondetur tunc sensus, et intellectus separabitur in promptuarium suum. Et queretur a multis et non invenietur.*' She cites an English translation that conveniently renders *separabitur* as 'withdraw'. This translation seems odd, given that the verb *separo* unambiguously means 'to separate or detach' (lit. 'to be cut in half'), and moreover, its passive construction in Latin does not correspond to the self-reflexive use in the English translation. Good additionally cites *2 Bar.* 49.36, which also speaks of Wisdom departing, but this text is in Syriac and so again it is not possible to show a direct link.

47. Good, 'ἀναχωρέω', p. 12.

Exploring intertextually, ἀναχωρέω is regularly connected to the exploitation of individuals within their respective social and political environments. Of its fourteen appearances across the LXX and deuterocanonical literature, a number of examples stand out for their mention of political rulers displacing marginal refugees. In Exod. 2.15, for instance, the term describes the action Moses takes after Pharaoh discovers he has killed an Egyptian, 'When Pharaoh heard of it, he sought to kill Moses. But Moses fled [ἀνεχώρησεν/וַיִּבְרַח] from Pharaoh. He settled in the land of Midian, and sat down by a well'. The Hebrew verb ברח means 'to run away or flee from danger'.[48] Likewise, in 1 Sam. 19.10, ἀναχωρέω denotes David's flight and escape from King Saul when Saul was actively seeking David's life. 'Saul sought to pin David to the wall with the spear; but he eluded Saul, so that he struck the spear into the wall. David fled [ἀνεχώρησεν/נָס] and escaped [διεσώθη/וַיִּמָּלֵט] that night'. Its use in conjunction with the verb διασῴζω ('to escape', lit. 'to save through') in addition to the temporal setting of the night magnifies the need to move or withdraw promptly because of an immediate hazard or danger. This time the LXX translates a different Hebrew verb, נוס, which roughly translates 'to rush to bring something into safety' (cf. Exod. 9.20) and/or 'to find safety for oneself',[49] also communicating a sense of urgency. The book of Tobit contains yet another example of a king who seeks to kill the protagonist. In this instance, Tobit explicitly displays the trait of fear before fleeing just as Joseph is said to fear (ἐφοβήθη) Herod's son Archelaus before withdrawing to Galilee (Mt. 2.22). 'Then one of the Ninevites went and informed the king about me, that I was burying them; so I hid myself. But when I realized that the king knew about me and that I was being searched for to be put to death, I was afraid [φοβηθείς] and ran away [ἀνεχώρησα]' (Tob. 1.19).

Also noteworthy is the verb's appearance in Ps. 114. The Psalm contains a hymn praising the God of the Exodus, 'Why is it, O sea, that you flee? [ἀνεχώρησας/תָנוּס] O Jordan, that you turn back?' (114.5). Again the LXX employs ἀναχωρέω to render the Hebrew verb נוס. Within this Psalm, the passage through the sea (cf. Exod. 14.29) is paralleled by the crossing of the Jordan (cf. Josh. 3.14-17), the beginning and end of the Exodus. The use of ἀναχωρέω within Mt. 2.13-23 is intertextually infused with this particular Psalm's ritual re-enactment of the Exodus and so indicates the text's identity-forming function in the life of Jesus, just as the Exodus functions as an identity-forming event for the Israelite people.

The term ἀναχωρέω is, therefore, richly layered with intertextual significance that intensifies the theme of displacement within the Matthean text. Its repetition within 2.13-23, in particular, draws attention to the socio-political

---

48. 'ברח', *HALOT*, I, p. 156.
49. 'נוס', *HALOT*, II, p. 681.

dimension of the narrative. Jesus' first major displacement is heralded by the gross manifestation of Herodian-sanctioned violence, to which we now turn.

The Infanticide in Bethlehem

In the second scene (2.16-18), Herod realizes that he has been made a fool (ἐνεπαίχθη) by the wise men and so goes about ordering the slaughter of all the children in and around Bethlehem who are two years old or under. Marianne Blickenstaff observes that the slaughter of the innocents fore-shadows the disruption of families later in the Gospel (e.g. 10.34-38; 12.46-50; 19.29).[50] Although on this occasion Jesus narrowly escapes death, the event foreshadows the violence that institutions of power will direct toward him right up to the end of his life (26.24, 39-42, 53-54, 59-60; 27.21, 24).

Conventional commentary on this text has tended to focus on whether the infanticide really took place, and if it did, to determine how many children were actually slaughtered.[51] Davies and Allison, for instance, note that, as a matter of historical fact, Herod's reign was marked by the massacres of many innocents (Josephus, *Ant.* 15.5-7, 50-87, 173-78, 232-36, 247-52, 260-66, 289-90; 16.361-94; 17.42-4, 167, 182-87), and he was widely known as a slaughterer of both the young and old.[52] Even so, there is no mention of the Bethlehem infanticide in Josephus or any other ancient source independent of Matthew. The infanticide is also regarded as a recon-figuration of Pharaoh's decree to kill all the Hebrew male children in the Exodus story (Exod. 1.15-22),[53] an allusion that warrants further exploration below. Alternatively, some scholars have sought to investigate the inherent

---

50. Marianne Blickenstaff, *'While the Bridegroom Is with Them': Marriage, Family, Gender and Violence in the Gospel of Matthew* (JSNTSup, 292; London: T. & T. Clark, 2005), pp. 147-48.

51. See, for example, R.T. France, 'Herod and the Children of Bethlehem', *NovT* 21.2 (1979), pp. 98-120. Brown curiously speculates that despite scholars' obsession with calculating the number of infants, because of the high infant mortality rate, if the total population in and around Bethlehem was around one thousand, with an annual birth rate of thirty, then the total number of male children under two years of age would probably be less than thirty. See Brown, *Birth*, p. 204.

52. Davies and Allison, *Matthew*, I, pp. 264-65; cf. Jan W. van Henten, 'Matthew 2:16 and Josephus' Portrayal of Herod', in *Jesus, Paul, and Early Christianity: Studies in Honour of Henk Jan de Jonge* (ed. Rieuwerd Buitenwerf *et al.*; Leiden: Brill, 2008), pp. 101-22; Francis Wright Beare, *The Gospel according to Matthew* (Oxford: Basil Blackwell, 1981), p. 82; Keener, *Matthew*, p. 110; Meier, *Matthew*, p. 14.

53. See, for instance, Carter, *Margins*, p. 85; Davies and Allison, *Matthew*, I, pp. 264-65; Craig A. Evans, *Matthew* (NCBC; Cambridge: Cambridge University Press, 2012), p. 60; Fenton, *Matthew*, p. 49; France, *Matthew*, p. 84; Harrington, *Matthew*, p. 45; Nolland, *Matthew*, p. 124.

theodicy problem within the text. How can it be justified that God brings salvation to Jesus but ends up allowing the extermination of numerous innocents? Surely if God was able to save Jesus through Joseph's dreams, and God is entirely just, then should not the other infants in and around Bethlehem have also been delivered from oppression?[54] This spectre of divine injustice haunts the sublimation of Jesus' lone salvation; his miraculous escape should not, as such, distract the dissenting reader from confronting the atrocity of infanticide in the text's ideological texture.

From a symptomatic understanding of homelessness, the infanticide exposes a mechanical basis to Joseph, Mary and Jesus' displacement. War, political instability and violence (followed closely by natural disasters) are primary reasons for refugeeism. The actions of Herod foregrounded in vv. 16-18, then, reverberate through the rest of the narrative, dictating the actions of other characters and exposing the obscene underside of Jesus' socio-political reality. Only after Herod's death is the region considered stable enough for Joseph to return to Israel, and even then the danger still resides.

On the surface of the narrative, it is unclear whether the actions of Herod are intended to bring about the end of Jesus. What is clear, however, is that the bestowing of gifts on Jesus by the magi (v. 11) is of grave concern to Herod. The infanticide is prompted by Herod's realization that he has been fooled (ἐνεπαίχθη). The verb ἐμπαίζω has two meanings: first, 'to subject to derision, ridicule, make fun of'; second, it means 'to trick someone so as to make a fool of the person, deceive, trick'.[55] Most translations opt for this second definition (the NRSV renders it as 'tricked', likewise, the NIV states that Herod has 'been outwitted'), but the first definition is equally important to understanding Herod's actions. Elsewhere in Matthew, the verb is used only with the first definition in mind. In Matthew 27, for example, the verb appears three times to describe the mocking of Jesus as a pretend king shortly before his crucifixion (27.29, 31, 41; cf. 20.19).

So too, in 2.16 Herod is humiliated by the magi (and also by Joseph and Jesus, who escape his acts of terror); the text communicates his loss of honour, power and social status within the symbolic order of first-century Palestine. Louise J. Lawrence notes how from an honour-and-shame perspective, 'Herod seems acutely aware of his exposure to judgment from others'.[56] Having missed his opportunity to derail the perceived threat, and having been dishonoured by the magi, Herod acts out in an attempt to regain his uncompromising authority as a reflection of his honour. He does so by

54. See Richard J. Erickson, 'Divine Injustice?: Matthew's Narrative Strategy and the Slaughter of the Innocents (Matthew 2:13-23)', *JSNT* 64 (1996), pp. 5-27.

55. 'ἐμπαίζω', *BAGD*, p. 323.

56. Lawrence, *Ethnography*, p. 120.

eliminating those he deems most expendable. The backhanded challenge of the magi is 'corrected' by Herod's aggressive response of subjective violence; the display of power enables Herod to retain his social standing through honour acquisition. Andries G. Van Aarde similarly contends that Matthew's infancy narrative can be interpreted from the perspective of the social pattern of challenge and response in terms of honour acquisition between two kings. While Herod retains ascribed honour from the Roman senate when it declared him 'King of the Jews', the text engages in an act of retroactive sublimation through its honouring of Jesus as God's beloved son.[57] In a display of anger and violence, 'Herod creates what he imagines is a geographical and temporal safety zone'.[58] These markers become scripted on bodies through subjection to extreme violence and also function to separate Joseph, Mary and Jesus from other members of their household and their wider social community.[59]

Besides his intention to rid the threat to his honour, what is Herod's motivation for killing the innocents? We should, of course, refrain from sensationalizing infanticide to the extent that it becomes divorced from its utility within the mundane, mechanical reality of everyday life in the ancient Mediterranean world. Archaeological discoveries suggest that in the Roman Empire infanticide was commonplace and a tolerated part of society.[60] While the mass killing of infants may seem abhorrent to modern Westerners, it was a practice routinely employed by societies with extreme poverty in order to conserve resources and reduce economic strain. Infanticide was also part of

---

57. Andries G. van Aarde, 'The Evangelium Infantium, the Abandonment of Children, and the Infancy Narrative in Matthew 1 and 2 from a Social Scientific Perspective', *SBL 1992 Seminar Papers* (Atlanta, GA: Society of Biblical Literature, 1992), pp. 435-53.

58. Carter, *Margins*, p. 86.

59. In the ancient world, the wider household functioned as the primary mediator of familial and social identity. Moxnes writes that 'the household was the most significant group of others. To be put outside of that location was to be marginalized and displaced.' See Moxnes, *Putting Jesus in his Place*, p. 67. Without access to employment or social networking the family unit is further alienated from the norms of everyday life in Judea. The irony, of course, is that despite Herod's hysteria, Jesus has no earthly power within this text. Both he and the infants Herod massacres are the most vulnerable and defenceless members of society. As mentioned above, the narrator gives no agency or voice to Jesus. Herod, however, benefits from the institutionalization of his power and is able to enact his fantasies of destruction with ease.

60. William V. Harris, 'The Theoretical Possibility of Extensive Infanticide in the Graeco-Roman World', *Classical Quarterly* 32.1 (1982), pp. 114-16; cf. Susan C.M. Scrimshaw, 'Infanticide in Human Populations: Societal and Individual Concerns', in *Infanticide: Comparative and Evolutionary Perspectives* (ed. Glenn Hausfater and Sarah Blaffer Hrdy; New York: Aldine, 2008), pp. 439-62. Scrimshaw provides an analysis of infanticide as a widespread social and political phenomenon.

a larger ancient tendency to devalue children. As de Ste Croix points out, '[e]xposure of infants, of course, has often been resorted to as a means of population control: by the rich or the moderately well-off in order to prevent the division of inheritances, and even more by the poor in their struggle for survival'.[61] The death of so many infants may not appear as repugnant to the elite when their social, moral and economic value is weighed against that of the ruling and even producing units of society.

Furthermore, as a prominent member of the wealthy elite, Herod's self-understanding of his social location is one of entitlement. From this viewpoint, Jesus is deemed undeserving of the extravagant financial and material assistance bestowed on him by the magi. Within a limited resource society, benefaction afforded to non-producing units is regarded as unsustainable. Accordingly, in Herod's eyes the infants are legitimately expendable, and their extermination helps to restore economic and social balance.

In fact, one might even suggest that, as a savvy political manoeuvre, their elimination enables the ideological–political order to continue functioning as normal. Žižek perceives that '[t]he standard way of disavowing an antagonism [in ideology] . . . is to project the cause of the antagonism onto a foreign intruder who stands for the threat to society, as such, for the anti-social element, for its excremental excess'.[62] The antagonism arising with the introduction of the infant Jesus, venerated by the magi as a potential contender to the throne, is resolved for Herod only by displacing this imbalance onto all the infants in and around Bethlehem. This remainder, also left abandoned within God's salvific plan, is identified by Herod as the nonproductive, expendable excess to the continued smooth functioning of the socio-political order.[63]

By bringing the reader's attention to the obstinacy of Herod's narrow rationalization, however, the text highlights the intrinsic social and political involvement that the elite establishment has in granting life or death to the general population. Joseph only narrowly manages to flee from oppression, and had divine intervention not occurred, Jesus would have been slaughtered along with the rest of the innocents. Jesus' lone redemption against this backdrop of mass carnage intrudes on the theological idealization of Jesus as God's son. The citation of Jeremiah, moreover, invokes weeping, lamenting and grieving for the wasted loss of life. The interruption in v. 18 of the text's narrative prose with poetic verse reveals a deep-seated antagonism evoking the guilt associated with Jesus' exceptionalism. In fact, Jesus' initial displace-

---

61. De Ste Croix, *Class Struggle*, p. 103.
62. Slavoj Žižek, *The Year of Dreaming Dangerously* (London: Verso, 2012), p. 23.
63. Never mind the long-term view that these infants constitute the next generation of workers sustaining the elite way of life; reactionary politics is often impulsive and inconsistent with respect of its own objectives.

ment occurs not because of divine providence, but as a remainder to the routine horror of infanticide and the irredeemable violence of divine injustice.

The Flight to Galilee

In the third scene Joseph has another dream, this time instructing him to return to the land of Israel (2.19-20). Upon returning, however, Joseph hears that Herod's son Archelaus is ruling over Judea (vv. 21-22). The combination of fear and another dream persuade Joseph to withdraw (ἀναχωρέω) to the town of Nazareth in the district of Galilee (vv. 22-23). This so-called return from exile is the most intriguing component of 2.13-23 when assessing the text's ideological texture. This is because a close reading of the text reveals that, despite our best yearnings for plot resolution, Joseph, Mary and Jesus never actually make it back to their hometown, Bethlehem. Instead, they experience a second exile to the north, to Galilee. This unexpected fracture in the text's narrative flow produces yet another effect of desublimation. The infancy narrative ends not with a romantic return to home place but with its exact opposite: a forced migration to the geographical, political and social margins of first-century Palestine.

Analysis of this final scene begins with a discussion of the inner texture and historical intertexture that is infused within the text. The narrative mirrors the first scene but ruptures at v. 22. Joseph is commanded by an angel in a dream to leave Egypt and return to the land of Israel. But instead of ending there, the text introduces Herod's son, Archelaus (lit. 'ruler of people'), whose characterization within the Matthean text is limited to the fearful (ἐφοβήθη) reaction he evokes in Joseph. In addition to associating Archelaus's rule with the hostile policies of his father, the text reconfigures another aspect of historical intertexture, namely, the death of Herod the Great and the division of his kingdom.[64] The appearance of Archelaus indicates to the reader that political turmoil still lingers within the region. Upon returning to the land of Israel, Joseph must once again negotiate his family's survival against the intrusion of external political realities.

In an attempt to reclaim the illusion of a unified narrative, however, interpreters employ a variety of creative explanations to account for this final

---

64. After Herod's death in 4 BCE Augustus Caesar resolved a dispute that broke out among three of Herod's surviving sons by dividing the kingdom among them. Philip received Batanea, Trachonitis and Auranitis. Antipas (14.1-12) received Galilee and Perea. Archelaus received the title 'ethnarch' and the territories of Judea, Idumea and Samaria. Archelaus's reign was incredibly short and disastrous. 'Both Jews and Samaritans petitioned Rome for his removal because of his brutal and insensitive rule. Augustus banished him to Gaul in A.D. 6, and his territory became a Roman province under the prefect Coponius'. See 'Archelaus', *HCBD*, p. 66; cf. Peter Richardson, *Herod: King of the Jews and Friend of the Romans* (Columbia, SC: University of South Carolina Press, 1996), pp. 21-22.

movement of Joseph, Mary and Jesus. Such strategies allow for uninterrupted *jouissance* in the world before the text by averting our gaze from
the second displacement prompted by Archelaus's abrupt appearance.
Davies and Allison, for instance, suggest that the move to Galilee is meant
to implicitly associate Jesus with the salvation of the Gentiles.[65] Similarly,
Graves suggests that Matthew is trying to emphasize Jesus' humble origins
or perhaps, because of Nazareth's mixed Gentile/Jewish population, is trying to appeal to a broad audience.[66] John P. Meier argues that Matthew cannot end his story with the return to Israel for although '[h]is tradition pre-
supposed that Joseph and Mary came from Bethlehem . . . everyone knew
that Jesus grew up at Nazareth and was called a Nazarene. Therefore Mt
must find a reason for a final shift in sacred geography'.[67] Meier goes on to
write, 'While fear of Archelaus would be a good reason for leaving Judea,
it is strange that safety would be sought in Galilee, which was ruled by
Herod's other son, Antipas, who later killed the Baptist'.[68] Meier's second
comment is symptomatic of interpreters who can find no narrative explanation for the move to Galilee; it curiously appears as a disjointed addition to
an otherwise harmonious narrative.

From the perspective of homelessness and displacement, however, Nazareth's insignificance makes it a suitable hiding place for the exiled. Escap-
ing to a small village far from the political centre of Judea means that Jesus
will be 'off the radar' of the ruling aristocracy. Itinerancy and distance from
the centre equal safety. Although the region of Galilee was integrated into
the economic network of the larger Roman world with roads connecting it
to the surrounding regions, most people traveling through Palestine would
have bypassed Galilee (though some would have passed nearby).[69] The text
alludes to the danger surrounding the more developed and urbanized area of
Judea. In such contexts, a socially uprooted individual (such as Jesus after
his forced excursion to Egypt) would be perceived as more of a threat to the
smooth, uninterrupted functioning of the ideological–political order.

Those who are forced to flee often have little choice over where they might
end up. Joseph, it seems, is presented with something of a dilemma. After
Herod dies, the divine messenger instructs him to return to Israel, presumably

65. Davies and Allison, *Matthew*, I, p. 208.

66. Graves, 'A Story Ignored', p. 73.

67. Meier, *Matthew*, p. 15; cf. Beare, *Matthew*, p. 84; Brown, *Birth*, p. 207; Davies
and Allison, *Matthew*, I, p. 274; Evans, *Matthew*, p. 61; Donald A. Hagner, *Matthew
1–13*, vol. 1 (WBC; Nashville, TN: Thomas Nelson, 1993), pp. 39-40; Nolland,
Matthew, pp. 126-27.

68. Meier, *Matthew*, pp. 15-16. However, Evans claims that the younger Antipas
was perhaps more 'tolerant' than Archelaus. See Evans, *Matthew*, p. 61.

69. Mark A. Chancey, *Greco-Roman Culture and the Galilee of Jesus* (SNTSMS,
134; Cambridge: Cambridge University Press, 2005), p. 20.

because it is safe, but when he gets there the danger has not fully subsided. So in order to fulfil the divine mandate, Joseph takes his family to the margins of Israel, creating a boundary of safety between Jesus and Judea. Jesus thus ends up in a liminal space: still residing in his homeland of Israel but estranged from his hometown of Bethlehem. Despite the fantasmatic desire for a harmonious ending, there is no genuine 'return from exile'. By the end of 2.13-23 Jesus remains displaced from his hometown, estranged from his wider household and forced to integrate into a new and different social environment (with a mixed Jewish/Gentile and rural population). Meier reasons that '[s]ince Bethlehem was Jesus' home town according to Mt, Galilee is a place of exile. It is in exile that Jesus will exercise his ministry. He will come home to Judea only to die'.[70] Having detected the unresolved ending of 2.13-23, in which the displaced Jesus remains detached from home place, I now move to an exploration of the text's intertexture, to discern how it provides further material for the text's potential desublimation.

Intertexture in the Flight to Egypt (Matthew 2.13-23)

As noted above, Mt. 2.13-23 contains an abundance of oral-scribal intertexture, a subset of intertexture that involves the reconfiguration, recitation and/or re-contextualization of other texts.[71] Brown notes that nowhere else in the Matthean text do explicit citations come in such abundance (they constitute about one-third of the content in 2.13-23).[72] Conventional interpretations often regard the citations of the OT and allusions to Moses as the driving force behind the narrative. Rather than dominating the text, however, the strategic use of intertexture enhances the narrative of displacement by giving it further depth and significance in the text's proclamation that Jesus is not only the Jewish Messiah but also a displaced outsider. It does this, specifically, by reciting and reconfiguring episodes of homelessness, displacement and exile central to the Jewish tradition. In this section I focus on the ways in which the intertexture of 2.13-23 enhances the narrative of displacement explicated above, first, by introducing a Moses typology that resounds through the Matthean text, and second, by examining the text's fulfilment-of-prophecy motif.

Moses Typology

In his study *The New Moses: A Matthean Typology*, Dale C. Allison identifies a number of intertextual links between the Matthean Jesus and the OT figure of Moses. The evangelist, he contends, reconfigures Jesus as the new

70. Meier, *Matthew*, p. 16.
71. Robbins, *Exploring the Texture*, pp. 40-58.
72. Brown, *Birth*, p. 219.

Moses, a long-awaited liberating figure who will save his people.[73] Many aspects of Moses' life are echoed in the flight to Egypt text: first, Herod's order to slaughter the infants in and around Bethlehem in 2.16-18 echoes Pharaoh's decree to expunge every male Hebrew child in Exod. 1.15-22; second, Jesus' displacement as an infant echoes Moses' displacement in Exod. 2.15; and third, Joseph's return to Israel with Mary and Jesus in Mt. 2.21 echoes Moses taking his wife and sons and returning to Egypt in Exod. 4.20.[74] The following table lists the intertextual allusions to Moses present within the wider infancy narrative of Matthew 1–2:

Parallels between Jesus and Moses[75]

A genealogy locates Moses within the line that runs from the patriarchs (Exod. 1.1-5; 6.14-20).	A genealogy places Jesus within the lineage coming from Abraham (Mt. 1.2-16).
In a dream, an angel prophesied of Moses that he would save the people (Josephus *Ant.* 2.210-16).	In a dream, an angel told Joseph that Jesus would save his people (Mt. 1.21).
At the time of Moses' birth, Pharaoh gave orders to do away with every male Hebrew child (Exod. 1.15-22).	The birth of Jesus was accompanied by Herod's slaughter of the infants (Mt. 2.16-18).
Pharaoh decided to kill the male Hebrew babies because he learned about the birth of the future liberator of Israel (Josephus *Ant.* 2.205-209).	Herod killed the infants because he learned about the birth of the king of the Jews (Mt. 2.2-18).
Pharaoh learned of the future deliverer from the sacred scribes (Josephus *Ant.* 2.205, 234).	Herod learned of the coming saviour from the chief priest and scribes (Mt. 2.4-6).
When Moses was a young man, he was forced to leave his homeland because Pharaoh wanted to kill him (Exod. 2.15).	As a child, Jesus was providentially taken from the land of his birth because Herod wanted to kill him (Mt. 2.13-14).
After the death of Pharaoh, Moses was commanded by God to return to Egypt (Exod. 4.19).	After the death of Herod, Joseph was commanded by an angel to return to Israel (Mt. 2.19-20).
Moses took his wife and sons and returned to Egypt (Exod. 4.20).	Joseph took his wife and son and returned to Israel (Mt. 2.21).

73. Dale C. Allison, *The New Moses: A Matthean Typology* (Minneapolis, MN: Fortress Press, 1993).

74. Luz points out that there are, in fact, numerous ancient parallels to the persecution and preservation of a royal child (and provides an extensive list for comparison). See Luz, *Matthew 1–7*, pp. 144, 52-55.

75. Adapted from Charles H. Talbert, *Matthew* (Grand Rapids, MI: Baker, 2010), pp. 37-38.

Allison contends that the new Moses typology functions to add authoritative support to Matthew's Jesus by evoking the influential presence of the past. While Jesus does not match expectations of the Jewish Messiah—his death as a criminal on a shameful Roman cross being the biggest scandal—the text is at pains to present him in continuity with the traditional Jewish story of liberation. 'A Jesus discontinuous with the Jewish tradition could not have been Israel's Messiah, for the latter was a feature of the former'.[76] Although Jesus is displaced by and within his own society, he still has a cultural home within the Jewish mythological tradition, itself interwoven with episodes of displacement and exile. While the Matthean Jesus is perceived as a marginal figure within first-century Palestinian society, the text recognizes this marginality as a central emblem within the Jewish tradition, and, in particular, within the prophetic stream originating with Moses.

Accordingly, the story of Moses as a displaced figure in the OT functions to supplement the narrative of displacement in Mt. 2.13-23 by providing another reading site of desublimation against the romanticization of Jesus' homelessness. While Moses was a liberator of the Hebrew people, he also lived as an alien within Egypt. Within the book of Exodus, Moses undergoes a number of cycles of homelessness and/or displacement, and his infancy is one of bloodshed and abandonment. Shortly after his birth, the Egyptian Pharaoh commands that all male Hebrew infants be killed by drowning (Exod. 1.15-22). Rather than sending him to be killed, Moses' parents set their child adrift on the Nile River wherein he is found and adopted by Pharaoh's kin. He then grows up as an outsider within the royal family of Egypt (2.1-22). As an adult, Moses agitates Pharaoh until he is finally forced to leave Egypt because of the violence set against him. After leading the exodus 'out of Egypt' under God's guidance and command (12–14), he becomes a wanderer in the desert with his people and never actually makes it to his (new) home place in the 'promised land'. Moses in fact dies in the desert as a homeless wanderer.

Fulfilment-of-Prophecy Motif
Matthew 2.13-23 also contains three mentions of fulfilled prophecy. The narrator reconfigures certain texts from the OT in light of the story being told about Jesus.[77] As discussed above, the focus on 'prophecy fulfilled' can feed Christian apologetic concerns about the accuracy of Scripture that may

---

76. Allison, *The New Moses*, p. 272.

77. For a detailed discussion of the prophecy citations, see George M. Soares Prabhu, *The Formula Quotations in the Infancy Narrative of Matthew* (Rome: Biblical Institute Press, 1976). For examples of their typical treatment within scholarship, see Brown, *Birth*, pp. 219-25.

detract from the socio-political elements encoded within the text. Horsley explains:

> Recognition of Matthew's distinctive use of 'formula quotations' . . . led to the claim that Matthew 2 . . . 'is dominated by geographical names', which are 'what is really important to him'. The purpose of Matthew in Chapter 2 was apologetic: how did Jesus the messiah come from Nazareth in Galilee and not from Bethlehem. However, the claim that the geographical names, even as emphasized by the formula quotations, dominate Matthew 2 seems highly questionable. What dominates the narrative is clearly the conflict between the newborn king of the Jews and the reigning king, Herod. The threatened Herod figures directly or indirectly at every point in the narrative except the actual visit of the Magi in verses 9-11 and the naming in verse 23.[78]

How, then, do the three prophecy citations in 2.13-23 function to supplement the narrative of displacement prominent in the text's other textures?

The first prophecy citation occurs in v. 15 and reads, 'Out of Egypt I have called my son'. The Matthean text shapes the displacement of Joseph, Mary and Jesus to Egypt and their subsequent return to home place in fulfilment of Hos. 11.1, 'When Israel was a child, I loved him, and out of Egypt I called my son'. The infant Jesus is identified with the nation of Israel collectively referred to as 'my son' in the Hosean text.[79] Return to home place is combined with a message of deliverance from the oppression of Egypt. Evans notes that '[t]he passage is not predictive, nor is it messianic'.[80] Instead, the text enhances the Moses typology discussed above. Just as God saved his people by calling them out of Egypt with the help of his prophet Moses, so he will once again save his people by calling his son, Jesus, out of Egypt. As Elaine M. Wainwright puts it, Jesus becomes a 'liberated liberator'.[81] By having Jesus repeat certain experiences of Israel's history, the text seeks to integrate Jesus into the wider story of his people as part of his cultural and traditional home place, in much the same way as was attempted by the genealogy. Just as there were ruptures in the genealogy signaling his displacement, however, Jesus' return to home place is disrupted by the introduction of Archelaus who, as we observed above, provokes the second displacement to Nazareth in Galilee.

---

78. Horsley, *Liberation of Christmas*, pp. 6-7.

79. For a discussion regarding the seemingly odd position of this particular quotation, see Martinus J. Menken, '"Out of Egypt I Have Called My Son": Some Observations on the Quotation from Hosea 11.1 in Matthew 2.15', in *The Wisdom of Egypt* (ed. Anthony Hilhorst and George H. van Kooten; Leiden: Brill, 2005), pp. 143-52.

80. Evans, *Matthew*, p. 58.

81. Wainwright, *Shall We Look*, pp. 60-66. Viljoen similarly argues that while Herod impersonates the foreign domination of Roman imperial ideology and exposes Jesus to unlimited power over, Jesus ultimately emerges as victor. See F.P. Viljoen, 'Power and Authority in Matthew's Gospel', *Acta theologica* 31.2 (2011), pp. 329-45.

The second prophecy citation follows Herod's murderous actions (2.16) and interrupts the narrative prose with poetic verse to reveal an underlying discomfort with Jesus' lone redemption:

> Then was fulfilled what had been spoken through the prophet Jeremiah:
> 'A voice was heard in Ramah,
>   wailing and loud lamentation,
> Rachel weeping for her children;
>   she refused to be consoled, because they are no more' (2.17-18).

As mentioned above, Jesus' initial displacement occurs not because of divine providence but as an excremental remainder to the routine horror of infanticide. Jeremiah 31.15, the OT text cited, originally referred to the destruction of the Northern tribes, particularly the descendants of Joseph and Benjamin, whose mother was Rachel, the wife of the patriarch Jacob (Gen. 30.22; 35.16-20). The Matthean text associates the slaughter of the children in Bethlehem with the conquest of Northern Israel in 722 BCE by the Assyrian Empire, evoking its disorienting effect on both the Northern and Southern Kingdoms. To draw a parallel with Jesus, the conquest resulted in the exile of its inhabitants (Jer. 31.16b, 17).[82] Jack R. Lundbom adds that if Jeremiah postdates the Babylonian destruction of Jerusalem in 586 BCE, then Rachel is most likely weeping for all of Jacob's children who were forced into exile.[83] Such a connection is particularly fitting given that Ramah was a staging area from which the exiles were deported to Babylon. Once again, the intertexture of the text evokes the themes of exile and estrangement from home place, bound up with immense grief, to supplement the narrative of displacement.

The third prophecy citation concerns Jesus' second displacement to Nazareth, 'There he made his home in a town called Nazareth, so that what had been spoken through the prophets might be fulfilled, "He will be called a Nazorean"' (Mt. 2.23). What is troubling for traditional exegetes is that the source of the prophecy citation cannot be found in the OT or other ancient texts. Davies and Allison suggest that because Nazareth itself was looked down upon as a town eligible of reproach (cf. Jn 1.46), the location itself might be regarded as an object of prophecy (specifically the material of the suffering servant in Isaiah 53 who is scorned and despised).[84] Even so, the text is possibly a summary and word-play on Judg. 13.5, 'For behold, you shall conceive and give birth to a son, and no razor shall come upon his

---

82. The following commentaries explicitly identify Jesus as a symbolic participant in Israel's exile: Davies and Allison, *Matthew*, I, pp. 267-68; Keener, *Matthew*, p. 112; Meier, *Matthew*, p. 15; Nolland, *Matthew*, p. 125.

83. Jack R. Lundbom, *Jeremiah 21–36* (Anchor Bible; New York: Doubleday, 2004), p. 437.

84. Davies and Allison, *Matthew*, I, p. 280.

head, for the boy shall be a Nazarite to God from the womb; and he shall begin to save Israel', and Isa. 11.1, 'a shoot [וְנֵצֶר] will spring from the stem of Jesse, and a branch from his roots will bear fruit', both involving key words resembling Nazareth. In Judges, the parents of Samson are promised a boy who will be a Nazarite. A Nazarite was a holy person who consecrated himself or herself to the service of God by taking a special vow requiring abstinence from wine and the cutting of one's hair (cf. Num. 6; Judg. 13.5-7; 16.17; Amos 2.11-2; 1 Macc. 3.49-52; Acts 18.18; 21.17-26; *m. Nazir*). The Matthean text, accordingly, consecrates its Jesus simulacrum to God's service.

As a charismatic leader, Jesus' experience of displacement will, in time, testify to his proclamation of the Kingdom of the Heavens and the need for righteousness and justice. In the Isaiah text, the prophet foretells the coming of a branch of the roots of Jesse, the father of David. Hence the prophets have foretold the coming Messiah 'will be called a Nazarene'.[85] In this sense, Jesus is once again integrated into his familial lineage, recalling the genealogy in Mt. 1.1-17, especially its emphasis on Jesus' Davidic ancestry which, as we observed above, evokes for the reader the suffering of displacement and exile.

Taken together, then, the heavy use of intertexture within 2.13-23 amplifies its narrative of displacement. The Moses typology reappears throughout the Matthean text to lend authoritative support to Jesus' mission and ministry (cf. Mt. 3.13-17, Exod. 14.10-31; Mt. 4.1-11, Exod. 16.1-17.7; Mt. 5–7, Exod. 19.1–23.33; Mt. 11.25-30, Exod. 33.1-23; Mt. 17.1-9, Exod. 34.29-35; Mt. 28.16-20, Deut. 31.7-9). Allison remarks that the passages in which Moses' tacit presence is the strongest display an order that, for the most part, mirrors the Pentateuch.[86] The prophecy fulfilment motif will also continue through the Matthean text (Mt. 3.3; 4.13-16; 5.17; 8.17; 12.17-21; 13.14-15, 35; 21.4-5; 26.54-56; 27.9-10) and each time implicitly reawakens Jesus' marginal self-identity formed during his infancy.

Conclusions

Jesus' identity as a displaced outsider is established from the very inception of the Matthean text. This chapter has argued that the effects of this initial

---

85. William F. Albright, 'The Names "Nazareth" and "Nazorean"', *JBL* 65 (1946), pp. 397-401; J. Spencer Kennard, 'Nazorean and Nazareth', *JBL* 66 (1947), pp. 79-81; Graeme Allan, 'He Shall Be Called — a Nazarite?', *ExpTim* 95.3 (1983), pp. 81-82; Rudolf Pesch, '"He Will Be Called a Nazorean": Messianic Exegesis in Matthew 1–2', in *The Gospels and the Scriptures of Israel* (ed. Craig A. Evans and W. Richard Stegner; Sheffield: Sheffield Academic Press, 1994), pp. 129-78.

86. Allison, *The New Moses*, p. 268.

displacement on Matthew's Jesus simulacrum include his uprooting from both home place and normalized social institutions. The genealogy (1.1-17), which gestures toward Jesus' future displacement, contains echoes of forced displacement, itinerancy and homelessness within the remembered history of the OT, thereby offering a reading site of desublimation against the romanticization of Jesus' homelessness in the world before the text. Furthermore, the flight to Egypt frames homelessness as an objective reality, inseparable from external political and social pressures. It is set during a period of significant political instability and turmoil. Joseph, Mary and Jesus are forcefully displaced as refugees to Egypt, and then again, upon their return to Israel, to the politically insignificant town Nazareth in Galilee.

Despite its retroactive heralding of Jesus as a prophetic saviour and liberated liberator, the Matthean text employs a number of rhetorical strategies that intensify the suffering associated with Jesus' infancy. When attention is drawn to these properties of the text, the reader is able to resist the idealization of the infancy narrative and instead focus on its obscene underside. The repetition of the key verb ἀναχωρέω, for instance, underscores the involuntary nature of displacement. Likewise, the divine injustice of Jesus' lone redemption against the mass carnage of infanticide intrudes on the theological idealization of Jesus as God's son. While the return to Israel provides the illusion of stability and wholeness, the text breaks expectations with the introduction of Archelaus, prompting a second exile to Galilee.

The location of Jesus within Matthew 1–2 must not be limited to just his geographical location (i.e. where he comes from), but should also include his social location, which is one of displacement, marginality and exteriority—that is, of being on the outside. Surely the formational event of a double-exile in 2.13-23 has something to say about Jesus' identity as an expendable itinerant who will later come into significant conflict with institutions of power. While Joseph intends to keep his wife and child safe, Jesus grows up away from his original home place in Bethlehem and forms a marginal self-identity. The theme of withdrawal for safety is continued in the beginnings of Jesus' mission, to which I now turn.

3

REACTION

The concepts of resistance and disruption are especially useful for a study on homelessness because so many of the Christian responses, while hospitable in intent, do not challenge institutional inequality and oppression. While Jesus exhibited compassion on an individual level, he also challenged oppressive structures and practices.

Laura Stivers[1]

[A] range of contemporary critical theories suggests that it is from those who have suffered the sentence of history—subjugation, domination, diaspora, displacement—that we learn our most enduring lessons for living and thinking.

Homi Bhabha[2]

Jesus' itinerant mission is almost always conceived of as a manifestation of his agency. The protagonist freely accepts his God-given mission to 'save his people from their sins' (Mt. 1.21). It is in the process of fulfilling this task that he 'chooses' to enact a so-called homeless lifestyle for himself and his disciples. While Jesus' itinerancy is an integral part of his mission, the reasons behind it are more complex than usually supposed. The Matthean text signals a number of social, political and economic factors that drive Jesus to the margins. As we have already seen, the infancy narrative in Matthew 1–2 introduces the reader to a saviour who is both geographically and politically displaced, and grows up in Nazareth away from his original hometown of Bethlehem. Homelessness and displacement are not usually conditions that people freely choose to enact. Rather, external factors, often far beyond their control, influence their ability to act and react within a particular social and economic environment. The same is true within the story world of Matthew's Gospel, in which Jesus' actions must always be understood in relation to other events, characters and external pressures that are encoded within the world of the text.

---

1. Stivers, *Disrupting Homelessness*, p. 8.
2. Homi Bhabha, *The Location of Culture* (London: Routledge, 1994), p. 172.

It is with this in mind that we approach the beginnings of Jesus' mission in 4.12-25. As we will see, dominant interpretations typically frame the beginning of Jesus' proclamation of the Kingdom of the Heavens and his calling of the first disciples as a primary manifestation of his agency. Such interpretations sustain the fantasmatic dimensions of neoliberal ideology by emphasizing the ease of social mobility over the influence of structural determinants. Jesus and his disciples, so it is presumed, arbitrarily decide to resist the dominant structures of the world by organizing themselves into a new counter-cultural religious movement. In fact, the calling narratives are often viewed as paradigmatic for all Christian disciples, a universally applicable narrative of radical orientation toward Jesus. But lurking within the text's gaps and neglected details lay textures of conflict and disruption. What good is it to speak of choice when one only has a limited array of options? Can one really move from the centre to the margins voluntarily? On the contrary, this chapter argues that a number of external socio-political realities are internalized in Jesus as an experience of perpetual uprooting and displacement. Jesus' itinerant mission begins as a *reaction* to his physical and social displacement within first-century Palestinian society.

This chapter follows the usual route of analysis: narrative features are discussed in tandem with intertextual components and social and cultural textures. At all points the ideological hermeneutic outlined in Chapter 1 informs the questions asked of the text and its interpretation. Before getting to the highlighted text (4.12-25), however, it is important to explore its wider literary context. What noteworthy events have transpired since the flight to Galilee at the end of the infancy narrative in 2.23?

Another Homeless Prophet (Matthew 3.1–4.11)

Matthew 3 introduces the character of John the Baptist, who features as another homeless figure within the Gospel of Matthew. The Baptist's meagre existence in the wilderness is apparent from his clothing and diet: he 'wore clothing of camel's hair with a leather belt around his waist, and his food was locusts and wild honey' (3.4).[3] These details allude intertextually to the OT figure of Elijah, who is also described as '[a] hairy man, with a leather belt around his waist' (2 Kgs 1.8). Carter writes that the Baptist's 'food denotes poverty, as well as his commitment to and trust in God by not being distracted from the reign because of concern with daily food (cf. Mt.

---

3. For a detailed study on the diet of John the Baptist, see James A. Kelhoffer, *The Diet of John the Baptist: 'Locusts and Wild Honey' in Synoptic and Patristic Interpretation* (Tübingen: Mohr Siebeck, 2005); cf. Moxnes, *Putting Jesus in his Place*, pp. 101-102.

6.25-34, 11). He is indebted to no one.'[4] In other words, John exists as an archetypal homeless prophet, detached from the household and normalized society, and sitting at the margins of the ideological–political order.[5] Moreover, according to the Matthean text, 'people from the regions of Jerusalem and Judea were going out to him, and all the region along the Jordan, and they were baptized by him in the river Jordan, confessing their sins' (3.5-6).[6]

Is it correct to think that John's apparent homelessness is also a remnant, symptomatic of existing arrangements of power in the first century? The narrative abruptly marks his appearance (παραγίνεται) in 3.1 and does not provide a background or origin story as we had with Jesus. Within the sacred texture of the text, the Baptist is characterized as the forerunner to Jesus whose proclamation, which involves both a call to repentance and anticipation of Jesus' preaching, readies the audience for the Jewish Messiah. The text appeals to Isa. 40.3 ('The voice of one crying in the wilderness, "Prepare the way of the Lord"') in its rationale for the Baptist's retreat to the wilderness.[7] His subordination to Jesus is also explicated in Mt. 3.11-12, 14 and 11.2-6. Davies and Allison note a high degree of parallelism between the Matthean portraits of John and Jesus: they say similar things (cf. 3.2 with 4.17, and 3.7 with 12.34 and 23.33, and 3.10 with 7.19); they are introduced in a similar fashion (cf. 3.1 with 3.13); they act by the same authority, which emanates from Heaven (21.23-32); they are prophets (11.9; 14.5); they are executed as criminals (14.1-12; 26–27); and they are buried by their own disciples (14.2; 27.57-61).[8] We can add to this list their shared characterization as displaced outsiders.

---

4. Carter, *Margins*, p. 95.

5. See Ellis Rivkin, 'Locating John the Baptizer in Palestinian Judaism: The Political Dimension', *SBL 1983 Seminar Papers* (Atlanta, GA: Society of Biblical Literature, 1983), pp. 79-85.

6. For more on John the Baptist from a historical perspective, see Ernst Bammel, 'The Baptist in Early Christian Tradition', *NTS* 18.1 (1971), pp. 95-128; Joan E. Taylor, *The Immerser: John the Baptist within Second Temple Judaism* (Grand Rapids, MI: Eerdmans, 1997); Walter Wink, *John the Baptist in the Gospel Tradition* (SNTSMS. 7; Cambridge: Cambridge University Press, 2006). For an analysis of the Baptist in Matthew's narrative, see Gary Yamasaki, *John the Baptist in Life and Death: Audience-Oriented Criticism of Matthew's Narrative* (JSNTSup, 167; Sheffield: Sheffield Academic Press, 1998).

7. This quote is also found within the DSS, leading some scholars to posit a connection between John and the Qumran community (or the Essenes) who withdrew to the wilderness out of concerns for religious purity, see 1QS 8.12-16; 9.19-20; cf. Otto Betz, 'Was John the Baptist an Essene?' *BR* 6.6 (1990), pp. 18-25; Craig A. Evans, *Ancient Texts for New Testament Studies: A Guide to the Background Literature* (Peabody, MA: Hendrickson Publishers, 2005), pp. 149-50.

8. Davies and Allison, *Matthew*, I, pp. 289-90. Meier argues that the emphasis on parallelism between Jesus and John the Baptist, with a few pointed statements about

In his analysis of the class struggle in the ancient Greco-Roman world, de Ste Croix constructs a spatial dichotomy between the city (πόλις) and the countryside (χώρα). Both terms connote class: on the one hand, and as will be explored in more detail below, the πόλις represents the concentration of political and economic power; the χώρα, on the other hand, refers to the vast stretches of farmed land, village communes and, of course, the non-elite role in the cycle of production. Underscoring this geographical distinction is an accompanying set of ideological perceptions: those inside the πόλις view the peasants of the countryside with a dismissive and undifferentiated contempt; from the perspective of those in the χώρα, however, the elite population of the city are brutal and exploitative, extant only because of their objectively violent system of extracting tribute. It is in the χώρα that de Ste Croix places the historical Jesus, who, until his fateful trip to Jerusalem, tends to avoid the πόλις.[9]

Now add to this the Baptist's appearance in the wilderness or desert (ἔρημος), and we can detect a rupture in the smooth functioning of the ideological–political and economic orders. John is positioned outside the main sites of agricultural production (χώρα) and consumption (πόλις), and instead within the dangerous and anarchic wasteland of the ἔρημος. The ἔρημος is infused with political overtones that communicate a sense of danger and lawlessness. For instance, in Acts 21.38 the ἔρημος is referred to as a gathering place of a band of revolutionaries. Woven into the text's intertexture is also the special significance that the wilderness has in the OT, given the forty years of homeless wandering by the Hebrew people (Exod. 33.12, 15; Num. 14.13; 16.31; Josh. 24.18).

The destitution of this remembered tradition is encapsulated especially well by Psalm 107:

> . . . Some wandered in desert wastes [בַמִּדְבָּר/ἐρήμῳ],
>> finding no way to an inhabited town;
> hungry and thirsty,
>> their soul fainted within them . . . (vv. 4-6).

The Matthean text champions the Baptist's outsider status. His immense popularity draws out from the cities and their surrounding regions the surplus population to the elite's requirements for economic production. Despite the prophetic nature of John's ministry and his calling from God to prepare the way, however, his marginal existence in the wilderness is best not romanticized. The text describes the fragmentation of regulating power

the Baptist's inferiority, reflects the Baptist's place in Matthew's three-part progression of salvation history (the OT, the time of Jesus, and the time of the church). See John P. Meier, 'John the Baptist in Matthew's Gospel', *JBL* 99 (1980), pp. 383-405.

9. De Ste Croix, *Class Struggle*, pp. 9-18.

structures in the centre over the margins by alluding to a growing resentment against the status quo. John's baptism signifies an interruption of
renewal and change. His hostile encounter with some of the Pharisees and
Sadducees who come for baptism in Mt. 3.7-10 demonstrates the political
tension that his prophetic speech and action readily invite. John is, accordingly, later arrested and beheaded by the ruling elite (4.12; 14.1-12).

Jesus appears on the scene in 3.13 to be baptized by John. Following
an exchange about whether it is appropriate for the inferior John to bap-
tize the superior Jesus (3.14-15), a baptism takes place and the Spirit of
God descends upon Jesus (3.16), driving him farther 'into the wilderness' to
experience yet another cycle of homelessness (4.1-11). Again, the intertexture of the text echoes the Exodus story of wandering in the Sinai desert; he
'fasted for forty days and forty nights' recalls the forty years the Israelites
spent sojourning. Davies and Allison remark that the inclusion of the 'Spirit
of God' as a driving force solidifies this intertexture as it 'was held to have
been particularly active among the Israelites during the exodus and the wilderness wanderings'.[10] The rupturing of the spatial dichotomy between the
countryside and the city is continued in the non-productive wasteland by the
devil's temptation of food (4.2-4), the promises of the city (4.5-7), and the
kingdoms of the world (4.8-11). It is immediately following this period of
testing and withdrawal in the wilderness that Jesus will begin his itinerant
mission.

Structuring the Beginning of Jesus' Mission (Matthew 4.12-25)

From a narrative perspective, Mt. 4.12-25 contains four distinguishable
scenes: first, the arrest of John the Baptist (vv. 12-16); second, the proclamation of the kingdom (v. 17); third, the calling of the first disciples
(vv. 18-22); and fourth, the inauguration of itinerant mission, healings and
the spread of Jesus' fame (vv. 23-25). Interpreters ought to exercise caution
in their structuring of the text, however. In recent years a structuring of Matthew that views the opening five words of 4.17 ('From that time Jesus began
. . . ') as constituting an introductory formula to a new major section of the
Gospel has gained some traction.[11] A consequence of this structuring is that

---

10. Davies and Allison, *Matthew*, I, p. 355.
11. Kingsbury adopts this threefold structure of Matthew: the presentation of
Jesus (1.1–4.16); the ministry of Jesus to Israel and Israel's repudiation of Jesus (4.17–
16.20); and the journey of Jesus to Jerusalem and his suffering death and resurrection
(16.21–28.20). He suggests that the formulaic phrase 'From that time on Jesus began to
preach . . .' (4.17; 16.21) initiates each new narrative block. See Jack Dean Kingsbury,
Matthew: Structure, Christology, Kingdom (Minneapolis, MN: Fortress Press, 1975);
cf. David R. Bauer, *The Structure of Matthew's Gospel: A Study in Literary Design*

Jesus' displacement to Capernaum becomes isolated from the proclamation of the coming kingdom.[12]

Key to this structuring is the much disputed formula Ἀπὸ τότε ['from that time'] in 4.17. Luz, for instance, points out that the inclusion of this clause is intended precisely to establish a connection with the preceding verses.[13] The Matthean text often uses the adverb τότε as a connective particle to link two events through an unspecified passage of time.[14] F. Neirynck argues that enough narrative connections exist between 4.17 and 4.12-16 to warrant its inclusion in the same paragraph.[15] Indeed, as will be argued below, it is the event of the arrest of the Baptist that prompts Jesus to withdraw to Capernaum, go about calling the first disciples and begin his itinerant mission. The event also carries through the narrative thread of the Baptist's outsider location into Jesus' own ministry.

If taken together, the beginnings of the Matthean Jesus' mission are best understood as a reaction to the arrest of the Baptist, in addition to the other social and economic threads that are encoded within the text. While religious motivations for Jesus' undertaking are certainly evident (and noted particularly by the eschatological context of proclamation of the kingdom),[16] these must be balanced against the various political, economic and social forces that drive his movements. A politicizing of these textures reveals that the arrest of the Baptist functions as a significant trigger for Jesus' *withdrawal* from Nazareth and the beginning of his ministry in Capernaum. As a result, the Matthean Jesus' itinerant mission is from its very inception symptomatic of underlying pressures within his wider ideological–political environment.

(Bible and Literature Series; Sheffield: Sheffield Academic Press, 1988). Carter also divides the text here in his structuring of Matthew into six sections: see Carter, *Margins*, p. 119. Nolland attaches v. 12 to the previous pericope (4.1-11): Nolland, *Matthew*, p. 170.

12. The arrest of the Baptist, it is presumed, brings to a close the John material introduced in Matthew 3, and Jesus' proclamation in 4.17 is seen to initiate a new chapter in Matthew's story of Jesus.

13. Luz, *Matthew 1–7*, p. 192; cf. Donald Senior, *Matthew* (Nashville, TN: Abingdon Press, 1998), p. 61.

14. Cf. A.H. McNeile, 'τότε in St. Matthew', *JTS* 12 (1911), pp. 127-28.

15. F. Neirynck, 'Απο Τοτε Ηρξατο and the Structure of Matthew', *ETL* 64 (1988), pp. 21-59.

16. Sim, for instance, argues that by opening Jesus' ministry with a call to repentance the text accepts the notion of free will and human responsibility for individual action. A tension between human responsibility and the inevitable onslaught of apocalypse is present in much of Jewish eschatological thought. See David C. Sim, *Apocalyptic Eschatology in the Gospel of Matthew* (SNTSMS, 88; Cambridge: Cambridge University Press, 1996), p. 91.

Jesus Withdraws (Matthew 4.12-16)

After hearing of John's arrest, Jesus, sensing danger, withdraws (ἀνεχώρησεν) from Nazareth and settles in Capernaum. The Matthean text locates Capernaum by the sea (θαλάσσης) in the area of Zebulun and Naphtali and includes another fulfilment citation from the prophet Isaiah. Immediately following this, Jesus begins his mission by proclaiming (κηρύσσειν) that people should repent (μετανοεῖτε) in preparation for the coming Kingdom of the Heavens (ἡ βασιλεία τῶν οὐρανῶν).

Commenting on Mt. 4.12-13, Luz supposes that

> Matthew does not provide information about the subjective motives of Jesus for his return. Jesus goes to Galilee for the sole and uncomplicated reason that it corresponds to the divine plan that he minister to 'Galilee of the Gentiles'. . . . This applies precisely to the move to Capernaum also. Matthew underscores through the allusions to the following quotation that the move corresponds to the divine plan. Why Jesus (biographically) left Nazareth and chose Capernaum as residence is of no interest to him.[17]

To recall a key discourse of neoliberalism, it is curious that Luz frames Jesus' movement in terms of a 'choice' to enact God's divine plan. Even though Jesus' actions have economic, social and political consequences, they are isolated from this context and treated as significant only insofar as they advance Jesus' soteriological role. A careful reading of the text, however, reveals that the beginning of Jesus' mission is not the result of an arbitrary choice. Rather, the pericope begins with Jesus 'hearing' (Ἀκούσας) of John's arrest. This sensory-aesthetic texture echoes Joseph's 'hearing' (ἀκούσας) of Archelaus ruling over Judea in 2.22. Jesus is prompted to withdraw once again to Galilee for safety and refuge.[18] The inclusion of these mitigating factors directly preceding Jesus' public ministry provides a point of desublimation in the text's ideological texture.

My previous discussion of the key Matthean verb ἀναχωρέω in Chapter 2, for example, identified how the term predominantly appears in connection with episodes of socio-political danger and describes the forced displacement of its subject. Carter maintains that while John's arrest causes Jesus to withdraw into Galilee, 'Jesus' withdrawal from the wilderness (around the Jordan) to Galilee is not for safety reasons (as in 2.12, 13, 14, 22)'.[19] He

17. Luz, *Matthew 1–7*, p. 194; cf. Senior, *Matthew*, p. 62.

18. Nolland argues that the move to Capernaum in v. 13 is probably not connected to the withdrawal to Galilee in v. 12; see Nolland, *Matthew*, p. 171. Evans describes the move somewhat romantically as Jesus' 'return' to Galilee, 'he does not take up residence in Nazareth, his hometown, but rather in Capernaum . . . a bustling fishing village in Jesus' day, with a population of about 1,000'. See Evans, *Matthew*, p. 88.

19. Carter, *Margins*, p. 113.

points out that Jesus withdraws into a dangerous territory, occupied by the Roman client Herod Antipas, and is made more dangerous by the Baptist's arrest.[20] The reader should, however, recognize the echo to the previous displacement in which Joseph avoids the centres of power in Judea by fleeing to (the still dangerous) Galilee. Sean Freyne, for instance, suggests that 'the frequent withdrawals of Jesus might be interpreted as indicative of his need for constant vigilance before the threat of Herod, especially since there seems to be a conscious avoidance of the Herodian towns of Sepphoris and Tiberias'.[21] This makes sense given the explicit depictions of displacement in 2.12, 13, 14, 22. The threat of Herod lingers in the background of the narrative and continues to drive the actions of Jesus. Carter himself notes how, with Jesus' relocation, the 'periphery' of Galilee symbolizes 'a new and non-localized centre' of divine presence.[22]

Other narrative elements provide further clues that Jesus' response to John's arrest is symptomatic of external socio-political realities. The passive verb παραδόθη (of παραδίδωμι), for example, which alludes to the Baptist's arrest or 'handing over' in 4.12, occurs a number of times toward the end of the Gospel with respect to Jesus' own arrest (26.2, 16, 21, 23, 24, 25, 45, 46, 48; 27.2, 3, 4, 18, 26) and thus makes a clear parallel between their shared fate: the final solution for deviants who disrupt normalized society is extermination.

While Jesus' move to Capernaum is motivated by self-preservation, another ideological dimension to be considered is that of 'withdrawal' as a subversive political act. It is within this semantic range that ἀναχωρέω in the context of Matthew 4 is most evocative (and might also tie into the practice of monastic 'withdrawal' from the world). As discussed in Chapter 1, Žižek distinguishes between two broad categories of violence in the world: *subjective violence*, a more visible form performed by a clearly identifiable agent, and *objective violence*, which includes both a 'symbolic' violence embodied in language and its forms and 'systemic' violence, or the consequences of the smooth functioning of our economic and political systems.[23] The Baptist's arrest, for example, is not directly attributable to any one subject (e.g. Herod); rather he and his disruptive/prophetic ministry of baptism is disposed of through objectively violent regulating mechanisms in order that society may return to its smooth, uninterrupted functioning.

20. Davies and Allison are also reserved about whether this instance of ἀναχωρέω carries with it the connotations of fear and flight, for the movement involves no change in Herodian jurisdiction. See Davies and Allison, *Matthew*, I, p. 376.
21. Freyne, *Galilee*, p. 222.
22. Carter, *Margins*, p. 113.
23. Žižek, *Violence*, pp. 1-2.

It is in addressing these less-than-obvious forms of systemic violence in the contemporary dominance of late capitalist-democracy that Žižek frames his argument not via a revolutionary 'call to arms' but rather through the *inaction* of sitting back and waiting, by means of a patient, critical analysis. There is no need for a fake sense of urgency for '[t]he threat . . . is not passivity, but pseudo-activity, the urge to "be active", to "participate", to mask the nothingness of what goes on. People intervene all the time . . . [t]he truly difficult thing is to step back, to withdraw.'[24] Similarly, he contends that 'the task today is to resist state power by withdrawing from its scope, subtracting oneself from it, creating new spaces outside its control'.[25] So too, Jesus' 'withdrawal' from society functions as a time of escape. His forty days in the wilderness (4.1-11) is a period of abstinence and testing. In v. 12, upon hearing of the Baptist's arrest, Jesus further disengages from everyday life in Galilee, excusing himself from involvement in the city/countryside cycle of production.[26] As we will see below, Jesus' announcement of a heavenly kingdom attempts to extend this space well outside the scope of societal control and is followed immediately by the subtraction of fishermen from their full participation in the reigning ideological–political and economic orders.

Geographical Intertexture

After his 'withdrawal' or 'escape' in 4.12, Jesus moves to 'Capernaum, by the lake, in the territory of Zebulun and Naphtali' (4.13). Josephus describes Capernaum as a κώμη, a village or small town in the countryside (Josephus, *Life* 1.403). In the first century, it functioned primarily as a seaside fishing village, on the northwest shore of the Sea of Galilee.[27] Jesus' settlement here is denoted by the verb κατοικέω, which can mean to live, dwell or settle (down) in an intransitive sense, but can also describe the action of inhabiting a body (as in the case of a spirit) or space for a limited period of time.[28] It appears frequently in the LXX (nearly seven hundred times) to denote the inhabitation or settlement of the land, but appears just four times in Matthew: first, in 2.23, when Joseph settles in Nazareth after being displaced from Judea by Archelaus; second, in 4.13; and finally, twice to refer

---

24. Žižek, *Violence*, p. 183.

25. Slavoj Žižek, *In Defense of Lost Causes* (London: Verso, 2008), p. 339.

26. As noted above, the practice of withdrawing from wider societal practices in order to progress one's social and political goals is also illustrated by the first-century Jewish sect of the Essenes (Josephus, *War* 2.113-19).

27. For archaeological discoveries that may shed light on Capernaum as a place of residence for the historical Jesus, see James F. Strange and Hershel Shanks, 'Has the House Where Jesus Stayed in Capernaum Been Found?', *BAR* 8.6 (1982), pp. 26-37; Henry I. MacAdam, 'Domus Domini: Where Jesus Lived (Capernaum and Bethany in the Gospels', *TR* 25.1 (2004), pp. 46-76.

28. 'κατοικεω', *BAGD*, p. 425.

to spirits inhabiting bodies (12.45; 23.21).[29] Jesus' settlement here is not permanent, however. In terms of the first element of Bouma-Prediger and Walsh's phenomenology of home, Capernaum does not function as a site of permanence with a sense of enduring residence nor does it feature as a point of orientation. In their sixth element, Bouma-Prediger and Walsh suggest a distinction between a 'resident' and an 'inhabitant'; the former is merely a temporary occupant whereas the latter entails becoming rooted in a particular place.[30] The Matthean Jesus *resides* in Capernaum but does not come to *inhabit* it as home place (and moreover, he later attacks it in 11.22-23).

Given the frequent repetition of uprooting from home place, it is reasonable to assume that the move to Capernaum renders a certain psychological change for Jesus. In considering the itinerancy of Jesus' ministry from the context of Jamaican migration, Paul Zilonka suggests that villages such as Nazareth usually foster strong kinship ties, and the personal psychological impact of this transfer of residence likely involves considerable trauma. He writes that

> [w]hen Jesus permanently moved away from his family, his 'roots', he was thrust into a new drama on the public stage. He would learn the deeper meaning of the proverbial statement, 'You cannot go home again'. Geographical changes, a change of neighborhood, leave permanent effects in the way a person thinks and acts.[31]

Zilonka admits that an exploration of such features associated with migration appear outside of the Matthean 'evangelist's purpose'. On the contrary, such features are interwoven into the social and cultural texture of the text and, as discussed in Chapter 5, come to a breaking point during Jesus' return to his hometown (13.53-58).

Within 4.12-25, the trauma associated with forced displacement is highlighted when Jesus' escape (ἀναχωρέω) to Capernaum is followed by another prophecy citation:

> Land of Zebulun, land of Naphtali,
>   on the road by the sea, across the Jordan, Galilee of the Gentiles—

---

29. The NRSV translation of κατῴκησεν in 4.13 as 'made his home in' is problematic in that it fuels the illusion that Capernaum is a place of safety and stability for Jesus, and yet upon arrival he immediately begins an itinerant ministry. Other English translations are more restrained than the NRSV: the KJV, for example, says that Jesus 'came and dwelt' there, and the NIV renders it as 'he went and lived' there. Such translations grant the impermanence of Capernaum in its function as a home place for Jesus. Some commentators speak in a more nuanced fashion of Capernaum as a 'home base' for Jesus' ministry; see Harrington, *Matthew*, p. 71; Nolland, *Matthew*, p. 171.

30. Bouma-Prediger and Walsh, *Beyond Homelessness*, pp. 61-62.

31. Paul Zilonka, 'The Pain of Migration', *TBT* 26.6 (1991), p. 354.

> the people who sat in darkness
>   have seen a great light,
> and for those who sat in the region and shadow of death
>   light has dawned (4.15-16).

Davies and Allison suggest that the prophecy fulfilment offers 'scriptural warrant for a geographical fact of Jesus' ministry, namely, his presence in Galilee'.[32] Focused on determining the importance of the location for Matthew's intended audience, they venture that the evangelist must have either a theological interest in Galilee or is trying to redeem the geographical particulars of Jesus' movements against some vocal Jewish objections (they prefer the latter).[33] However, the prophecy citation can also function to further desublimate Jesus' displacement to Capernaum. As noted earlier, the Matthean text often employs prophecy citations to supplement a narrative of displacement as characters encounter hostile political circumstances. In light of this text's possible function as a counter-narrative to Roman imperial power, for example, Carter points out that the identifiers of the lands of 'Zebulun and Naphtali', 'across the Jordan' and 'Galilee of the Gentiles' locate Jesus not merely in Capernaum but in the promised land that God gave to the people and over which God has sovereignty. This challenges the Roman and Herodian legal claims to possession of Galilee.[34] The citation embeds Jesus within his cultural-religious home place and simultaneously confronts the Roman territorial claims of his wider ideological–political constellation.

The citation is drawn from Isa. 9.1-2 (although it is different from both the LXX and MT versions) and consists of the beginning of a poem declaring a new age and a new ruler, a promise of hope in the aftermath of displacement and defeat. Jesus' arrival in Capernaum is, accordingly, interpreted as the fulfilment of Isaiah's promise of deliverance, originally addressed to the devastated regions of northern Palestine of his day. The prophecy most likely concerns the historical situation described in 2 Kgs 15.26 and 1 Chron. 5.26, in which the Israelites from Naphtali are taken captive by the Assyrians during 733–732 BCE.[35] The intertexture evokes the suffering

32. Davies and Allison, *Matthew*, I, p. 379.

33. Davies and Allison, *Matthew*, I, p. 380. Beaton notes how the structuring of the wider pericope can have an impact on the interpretation of this prophecy citation. When the pericope is not broken at 4.17, and its wider literary context is taken into account, then the citation is able to 'move beyond a purely geographical proof-text'. See Richard Beaton, *Isaiah's Christ in Matthew's Gospel* (SNTSMS 123; Cambridge: Cambridge University Press, 2002), p. 105.

34. Carter, *Roman Empire and the NT*, p. 105.

35. Only some commentators make the explicit connection to 2 Kgs 15.26; see Carter, *Margins*, p. 115; Davies and Allison, *Matthew*, I, p. 380; France, *Matthew*, p. 143.

that goes along with their deportation but reconfigures it so as to associate Jesus with their hopes and desires of liberation. In the Isaiah text, a son from the house of David who brings salvation is promised (Isa. 9.6-7).[36] In the Matthean text, this promise is applied to the mission of Jesus, who, as a son from the house of David (Mt. 1.1), is retroactively heralded as a liberated liberator.[37] This rich use of intertexture not only amplifies Jesus' strategy of withdrawal in the face of perceived danger but draws the reader's focus onto the setting of the text. Having explored the geographical references above, I now briefly identify the text's topographical features.

The Setting of the Sea of Galilee

Topographical features within Mt. 4.12-22 evoke for the reader the socio-economic environment in which the beginning of Jesus' public activity is embedded. Reference to the sea (θάλασσαν) is made four times and functions as an element of the rhetography of the text's inner texture, inviting the reader to create a graphic image of the protagonist's surroundings.[38] Robbins describes the rhetography of the text as communicating a certain reality that functions to construct a familiar context of meaning.[39] Within the Gospels, sensory data is usually punctuated: the textures, sounds, smells and tastes engendered by the sea are left to the reader's imagination. Most first-century readers would be familiar not only with the aesthetics of the landscape evoked by the sea but also its economic utility. The Sea of Galilee (which is actually a freshwater lake) is the largest topographical feature in Palestine and is fed primarily by the river Jordan and a number of underground springs. During antiquity the lake gave rise to a number of settlements and villages with plenty of trade and ferrying by boat.[40]

Within the Matthean text, after hearing of the Baptist's arrest, Jesus temporally resides by the sea (θάλασσαν) in the small peasant town of Capernaum. The mention of water further strengthens the connection of Jesus to John, who was baptizing in the river Jordan. Carter suggests that the location 'by the Sea of Galilee' continues an emphasis on places away from the

---

36. For a more detailed exploration of the context behind this prophecy citation, see Beaton, *Isaiah's Christ*, pp. 102-19; Carter, *Roman Empire and the NT*, pp. 93-107; Soares Prabhu, *Formula Quotations*, pp. 107-35.

37. Wainwright, *Shall We Look*, pp. 101-18.

38. The toponym ἡ θάλασσα τῆς Γαλιλαίας is incredibly rare outside of the NT. Notley suggests that the origins of the phrase may have something to do with the Isaiah prophecy citation in Mt. 4.16-17. See R. Steven Notley, 'The Sea of Galilee: Development of an Early Christian Toponym', *JBL* 128 (2009), pp. 183-88.

39. Vernon K. Robbins, 'Rhetography: A New Way of Seeing the Familiar Text', in *Words Well Spoken: George Kennedy's Rhetoric of the New Testament* (ed. C. Clifton Black and Duane F. Watson; Waco, TX: Baylor University Press, 2008), p. 81.

40. Freyne, *Galilee*, p. 174.

powerful centre; the connection of the sea to the region of 'Galilee under the Gentiles' (4.12-16) evokes the 'places of oppressive darkness and death in which the light of God's saving presence now shines'.[41]

After the prophecy citation in vv. 15-16 (which also makes reference to the sea) and Jesus' proclamation of the nearing kingdom, Jesus walks by the Sea of Galilee and calls his first disciples who were 'fishing into the sea' [ἀμφίβληστρον εἰς τὴν θάλασσαν] (v. 18). The metaphor of fishing is then anthropomorphized by Jesus, 'Follow me and I will make you fish for people' [. . . ποιήσω ὑμᾶς ἁλιεῖς ἀνθρώπων] (v. 19). Resseguie suggests that in the NT the sea or lake is presented as 'a place of spiritual awakening to Jesus' transcendence and to the disciples' own fragile faith'.[42] In this text, however, the focus is also on the lake's economic utility in the cycles of production between the countryside and city. As will be discussed later, the emphasis on the occupation of these first disciples, combined with the topographical setting, draws attention to the socio-economic context within which these men 'choose' to leave their households and follow Jesus. Indeed, the entire region, including its topographical features (such as the Sea of Galilee), was not only under the jurisdiction of Herod but also Rome's claim of total ownership.[43] As such, the political economy was regulated in ways that favoured the institution of Rome and its elite population and tended to exploit the labour of the rest.[44] The setting, then, encodes a layered ideological–political complexity that permeates through the various textures of the text.

Heralding the Kingdom (Matthew 4.17)

Jesus' public ministry begins with a 'light [which] has dawned' (v. 16). Awakening to the reality of his marginal predicament, Jesus proclaims, 'Repent, for the kingdom of heaven has come near' [μετανοεῖτε, ἤγγικεν γὰρ ἡ βασιλεία τῶν οὐρανῶν]. His words not only echo the Baptist's proclamation in 3.2 but mark the dawning of a messianic age. The text employs the verb κηρύσσειν (the present active infinitive of κηρύσσω) to denote Jesus' activity of making a public declaration. His speech is akin to the official activity of heralds but also echoes the speech emanating from a

---

41. Carter, *Margins*, p. 121.
42. Resseguie, *Narrative Criticism*, 97.
43. The Sea of Galilee was passed down as inheritance among the Herods who functioned as puppet kings and were allied to Rome. Around the time of the historical Jesus, Antipas was said to be in control of the region; see Josephus, *Ant.* 18.36-38; *War* 2.168.
44. Carter, *Roman Empire and the NT*, pp. 8-13.

divine oracle, like that of the Hebrew prophets.[45] The proclamation contains a sense of immediacy; an imperative to repent (μετανοεῖτε) and the inclusion of ἐγγίζω leading the second clause highlight the immanent closeness of the kingdom's realization.[46] As mentioned above, the adjoining text in v. 17, 'From this time' [Ἀπὸ τότε], connects the proceeding clause to the on-going theme of displacement. Consequently, Jesus' proclamation is linked narratively to his withdrawal or escape after the arrest of the Baptist. This disrupts the sublimation of Jesus' break from home place as a lifestyle choice. Instead, the beginning of Jesus' mission is constructed in the context of forced migration; his proclamation is situated as a *reaction* against the intrusion of external political realities.

From a revolutionary perspective, the dawning of new light in the shadow of death (16b) evokes within the text's ideological texture the Marxist concept of class consciousness. Georg Lukács argues that becoming conscious of one's concrete social position and its revolutionary potential changes being itself—that is, it transforms a passive working class into the proletariat as a revolutionary subject.[47] As discussed in Chapter 1, Jesus' symbolic descent into the expendable social strata, outside of the dominant mode of production, makes him a potential revolutionary agent; with nothing to lose except his life, he possesses an innately destructive attitude toward the existing social order. While in exile, subtracted from the χώρα, Jesus becomes attuned to the objective nature of political and economic exploitation. His homelessness has occurred not because of individual moral or economic failure but as an excremental remainder to the symbiotic functioning of the wider ideological–political edifice. The text retroactively transforms his abject social reality into a theological locus for organizing revolutionary power.

In what follows I explore the rhetorical and sociological meaning and meaning effects produced by Jesus' proclamation in both the context of the Matthean text and specifically in terms of homelessness. This is achieved by discussing the social and cultural rhetography evoked by the proclamation of the Kingdom or *basileia*, and then considering the intended audience of Jesus' injunction to repent.

A Kingdom for the Homeless
The phrase βασιλεία τῶν οὐρανῶν appears twenty-three times in the Matthean text and functions as an evocative and counter-cultural epithet of the prophetic imagination. The kingdom or *basileia* presents an alterna-

45. 'κηρύσσω', *BAGD*, p. 543.
46. Davies and Allison, *Matthew*, I, p. 392.
47. Georg Lukács, *History and Class Consciousness: Studies in Marxist Dialectics* (trans. Rodney Livingston; London: Merlin, 1971).

tive vision of reality, disrupting the Real that frames and sustains dominant arrangements of power in society. Within such a vision the expendable
homeless population, those at the very bottom of first-century society, are
heralded a central place.[48]

In his book *Heaven and Earth in the Gospel of Matthew*, Jonathan T.
Pennington discusses the meaning of the *basileia* within his wider thesis
concerning Matthew's thematic use of heaven and earth. He argues that the
basileia, which has a variety of meanings including but not limited to the
rule or reign over a kingdom in a spatial sense, is both from heaven and
heavenly.[49] The phrase communicates both a spatial sense of God's kingdom in heaven and from heaven as well as a qualitative sense that God's
kingdom is heavenly. This naturally contrasts with the counterpoint of
earthly kingdoms and earthly ways of governance.[50] As such, the expression '*basileia* of the heavens' (βασιλεία τῶν οὐρανῶν) is used as part of the
thematic contrast between God's kingdom and the kingdoms of this world.
Pennington posits that 'the "of heaven" part . . . is not accidental or reveren-
tially circumlocutionary, but serves a very powerful literary and rhetorical
purpose: to contrast the world's kingdoms with God's'.[51]

Elaborating on the theology of the kingdom, Pennington remarks that the
social and cultural texture of Matthew

> repeatedly shows that the social order of the kingdom of heaven is very
> unlike the present earthly order, and that the latter will eventually be
> replaced by the former (6:9-10). In addition to radical teachings . . . Mat-
> thew depicts the heavenly kingdom as one in which the mourning and
> poor in spirit are blessed (5:3, 4, 10-12), while those who are meek stand
> to inherit the earth (5:5). Equally topsy-turvy, the nature of the kingdom

48. Evans, for instance, argues that Jesus' vision of the *basileia* includes the
redemption and restoration of Israel from its enduring exile. See Craig A. Evans,
'Aspects of Exile and Restoration in the Proclomation of Jesus and the Gospels', in
Exile: Old Testament, Jewish, and Christian Conceptions (ed. James M. Scott; Leiden:
Brill, 1997), pp. 299-328.

49. Pennington responds to the translation of *basileia* as 'empire' when read against
the NT background of its Roman imperial context. Several scholars, including Carter,
have begun to use this translation as a means of demonstrating how Matthew's Gospel might function in conscious opposition to Caesar and the injustices of the Roman
Empire. Pennington suggests that such readings 'in a faddish way tend to overplay
the Roman card and construe all texts through this lens'. In doing so, these readings
might miss out other important nuances within the semantic cluster. See Jonathan T.
Pennington, *Heaven and Earth in the Gospel of Matthew* (NovTSup, 126; Leiden: Brill,
2007), p. 302.

50. Pennington, *Heaven and Earth*, p. 328.

51. Pennington, *Heaven and Earth*, pp. 337-38. See further Robert Foster, 'Why on
Earth Use "Kingdom of Heaven"? Matthew's Terminology Revisited', *NTS* 48 (2002),
pp. 487-99.

of heaven is such that the one who is lowly like a child will be the greatest therein (18:1-4; cf. 19:13-15), while the leaders in God's community should be the slaves of all (20:25-28; cf. 23:11). Those who give up everything for the heavenly kingdom will gain all back and more (19:26-29)—the first shall be last, and the last first (19:30).[52]

In his exploration of the political dimensions of *basileia* imagery in Matthew, Carter likewise suggests that '[t]he empire of the heavens is God's saving presence. God's reign has come near.'[53] But what does this 'empire' of the heavens look like? Carter, who reads the entire Matthean text as a counter-narrative to Roman imperial power, suggests that it functions as a 'tensive, open-ended, expanding symbol'. He continues:

> In a world dominated by Roman rule, Jesus will manifest God's empire in proclamation (4:17), in creating an alternative community (4:18-22), in acts that transform misery and brokenness (4:23-25) in anticipation of the full establishment of God's reign over all imperfection, sickness, and want (13:39-43, 49-50; 19:28; chs. 24–25). The proclamation that soon the world will acknowledge God's sovereignty, not Rome's, threatens the status quo but encourages the gospel's [marginal] audience.[54]

By proclaiming the *basileia* as a form of counter-cultural rhetoric, the subjects of the Roman imperial order are compelled to confront the fact that it exists, and exerts power, only insofar as it is accepted as such by its subjects.[55]

Before moving to the next section, it is worth briefly exploring how the *basileia* pertains to the issues of home and homelessness. In his book on the historical Jesus, Halvor Moxnes situates the kingdom within the category of 'imaginary places' that function as a vision of how a real place might be imagined differently. In his words, the kingdom opens up a 'third-space' of representation or imagination that presents plans for alternative ways of structuring places and material practices from that of the ideologies domi-

---

52. Pennington, *Heaven and Earth*, p. 340.
53. Carter, *Margins*, p. 119.
54. Carter, *Margins*, p. 120.
55. Jesus' use of imperial language to counter imperial language in some ways legitimizes (or can be used to legitimize) such discourse in the world before the text, as is illustrated by the many forms of imperial Christianity throughout history that have employed the language of kingdom to ground oppressive arrangements of power. See Schüssler Fiorenza, *The Power of the Word*, pp. 35-68; Elisabeth Schüssler Fiorenza, 'Reading Scripture in the Context of Empire', in *The Bible in the Public Square: Reading the Signs of the Times* (ed. Cynthia Briggs Kittredge, Ellen Bradshaw Aitken and Jonathan A. Draper; Minneapolis, MN: Fortress Press, 2008), pp. 157-71. For a critical survey of the recent use of 'empire studies' in NT scholarship, see Diehl, 'Anti-Imperial Rhetoric', pp. 9-52; Stephen D. Moore, 'The "Turn to Empire" in Biblical Studies', *Search* 35.1 (2012), pp. 19-27.

nated by the elite; it thus works as a poignant criticism of present conditions.[56] Moxnes further suggests that for those 'who had been uprooted from
their place of identity, the sayings about the kingdom . . . served to reinstate
them in a location that could give them a new identity'.[57] One of the 'imagined places' for the kingdom was located in the house and household. As
discussed below, Jesus' first disciples are dislocated from their households
and become (up)rooted in a new social location among fictive kin.

What might this mean with respect to Jesus' homelessness? Aside from the
homeless population functioning as a symptom of the reigning ideological–
political order (revealing its structural deficiencies that remain beneath the
surface), the conceptual spaces opened by the proclamation of the *basileia*
facilitate the raising of questions about the objective violence that underscores social reality. In modern liberal societies, for example, the homeless
are predominantly depicted as moral and economic failures, or worse, as victims incapable of effecting political change by themselves (without the help
of the 'more fortunate'). Similarly, in first-century Palestine, expendables, at
the very bottom of the social hierarchy and outside of the dominant modes of
economic production, were seen to lack intelligence or moral character and
fell outside the purview of social responsibility.[58] Jesus' proclamation of the
basileia, however, traverses the fantasy that homelessness exists as a private,
individualized responsibility. Rather, it confronts the reality that homelessness is a product of systemic violence inherent within existing arrangements
of social, political and economic power.

Who Should Repent?
Because Jesus' proclamation involves the potential re-ordering of the wider
ideological–political constellation, we ought to investigate the intended
character groups designated by Jesus' injunction to repent. This section
argues that within Matthew, 'repentance' signifies not merely a private religious encounter but rather a corporate activity of social and political transformation.

According to *BAGD*, the verb μετανοέω (and its related noun form
ἡ μετάνοια) in its basic sense describes the changing of one's mind. It also
conveys the idea of a total reorientation of behaviour, 'to feel remorse' and/
or 'to be converted' in a variety of relationships and in connection with

---

56. Moxnes, *Putting Jesus in his Place*, pp. 108-109. For more on critical spatial
theory, see Henri Lefebvre, *The Production of Space* (trans. Donald Nicholson-Smith;
Oxford: Blackwell, 1991); Edward W. Soja, *Thirdspace: Journeys to Los Angeles and
Other Real-and-Imagined Places* (Malden, MA: Blackwell, 1996).

57. Moxnes, *Putting Jesus in his Place*, p. 124.

58. Lenski, *Power and Privilege*, pp. 180-84.

varied responsibilities of the moral, political, social and religious spheres.[59] This second meaning, in connection with a return to God, becomes more apparent within a Semitic context. As Geza Vermes puts it,

> In the Semitic mentality of Jesus the Jew, it [repentance] implied not a change of mind as the *metanoia* of the Greek Gospels would suggest, but a complete reversal of direction away from sin, in accordance with the biblical and post-biblical Hebrew dual concept of 'turning', viz. 'turning away from' or 'returning to', conveyed by the verb *shuv* and the noun *teshuvah*.[60]

Contemporary theological understandings of repentance typically assume a *subjective* logic. Because no specific character groups are designated within Jesus' call to repent, the imperative tends to be read in generic ways that place the burden of responding to moral failure on individuals (inadvertently re-inscribing a neoliberal emphasis on personal responsibility).[61] With the exception of the generic proclamations in Mt. 3.2 and 4.17, however, the Matthean text uses the verb only in an *objective* sense (i.e. independent of a single conscious entity or subject).[62]

Repentance as a theme is not as strong within Matthew as it is in Luke: μετάνοια occurs only twice (Mt. 3.8, 11), both times in relation to the Baptist (compared to five in Luke); μετανοέω occurs five times (compared to nine in Luke), once from the Baptist (3.2), and four times from Jesus (4.18; 11.20; 11.21; 12.41). The Baptist declares that the Pharisees and Sadducees coming for baptism—scathingly referred to as a 'brood of vipers!'—must 'bear fruit worthy of repentance [μετανοίας]' (3.7-8). Jesus then continues in the tradition of the Baptist's teaching and ministry with his proclamation in 4.17, using the same language, 'Repent [μετανοεῖτε], for the kingdom of heaven has come near'. Davies and Allison write that 'Israel is called to turn to God and away from sin, to arise in moral earnestness from a sinful

59. 'μετανοέω', *BAGD*, p. 640.

60. Geza Vermes, *The Religion of Jesus the Jew* (London: SCM, 1993), p. 191; cf. James G. Crossley, 'The Semitic Background to Repentance in the Teaching of John the Baptist and Jesus', *JSHJ* 2.2 (2004), pp. 138-57. Crossley argues that the Greek alters the Aramaic to also include gentiles.

61. See especially Evans, *Matthew*, pp. 71, 90; Davies and Allison, *Matthew*, I, pp. 388-89; Harrington, *Matthew*, p. 51. While Carter focuses on the turning around of individual lives, he does point out that the call 'assumes that life as it is currently constructed by the ruling elites . . . is not how God wants it to be. The call expresses the divine will for change and is a means of averting judgment and disaster'. See Carter, *Margins*, p. 93.

62. Interestingly, repentance within Matthew does not appear to be a prerequisite to following Jesus. When Jesus goes about instructing pairs of individuals to follow him (18–22) he does not ask them to repent. This further strengthens the claim that for Matthew, repentance is a corporate, political act, over and above an individual, and moralistic act of piety.

slumber and to gain a wakeful heart and sober thought'.[63] Note here the corporate dimension: the call invokes all of Israel to change, including its social and political structures.

Similarly, the mention of repentance in 11.20-24 is also connected to corporate entities. On this occasion Jesus reproaches the cities (πόλεις) in which some of his deeds of power in earlier chapters had been carried out 'because they did not repent' [μετενόησαν]. The term πόλις denotes a 'population centre of varying size'. Within the Greco-Roman world the term generally held strong political associations, particularly in terms of the city-state.[64] In *The City in Biblical Perspective*, for instance, J.W. Rogerson defines cities as places where power and resources are concentrated. While in the ancient world most people did not live in cities, they were (like their modern equivalents) 'the centres where justice was administered, trade carried on, records kept, scribes trained, armies recruited, labour organized, power exercised'.[65] This implies that Jesus expected these centres of power to repent, in all their systemic and symbolic capacity, and by not doing so they open themselves to God's wrath (11.23-24). Two of the cities mentioned, Chorazin and Bethsaida, were located in upper Galilee, north of the Sea of Galilee. Excavations at Chorazin have revealed a 'medium-size town' that would have existed during the first century.[66] Bethsaida, meaning 'house of fishermen', was a commercial hub given city status by the tetrarch Herod Philip and named 'Bethsaida-Julias' in honour of Emperor Augustus' daughter.[67]

This corporate dimension to repentance is also found in the final Matthean occurrence of μετανοέω in 12.41. Responding to the scribes and Pharisees' request to see a sign, Jesus remarks,

> An evil and adulterous generation [γενεά] asks for a sign, but no sign will be given to it except the sign of the prophet Jonah. For just as Jonah was three days and three nights in the belly of the sea monster, so for three days and three nights the Son of Man will be in the heart of the earth. The people of Nineveh will rise up at the judgment with this generation [γενεᾶς] and condemn it, because they repented [μετενόησαν] at the proclamation of Jonah, and see, something greater than Jonah is here! (Mt. 12.39-41).

Ninevah refers to a city-state that repented at the proclamation of Jonah (Jon. 3). The repeated emphasis on 'generation' (γενεά) further strengthens the case for repentance understood in a corporate sense. Jesus confronts

63. Davies and Allison, *Matthew*, I, p. 306.
64. 'πόλις', *BAGD*, p. 844.
65. J.W. Rogerson and John Vincent, *The City in Biblical Perspective* (BCCW; London: Equinox, 2009), p. 4.
66. Z. Yeivin, 'Ancient Chorazin Comes Back to Life', *BAR* 13.5 (1987), pp. 22-36.
67. Harrington, *Matthew*, p. 163.

Israel as a collective body (although the Pharisaic scribes take on a representative role in their generation's injustice and unbelief), and his condemnation can be likened to the Hebrew prophets' theodicizing about the generation sent into Babylonian exile.[68]

The biblical background of Jesus' threats against these unrepentant cities is found in Isaiah and other prophetic writings. Jesus' comparison of Chorazin and Bethsaida to Tyre and Sidon (11.21) evokes intertextually the oracle against these cities in Isa. 23.2-4: 'Be still, O inhabitants of the coast, O merchants of Sidon. . . . Be ashamed, O Sidon, for the sea has spoken' (cf. 23.12; Ezek. 28.1-26). Moreover, the link between Sodom and Capernaum in Mt. 11.23 evokes Isa. 1.9-10a, which calls on Sodom as an example of both a destroyed and sinful city with exploitative rulers, 'If the Lord of hosts had not left us a few survivors, we would have been like Sodom, and become like Gomorrah. Hear the word of the Lord, you rulers of Sodom!' In both these examples the cities are judged collectively, in tandem with the holders of political office.

As with the major OT prophets, then, the Baptist's and Jesus' calls to repentance are based on the conviction that radical change must occur on a societal level.[69] The prophets warned against systemic violence present within the religious, social and political structures of ancient Israel.[70] According to de Ste Croix (citing Jones), 'The cities were . . . economically parasitic on the countryside. Their incomes consisted in the main of the rents drawn by the urban aristocracy from the peasants. . . . The splendours of civic life were to a large extent paid for out of these rents, and to this extent the villages were impoverished for the benefit of the towns.'[71] Repentance, for the Matthean text, then, appears to have more to do with the reorientation of these structures than with individual piety. This brings

---

68. For more on this intertexture, see Richard Alan Edwards, *The Sign of Jonah in the Theology of the Evangelists and Q* (London: SCM, 1971); G.M. Landes, 'Matthew 12.40 as an Interpretation of "The Sign of Jonah" against its Biblical Background', in *The Word of the Lord Shall Go Forth* (ed. C.L. Meyers and M. O'Connor; Winona Lake, IN: Eisenbrauns, 1983), pp. 665-84.

69. Crossley argues, via a lengthy discussion of the use of 'sinners' across ancient Jewish texts, that those called to repent are not the poor, the exploited, the uneducated, or the ordinary folk, but rather the wealthy and exploitative benefactors of existing arrangements of social and political power. See James G. Crossley, *Why Christianity Happened: A Sociohistorical Account of Christian Origins (26–50CE)* (Louisville, KY: Westminster John Knox, 2006), pp. 75-96.

70. See Walter Brueggemann, *The Prophetic Imagination* (Minneapolis, MN: Fortress Press, 2nd edn, 2001); see also for the first century Richard A. Horsley and John S. Hanson, *Bandits, Prophets, and Messiahs: Popular Movements in the Time of Jesus* (Minneapolis, MN: Winston, 1985).

71. De Ste Croix, *Class Struggle*, p. 13.

us back to the meaning produced by Jesus' proclamation of the *basileia* if understood as a reaction against socio-political displacement: repentance in the Matthean text involves the turning away from sin and toward God not merely of *individuals* but rather of *entire political systems*, including especially those city-states perpetuating asymmetrical social and economic relations.

Forming an Alternative Community (Matthew 4.18-25)

The first action Jesus takes after heralding the *basileia* is to form a community of disciples.[72] Walking by the Sea of Galilee, Jesus calls two pairs of fishermen to leave their boats and follow him. Barton notes how the emphasis on brothers (ἀδελφούς) in 4.18-22, repeated twice, links to the notion that following Jesus involves joining a community 'best understood as a brotherhood'.[73] A comparison might be made to the contemporary homeless population, which will often form small communities or networks that function as surrogates for family and home place.[74]

From a symptomatic understanding of homelessness, the call of the first disciples necessitates another careful reading against the grain of the text. Analysing the pericope through the social-scientific model of collectivism and kinship, for example, Lawrence observes that

> [t]he disciples illustrate an individualistic and personal decision that opts for a 'universal' collectivist goal rather than a concern for the nuclear 'in-group' alone as defined by the amoral familism model. In some ways, these brothers show individualistic traits, their attachments are not fixed. . . . This example shows that there is a certain synthesis between individualistic and collectivist traits in Matthew's world.[75]

In this respect, the call of the first disciples can potentially facilitate an individualistic understanding of homelessness in the world before the text. For example, conventional interpretations frequently construct 4.18-22 as a model of faithful conversion to Christian discipleship. Jesus goes about calling two pairs of brothers to leave their former lives and re-orient themselves around him and the *basileia*. Keener, for instance, suggests that the

---

72. Wilkins suggests that the Matthean motif 'Jesus, Immanuel, with his People' underlines a bond between Jesus and his disciples. See Michael J. Wilkins, *The Concept of Disciple in Matthew's Gospel* (NovTSup 59; Leiden: Brill, 1988), p. 150. Cf. Mt. 10.24, which stresses the disciples' solidarity with Jesus in persecution, authority and mission.

73. Barton, *Discipleship and Family Ties*, p. 129.

74. Shiloh Groot and Darrin Hodgetts, 'Homemaking on the Streets and Beyond', *Community, Work and Family* 15.3 (2012), pp. 255-71.

75. Lawrence, *Ethnography*, p. 241.

purpose of 4.18-22 is to 'demonstrate people's proper response to God's rule . . .', but more than this, the text 'provides Matthew's community [and by extension all Christians?] several examples of servant leadership and radical discipleship'.[76] Hagner similarly stresses that 'the calling of these disciples serves as a model of the nature of true discipleship generally. The call of God through Jesus is sovereign and absolute in its authority . . . [a]s the first disciples were called and responded, so are Matthew's readers called to respond.'[77] Likewise, Davies and Allison claim the text 'serves an aetiological function, for it recounts the acts whereby Jesus began to make men into missionaries. This means that we have before us the birth of the Christian mission. Also before us is the birth of the church, the decisive moment when people first threw in their lot with the cause of Jesus.'[78]

This paradigmatic framing of 4.18-22, influenced by dominant theological interests in the world before the text, can function to unnecessarily obscure other possibilities of meaning. In fact, the application of a feminist hermeneutics of suspicion reveals a glaring ideological inconsistency: the emphasis on only male disciples filters out women, who do not feature here.[79] Moreover, Beare remarks that events likely did not occur so abruptly as they do in the narrative, 'Jesus is out for a stroll on the lakeshore when he happens upon some fishermen who have never laid eyes on him before, calls upon them to join him, with the promise that he will make them 'fishers of men'; and they leave their work and their property on the spur of the moment and go off in his company'.[80] As we will see below, the predominant focus on these characters as (sublime) examples of faithful discipleship has meant that elements of the text's social and cultural texture have remained relatively underexplored.

Existing studies that attempt to accentuate the socio-political context of the text can also serve the interests of dominant ideologies. In his discussion of the ways in which 4.18-22 raises the issue of the disciples' relationship to wider society, for example, Carter describes their characterization as 'voluntary marginal'. He elaborates that this consists of their 'choosing' to live a liminal existence in alternative households because of existing ideology,

76. Keener, *Matthew*, p. 149.

77. Hagner, *Matthew*, I, p. 78.

78. Davies and Allison, *Matthew*, I, p. 404.

79. In attempting to redeem the text's aetiological function for wo/men, Wainwright argues that the crowd in Mt. 4.25 is similar to the calling of the four fishermen in 4.18-22 except that the crowd's following does not include gender differences. Elaine M. Wainwright, *Towards a Feminist Critical Reading of the Gospel according to Matthew* (BZNW, 60; Berlin: de Gruyter, 1991), pp. 80-81.

80. Beare, *Matthew*, p. 117.

commitments and visions of reality.[81] In his commentary, Carter draws on the social-scientific criticism of Dennis Duling to construct a binarism of 'voluntary marginality' versus 'involuntary marginality'.[82] This construction, however, does not correspond to the reality that marginalization is always a dynamic process involving a combination of internal and external pressures and influences. While such models are intended to simplify, the lack of nuance and stark contrast between so-called voluntary and involuntary categories functions to affirm the logic of neoliberalism; if marginality is voluntary, then the responsibility for its consequences lies with the individuals affected. Marginality in all its complexity always involves subjective, inter-subjective and objective processes interacting with one another. Even purposeful or strategic ideologies and commitments that are marginal are always produced within a specific context. While it is reasonable to infer that by joining Jesus the disciples move farther to the periphery, the implicit assumption among many interpreters is that these characters do not already occupy a marginal space. It is with this observation in mind that I explore the socio-economic location of these characters in more detail.[83] The label 'in/voluntary' is employed below as a means of fragmenting these categories when discussing the disciples' 'decision' to join Jesus' itinerant mission, and should assist with the desublimation of homelessness in the text's ideological texture.

Fishing for Fishermen

Repetitive texture indicates that the shared occupation of Jesus' new followers is a major topic in the discourse of 4.18-22: the casting nets (τὰ δίκτυα) used to catch fish are mentioned three times; the occupation and activity of fishing appears twice (ἁλιεῖς); boat (πλοίῳ/πλοῖον) is used twice; and the sea/lake (θάλασσαν) is mentioned twice. Furthermore, the wordplay in v. 19 is generated by their occupation: Jesus declares that he 'will make you fish for people'.[84] An emphasis on the shared occupation of these characters

---

81. Warren Carter, 'Matthew 4:18-22 and Matthean Discipleship: An Audience-Oriented Perspective', *CBQ* 59 (1997), pp. 58-59.

82. Carter also dialogues with theorists of marginality in his commentary. See Carter, *Margins*, pp. 43-45; cf. Duling, *Marginal Scribe*, pp. 125-28.

83. In his theory of the fetishism of commodities, Marx argues that social relations between human beings are governed by the apparently autonomous interactions of the commodities they produce. Given that the Matthean text explicitly ties in this discipleship narrative to the disciples' economic activity, we cannot ignore this context in assessing their 'decision' to follow Jesus. See Karl Marx, *Capital: A Critique of Political Economy*, vol. 1 (Moscow: Progress Publishers, 1887).

84. Davies and Allison note that this phrase has no real parallel in rabbinic or Hellenistic literature. See Davies and Allison, *Matthew*, I, p. 398. For a more detailed study

alerts the reader to the fishing industry of first-century Palestine as it is encoded in the text's social and cultural texture.

Does the disciples' shared occupation as fishermen mean they enjoy relative economic security or perhaps even prosperity? Harrington, for example, suggests that '[i]n light of the importance of the fishing business at the Sea of Galilee it is clear that the first followers of Jesus were leaving behind a secure and stable lifestyle'.[85] Similarly, in documenting the extensive and economically significant fishing industry in Galilee, Keener deduces that by leaving their livelihood these first disciples are making a major economic sacrifice. He claims that successful fishermen, even if not high on the social scale, were far better off than the peasantry.[86] Such interpretations intend to heighten the dramatic sacrifice these characters make in following Jesus, thereby heightening their function as role models of individual discipleship.

De Ste Croix, however, suggests that within the ancient economic system of the Greco-Roman world, fishermen originate from and remain among the broader peasant population.[87] Recent social-scientific scholarship has also seriously challenged the belief that fishermen were financially secure. In examining the fishing industry as a subsystem within the political and domestic economy of first-century Galilee, K.C. Hanson identifies the 'relationships between the various players within the sub-system: the Roman Emperor; Herod Antipas; the tax administrators; the brokers, tax collectors, and toll collectors; the fishing families; the hired laborers; the suppliers of raw goods and other products; fish processors; and shippers and carters'.[88] Hanson cautions that although fishing was an important component of the Galilean economy, 'it was not the "free enterprise" which modern readers of the New Testament may imagine. Even fishers who may have owned their own boats were part of a state regulated, elite-profiting enterprise, and a complex web of economic relationships', including heavy taxation that extracted wealth produced by the local industry and funnelled it directly to support the lifestyle of projects of elite society.[89]

of this phrase, see Wilhelm H. Wuellner, *The Meaning of 'Fishers of Men'* (Philadelphia, PA: Westminster, 1967).

85. Harrington, *Matthew*, p. 72. Davies and Allison suggest that Peter, Andrew, James, John and Zebedee appear to have belonged to the same fishing partnership, which included a number of hired servants (cf. Mk 1.16-20; Jn 21.1-3). As such, they believe they were probably 'from the (lower) middle class'. See Davies and Allison, *Matthew*, I, p. 397; cf. Jerome Murphy-O'Connor, 'Fishers of Fish, Fishers of Men', *BR* 15.3 (1999), pp. 22-49.

86. Keener, *Matthew*, pp. 151-53.

87. De Ste Croix, *Class Struggle*, pp. 269-70.

88. K.C. Hanson, 'The Galilean Fishing Economy and the Jesus Tradition', *BTB* 27.3 (1997), p. 99.

89. Hanson, 'The Galilean Fishing Economy'.

Hanson points out that the economic structures of the ancient Mediterranean 'were not independent systems with "free markets," free trade, stock exchanges, monetization, and the like, as one finds in modern capitalist systems'.[90] Rather, the mechanisms of the political economy in the ancient Mediterranean were structured in terms of the flow of benefits upward to the urban elites, and especially the ruling families (one might point out, of course, that the same is true within capitalism). Similarly, Freyne notes how by Hellenistic times the ruler, as holder of the estate, made a large amount of profit, whereas the fishermen made very little. The fishing rights were farmed out at a very high rate (between 30 and 40 percent of the total catch), indicating the tight imperial control of all aspects of the economy.[91] Readers ought, therefore, to refrain from imagining individuals who 'go to work'; rather their activity was embedded in various and complex domestic-economic and political-economic relationships, including peasant families and households. Hanson also forcefully argues that families of fishermen would fit broadly into the 'peasant' strata of society and not in some kind of bourgeois-idealized 'middle class'.[92]

Given all this, we might ask to what extent the conditions of these disciples' employment influence their 'decision' to leave their livelihoods and to follow Jesus? At best these fishermen had a precarious existence, marginal in economic security to landed peasants and the small minority of urban elites. It is not much of a stretch, then, to imagine a scenario in which their hardship provoked them to abandon work and live as drifters, especially if they were heavily indebted. Indeed, the withdrawal of Jesus in 4.12 sets the scene for the in/voluntary withdrawal of the fishermen from their boats and from full participation in the reigning ideological–political order. Upon encountering Jesus' proclamation, the fishermen themselves become conscious of their marginal predicament, caused not through moral or economic failure, but as a consequence of the smooth, uninterrupted functioning of society.

The social and cultural texture of the call of Matthew in 9.9 similarly confirms that those Matthew's Jesus calls as disciples already occupy the

90. Hanson, 'The Galilean Fishing Economy', p. 100.

91. Freyne is referring specifically to the Egyptian economy, but suggests that similar conditions would have been likely in Palestine. See Freyne, *Galilee*, p. 174. A connection between fishing and paying taxes is made in Mt. 17.24-27.

92. He writes, 'The fishers could hardly be classed as "entrepreneurs" in such a highly regulated, taxed, and hierarchical political-economy. While the boat owners/fishers may or may not have also been involved in fish processing this would not have made them wealthy, and certainly not "middle class", as many authors have contended, since the whole conceptualization of a middle-class is anachronistic relative to Roman Palestine. The "surplus" went to the brokers and the ruling elite.' See Hanson, 'Fishing', pp. 108-109.

margins of society (this time not so much on the economic as the social margins). In this text, Jesus sees Matthew at his place of work in the tax booth (τελώνιον). The language echoes the two scenes in 4.18-22 with Jesus' command to follow (ἀκολούθει), after which Matthew gets up and follows him. This character's occupation is not to collect taxes on land or from individuals, which would be collected by the Roman or local administration, but tolls on transported goods. He would be contracted to collect a certain quota, and lived on a marginal surplus. Carter posits that tax collectors belonged to the retainer class (below the wealthy elite but above landed peasants); however, they had little respect or social status.[93] Tax collectors were perceived as godless and without honour by fellow Jews. This explains the Pharisees' negative reaction to Jesus dining with 'tax collectors', in the house, lumping them together with 'sinners' as an inappropriate domestic setting in the verses immediately following Matthew's call (9.10-12). Hagner surmises that '[t]ax collectors, or tax farmers, in that culture were despised as greedy, self-serving, and parasitic. They grew rich at the expense of the poor by extorting from them more than was required by their superiors in order to fill their own pockets.'[94] Again, it is problematic to suggest that Matthew becomes 'voluntarily marginal' as he, along with the fishermen, is already marginal within his social context. Furthermore, even if he was slightly better off economically than the fishermen, he is nonetheless a visible symbol of the exploitative system in which all first-century subjects of the Roman Empire were entrenched.

A further noteworthy point is that by leaving their households and following Jesus, the disciples (whether fishermen or other characters) move further to the margins of first-century Palestinian society. Given the context of an honour-and-shame-saturated culture, the male disciples' displacement from the household means that their identities as householders and/or sons of the household are strained.[95] For Jesus and the disciples to be 'without a house, in no-place, was therefore to be deprived of a role either as a householder, which given his age would have been his normal position, or as a son in a household'.[96] Accordingly, their already precarious social standing within the wider socio-symbolic order is threatened. Moxnes points out that

93. Carter, *Margins*, p. 218; cf. Lenski, *Power and Privilege*, pp. 243-48.

94. Hagner, *Matthew*, I, p. 238.

95. Neyrey suggests that Jesus' constant mobility and 'absence from home and household' is problematic within his first-century context; however, Matthew's explanation for this is tied to Jesus' obedience to his heavenly Father. There is no doubt a tension here between embedded social conventions and the Matthean text's negotiation of Jesus' deviant identity. See Jerome H. Neyrey, 'Jesus, Gender, and the Gospel of Matthew', in *New Testament Masculinities* (ed. Stephen D. Moore and Janice Capel Anderson; Semeia Studies; Atlanta, GA: Society of Biblical Literature, 2003), pp. 54-55.

96. Moxnes, *Putting Jesus in his Place*, p. 96.

the call-to-discipleship narratives are about leaving a place of social identity that defines, secures and structures their identity. He writes, 'The young male followers of Jesus had left their established, if inferior, position in the male world and were in a liminal situation'.[97]

Similarly, Malina and Neyrey develop the idea that by following Jesus the disciples enter into deviant space and contend that '[a] first indication of such [deviant] social activity is to be found in physical mobility'.[98] They write:

> Travel on pilgrimage or business, as well as visits to relatives and the like, would be expected, usual and non-deviant. Such travel presupposes a return home, a solid and stable base from and around which boundaries of geographical stability are drawn. However, general geographical mobility, random wandering and moving from place to place all symbolize a break with previous social location and rank. The meaning symbolled by this sort of wandering life, this sort of geographical mobility, would be negatively perceived by first-century Mediterraneans precisely because for them, stability, roots, sedentary living and a stable center were the ideal. These people shared great aversion to geographical mobility that would make one a stranger and foreigner to others. Continued geographical mobility except in the case of forced movement, such as enslavement and exile, or necessity, such as emigration due to famine, war or some other calamity, was a deviant type of behavior.[99]

The last sentence of this quote is, of course, incredibly problematic. Malina and Neyrey appear to be saying that ad hoc geographical movement, without a legitimate reason, is deviant, but if one has a good reason (such as in the case of forced migration) then it is not deviant. The problem with this view is that Jesus' itinerancy in the Matthean text is both thrust upon him by external pressures and also perceived by others as deviant behaviour.

Regardless, the withdrawal of the fishermen from their boats complements the withdrawal of Jesus following the arrest of the Baptist in v. 12. Just as Jesus is thrust to the outside, so too, the already marginal social location of the first disciples is exacerbated. An emphasis on the deviant aspects of their shared itinerancy within the text's social and cultural texture, then, should provoke an effect of desublimation in the text's ideological texture. This inner group of followers represents the formation of an alternative community of displaced brothers, banded together as a surrogate home place of fictive kinship. Jesus features as the locus around which their revolutionary activity is mobilized; his vision of the *basileia* compels them into conscious in/voluntary action. The Matthean text is keen to expand upon

97. Moxnes, *Putting Jesus in his Place*, p. 96.
98. Malina and Neyrey, *Calling Jesus Names*, p. 22.
99. Malina and Neyrey, *Calling Jesus Names*, p. 22.

this early success of Jesus' challenge to the dominant ideological–political order, and so follows the call of the first disciples by narrating the positive reception of Jesus' call to action among the crowds.

An Itinerant Movement Begins

The final three verses of our highlighted pericope (4.23-25) provide an overview of and introduction to Jesus' public activity within Galilee. This brief section builds upon the proclamation in 4.17 and describes both the nature of Jesus' prophetic activity and the response with which he is met. His activity includes preaching the good news of the *basileia* and curing sickness among the people (cf. 9.35; 10.1).[100] Jesus' response earns him fame among those located on, and sympathizers with, the margins of the first-century Palestinian ideological–political order. The reader is told that '[r]eports about him spread out into the whole of Syria'.[101] Moreover, 'great crowds followed him', and set the scene for the Sermon on the Mount beginning in Matthew 5.

Matthew 4.23 includes the first use of 'gospel/good news' (εὐαγγέλιον) in Matthew to summarize Jesus' message of the approaching *basileia*. But for whom is the 'good news' intended? The analysis thus far would suggest that Jesus' itinerant mission offers hope of emancipation for those who are already dispossessed in some way; the *basileia* he proclaims alludes to a vision of a more equitable social reality. In line with the prophetic stream of the Israelite tradition, those in positions of power, and institutions of power such as the πόλις ('city'), are ordered to 'repent', to change their direction or face the consequences of cosmic destruction on the Day of Judgment.

The text describes in hyperbole the growth of Jesus' movement by identifying 'great crowds' (ὄχλοι πολλοί) following him from Galilee but also from centres of power, including Jerusalem and the Decapolis. The term Δεκάπολις literally means 'ten cities' and refers to the ten cities of Hellenistic culture east of Galilee and Samaria. Pliny the Elder provides the following list: Damascus, Philadelphia, Raphana, Scythopolis, Gaddara, Hippos, Dion, Pella, Gerasa and Canatha (*Nat.* 5.74). The emphasis on centres of power indicates a widespread movement of withdrawal from normal-

100. Evans suggests that the reference to curing diseases in v. 23 probably alludes to Deut. 7.15 and suggests that the text frames Jesus' ministry of healing as being in fulfilment of promises linked to the renewal of the Promised Land (cf. Isa. 26.19; 29.18; 35.5-6; 61.1; *4 Ezra* 8.53). See Evans, *Matthew*, p. 95.

101. Some redaction critics argue that the addition of 'Syria' to the Markan counterpart of this text in Mk 1.28 is because the evangelist is thought to come from this region, such as Antioch. See G.D. Kilpatrick, *The Origins of the Gospel according to St. Matthew* (Oxford: Oxford University Press, 1946), p. 131; cf. Evans, *Matthew*, p. 95; Luz, *Matthew 1–7*, p. 167 n. 16.

ized society in the countryside and suggests growth of a counter-cultural
resentment that can be traced back to the instability of these ruling political institutions. The narration of this mass withdrawal amplifies Jesus' own
displacement, which has resulted as an excess to the smooth, uninterrupted
functioning of the ideological–political order.

Conclusions

This chapter has argued that the narrative of displacement established in
Matthew 1–2 continues through the beginnings of Jesus' public activity.
Jesus' apparent decision to begin an itinerant mission is, in fact, precipi-
tated by external forces, most prominently, the arrest of John the Baptist. In
Matthew 3, the Baptist appears on the outside in the wilderness, dispensing
prophetic speech and acts and drawing crowds out to him. By the end of
Matthew 4, Jesus is having a similar influence, but on a much greater scale.
Indeed, despite coming from a dysfunctional background, Jesus' immense
popularity, as summarized by 4.23-25, provides the backdrop to the subsequent narrative events of teaching and healing. While the disciples, introduced in 4.18-22, serve as an inner circle to Jesus, the crowds in 4.23-25
add an outer periphery to his itinerant network.

The external socio-political realities of Jesus' infancy are internalized in
the character of Jesus as he engages his wider ideological–political environment. After being displaced to Capernaum, Jesus publicly announces the
basileia; an imaginary counter-cultural space in which the ordering of society is reversed. Within this symbolic revolution, displaced subjects, such as
Jesus, are afforded honour and uplifting, whereas the elite and retainers of
the status quo are dishonoured and dethroned. The vision is accompanied
by an injunction to repent, not directed at individual men and women, but
rather to the entire ideological–political order, and in particular the cities'
extractive role in the cycles of production. Such prophetic dissent unsettles
the sensibilities of the normalized population, and Jesus will ultimately be
suppressed through lethal violence.

Jesus' first disciples are fishermen who abandon their fishing boats and
their livelihoods to follow him. Their withdrawal is not arbitrary, but rather
is integrated with their occupation and social standing as it is encoded within
the text. An emphasis on the socio-economic realities specific to the fishing
industry in first-century Palestine adds much needed complexity to the disciples' in/voluntary decision to leave the house and/or household structure.

Rather than presenting Jesus and his first disciples as individual,
free-roaming moral agents, able to make isolated economic choices, the
Matthean text embeds these characters within a wider social and political
context within which they are in constant negotiation. Far from 'choosing' to become homeless and begin an itinerant ministry, Jesus is already a

displaced and uprooted individual. Rather than condemning or celebrating him for this, the Matthean text points to the underlying resentment that the character of Jesus is able to provoke among the disciples and the crowds. In the next chapter, I consider a pericope in which two more would-be disciples engage Jesus in a dialogue about the desperation, destitution and offensiveness of an itinerant existence.

4

DESTITUTION

The puzzling aspect with many of the sayings of Jesus is that they speak about breaking with the household and moving away from it, but do not mention any socialization into a new location.

Halvor Moxnes[1]

These things were of themselves terrible and grievous; how could they be otherwise? Surely it was most miserable for men to become beggars . . . without having done any wrong, and to be rendered houseless and homeless, being driven out and expelled from their own houses, that thus, being compelled to dwell in the open air day and night, they might be destroyed by the burning heat of the sun or by the cold of the night.

Philo[2]

Matthew 8.20 contains a statement frequently cited as evidence for Jesus' supposed homelessness. Alluding to the material and psychological strain of his ministry, Jesus laments that '[f]oxes have holes, and birds of the air have nests; but the Son of Man has nowhere to lay his head'.[3] The bleak and restless tone evoked by the saying, which confesses both the destitution and desperation that typically accompany experiences of homelessness, traverses the romanticization of Jesus' homelessness in the text's ideological texture. As was discussed in the previous chapter, Jesus' ministry begins as a *reaction* against inhospitable socio-political circumstances, namely, the arrest of John the Baptist. His internal and subjective experience of homelessness is thus a condition of the objective processes of social reality. Jesus' 'decision' to go rogue, call like-minded disciples to follow him, and begin an itinerant ministry is symptomatic of underlying pressures and constraints. Like Mt. 4.12-25, the text of 8.18-22 is also concerned with Jesus' itinerant mission and the expectations placed upon those who follow him.

---

1. Moxnes, *Putting Jesus in his Place*, p. 49.
2. Philo, *Leg. Gai.* 18.123.
3. Parts of this chapter appear as Robert J. Myles, 'Probing the Homelessness of Jesus with Žižek's Sublime Object', *Bible and Critical Theory* 9.1 (2013), pp. 15-26.

This chapter begins by setting the highlighted pericope within its wider literary context. What narrative events precede the well-known saying about Jesus' homelessness in 8.20? This involves briefly tracking the teaching, healing and deeds of power that have taken place since the beginning of Jesus' ministry in 4.22-25. After this, I focus my attention on the saying of Jesus in 8.20, probing it with a hermeneutic of radical desublimation, to determine how best to understand Jesus' homelessness as it is constructed within the various textures of the Matthean text. Following this, problems arising from the conflation of the English terms 'house' and 'home' are discussed as they pertain to meaning and reality effects in the world before the text. Finally, I turn to the would-be disciples of Jesus in 8.18-22. How do these few short verses supplement the call to discipleship in 4.18-22? Social and cultural constraints on the eager scribe and the grieving disciple are considered, including an assessment of their respective capacity to make choices and follow Jesus. Ultimately, this chapter will demonstrate how the verses surrounding 8.20 function to amplify the destitution, desperation and offensiveness that accompany Jesus' homeless existence. This, then, interrupts the romanticization of Jesus' homelessness as a sublime object: the text fosters the desublimation of the Thing, the blind spot in our ideology, by reducing Jesus' homelessness to the indignity of its abject reality.

Teaching, Healing and Deeds of Power (Matthew 5–8)

Matthew 8.18-22 is situated in the midst of Jesus' public activity alongside episodes of teaching, healing and deeds of power. From the beginnings and initial growth of Jesus' itinerant mission in 4.23-25, the Matthean text depicts a number of episodes illustrating both its public nature and the spread of his fame and notoriety.

Matthew 5–7 contains the Sermon on the Mount, an extended discourse of teaching from Jesus to the crowds (οἱ ὄχλοι) and his disciples (οἱ μαθηταί). The mountain setting lends Jesus' teaching an added level of authority, recalling Moses ascending Mount Sinai where he received the law from God (Exod. 31.18). In this respect, the text also continues its casting of Jesus as the new Moses in their respective roles as ethical teachers and lawgivers, but also as displaced persons.[4] Jesus' teaching concerns the 'good news' of the *basileia*. Carter suggests that the sermon is not 'a comprehensive manual or rule book, not a step-by-step "how to" book. Rather, it offers a series of illustrations, or "for examples," or "case studies" of life in God's empire, visions of the identity and way of life that result from encountering God's present and future reign.'[5]

4. Dale C. Allison, 'Jesus and Moses (Mt 5:1-2)', *ExpTim* 98.7 (1987), pp. 203-205.
5. Carter, *Margins*, p. 128.

The sermon begins, for example, with a sequence of nine beatitudes promising eschatological fullness of life in God's kingdom for those who are suffering within the current ideological–political order, namely, the poor in spirit (Mt. 5.3);[6] mourners (v. 4); the meek (v. 5); those hungering for righteousness (v. 6); the merciful (v. 7); the pure in heart (v. 8); peacemakers (v. 9); and finally, those persecuted for righteousness' sake (v. 10). The beatitudes are mostly reconfigurations of OT texts from the wisdom and prophetic literature, with an emphasis on 'righteousness' (δικαιοσύνη).[7] Within the Matthean text, δικαιοσύνη refers to the proper conduct of humanity before God.[8] The term denotes the practice of judicial responsibility, with a focus on justice, equitableness and fairness.[9]

In many respects, the beatitudes also function to expose the obscene underside of the symbolic order by confronting dominant arrangements of power and cultural values in first-century Palestinian society. Neyrey, for example, argues that the beatitudes are an attempt at publicly acknowledging those who have been dishonoured within the wider value systems of ancient Mediterranean society, such as the poor, the meek and the oppressed. The repeated term μακάριος, usually translated 'blessed' or 'happy', is instead rendered as 'honourable'. Neyrey also posits that reference to the 'poor' (πτωχοί) in 5.3 refers not to the economically deprived, as such, but rather to destitute beggars. Not only are these people poor, but they are miserable, dependent and humiliated, lacking 'sufficiency and most other economic and social resources, such as social standing'.[10]

The Anxiety of Poverty (Matthew 6.25-34)

During the mid-point of the sermon, Jesus exhorts his audience not to worry about life, what they will eat, drink or wear, for God will provide these things so long as they strive for the righteousness (δικαιοσύνη) of God and the *basileia*. While Mt. 6.19-24 focuses on treasure, with Jesus arguing that his followers should lay up treasure in heaven and not on earth, 6.25-34

---

6. Engels identifies the original revolutionary potential of this beatitude, which has since become tamed, and contends that the lower classes in a society tend to be more closely aligned with progress. See Karl Marx and Friedrich Engels, 'Letters from London', in *Collected Works* (London: Lawrence & Wishart, 1975), p. 380.

7. While the beatitudes stand in the tradition of Jewish wisdom, Brooke notes they also contain novel elements, such as eschatology, judgment and reward. See G.J. Brooke, 'The Wisdom of Matthew's Beatitudes (4QBeat and Mt. 5:3-12)', *Scripture Bulletin* 19.2 (1989), pp. 35-41.

8. Benno Przybylski, *Righteousness in Matthew and his World of Thought* (Cambridge: Cambridge University Press, 1980), pp. 78-99.

9. 'δικαιοσύνη', *BAGD*, p. 247.

10. Jerome H. Neyrey, *Honor and Shame in the Gospel of Matthew* (Louisville, KY: Westminster John Knox, 1998), p. 171; cf. Lawrence, *Ethnography*, pp. 189-94.

centres on the anxiety that goes hand in hand with poverty and the deviancy associated with the itinerancy of Jesus and his disciples. The sixfold repetition of 'worry' (μεριμνάω) in 6.25-34 adds a thematic thrust to the anxiety of poverty. According to *BAGD*, the term denotes a condition of apprehension, anxiety and/or undue concern.[11]

During his exhortation, Jesus remarks,

> Look at the birds of the air; they neither sow nor reap nor gather into barns, and yet your heavenly Father feeds [τρέφει] them. Are you not of more value than they? ... And why do you worry [μεριμνᾶτε] about clothing [ἐνδύματος]? Consider the lilies of the field, how they grow; they neither toil nor spin, yet I tell you, even Solomon in all his glory was not clothed [περιεβάλετο] like one of these (6.26-29).

Food, drink and clothing are, as with the provision of shelter, basic necessities of human existence. Verses 28-30 repeat the content of 6.26, adding rhetorical force to a deeply rooted anxiety. The slightly disparaging allusion to King Solomon recalls intertextually his proverbial splendour and grand kingdom (1 Kgs 9.26–10.29; 2 Chron. 9.13-28; Josephus, *Ant.* 8.39-41). Davies and Allison note that belief in the care of the heavenly Father for all creatures is 'thoroughly Jewish' (cf. Job 12.10; 38.41; Ps. 147.9; 104).[12] Accordingly, Jesus directs the gaze of his audience toward nature. God feeds the birds, he clothes the fields with flowers, and so Jesus' audience need not worry, for presumably God cares even more for them.

Talbert points out that both in Jewish tradition (e.g. Prov. 6.6-11; Job 38.41; Ps. 147.9; *Pss. Sol.* 5.9) and in Greek philosophy there is often an assumption that human behaviour can be learned from animals.[13] Rabbi Simeon ben Eleazar, for instance, is said to have uttered a similar epithet (however his main point was different), 'Have you ever seen a wild animal or a bird practicing a trade? Yet they have their sustenance without care' (*m. Qidd.* 4.14). Jesus' argument moves beyond this, of course, to suggest that God cares even more for humans. Aside from opening himself to ecological critique,[14] the Matthean Jesus shifts the burden and responsibility

---

11. 'μεριμνάω', *BAGD*, p. 632. Within 1 Macc. 6.10 and Sir. 42.9 it is associated with sleeplessness.

12. Davies and Allison, *Matthew*, I, p. 650. See also Philo, *Spec. Leg.* 2.198, which reads: 'we do not ascribe our preservation to any corruptible thing, but to God the Parent and Father and Saviour of the world and all that is in it, who has the power and right to nourish and sustain us by means of these or without these'.

13. Charles H. Talbert, *Reading the Sermon on the Mount: Character Formation and Decision Making in Matthew 5–7* (Grand Rapids, MI: Baker, 2004), p. 127.

14. By measuring the value of people and/or Jesus' followers above that of animals and the earth, the text reveals its anthropocentrism. For a lucid outline of an ecological hermeneutic for biblical interpretation, see Norman C. Habel, 'Introducing Ecological

of provision from the individual to God. The basic necessities of life are, in fact, available: there is enough food and drink in the world that nobody need go hungry nor thirsty; there are materials available for clothing (i.e. John the Baptist wears clothing made of camel hair, Mt. 3.4); and so on. The problem of hunger and thirst arises, however, because the arrangements of power across society mean that its subjects have differing levels of access to these resources.

Such a critique of the distribution of resources can be enhanced by looking to the text's social and cultural texture.[15] Within an ancient agrarian society, the ideological perception of the limited good was naturalized as part of everyday existence, especially among the lower peasant classes. Social-scientific critics contend that most people depicted in the NT would

> view their social, economic, and natural universes—their total environment—as one in which all of the desired things in life such as land, wealth, health, friendship and love, manliness and honor, respect and status, power and influence, security and safety, *exist in finite quantity* and *are always in short supply*, as far as the peasant is concerned.[16]

Jesus' teaching, then, appears to challenge the received wisdom that access to resources is, in fact, limited by nature (or the 'market' in today's terms). Rather, the distribution of resources is controlled by the city/countryside cycle of production and sustained by the wider ideological–political apparatus. Jesus' exhortation provides not only an imaginary means of escape for the oppressed (by relegating the provision of bare necessities to God), but in fact antagonizes the disorder of the dominant economic system that extracts a heavy rate of surplus and causes widespread desperation and destitution.

Jesus concludes this section of the sermon by returning to the saying with which the section began, 'So do not worry about tomorrow, for tomorrow will bring worries of its own. Today's trouble is enough for today' (Mt. 6.34). Evans points out how this language is intertextually reminiscent of the wisdom tradition (cf. Prov. 27.1; *b. Sanh.* 100b; *b. Ber.* 9b).[17] No doubt Jesus' wisdom draws not only from his immersion in Jewish tradition but

Hermeneutics', in *Exploring Ecological Hermeneutics* (ed. Norman C. Habel and Peter Trudinger; Atlanta, GA: Society of Biblical Literature, 2008), pp. 1-8.

15. James P. Grimshaw suggests that Mt. 6.25-34 not only affirms the material need for a community that is hungry, but connects food to the larger social, natural and theological context. See James P. Grimshaw, *The Matthean Community and the World: An Analysis of Matthew's Food Exchange* (New York: Peter Lang, 2008), pp. 63-78.

16. George M. Foster, 'Peasant Society and the Image of Limited Good', *American Anthropologist* 67.2 (1965): 296; cf. Neufeld and DeMaris (eds.), *Understanding the Social World*, p. 237.

17. Evans, *Matthew*, 161; cf. J.G. Griffiths, 'Wisdom about Tomorrow', *HvTSt* 53 (1960), pp. 219-21.

also his experience as a displaced outsider. In their taxonomy of the social effects of marginalization, Hall, Stevens and Meleis observe that

> [a]s a consequence of stigmatized differentiation, disempowerment, and secrecy, marginalized persons have subjective experiences that distinguish them from more centrally located community members. The inner worlds of marginalized persons mirror the contradictions and pressures external to themselves and create the necessity for continual, purposeful introspection.[18]

The authors go on to state that marginalized persons, by necessity, live 'examined lives'. Jesus' exhortation not to worry about the provision of bare necessities reveals a way of coping in an unjust society. With the capacity for introspection, of course, comes the understanding that this sense of alienation and/or destitution is neither imagined nor the result of personal failure. Jesus' subjective experience of marginalization is symptomatic of the objective violence of social reality. His advice is to get on with the task at hand (namely, to strive for righteousness and the *basileia*) and not to anxiously privatize one's suffering and destitution. As will be discussed in more detail below, a tension emerges between this advice and Jesus' lament of homelessness in 8.20. Indeed, the restlessness of Jesus appears to directly contradict his earlier exhortation not to worry or be anxious (μεριμνάω).

Illness in the House/Household (Matthew 8.1-17)
Following the Sermon on the Mount and preceding Jesus' lament are three episodes of healing: first of a leper (8.1-4), followed by a centurion's servant (8.5-13), and finally the mother-in-law of Peter the disciple (8.14-15). These episodes are interwoven with details of Jesus' movements: after delivering his sermon, Jesus descends the mountain to heal the leper (8.1); after healing the leper he returns to Capernaum (8.5); and prior to healing Peter's mother-in-law he enters Peter's house/household (8.14). By this stage Jesus' ministry has centred on and around Capernaum, the location to which he withdrew from Nazareth in 4.13. The rhetorical strategy of citing Isaiah in vv. 17-18, 'He took our infirmities and bore our diseases', implicitly recalls the marginal identity formed during Jesus' infancy and his role as a liberated liberator.

Within 8.1-17, Jesus shows compassion to those who, like him, are located outside the bounds of social normalcy. Leprosy, for instance, is a skin disease that made one unclean and ostracized from societal participation (Lev. 13.1-59; Num. 5.1-4). Jesus' declaration that the sufferer is now clean enables the man to re-integrate into the community. Similarly, the centurion's servant is ostracized from the wider world; the man (or boy) is

---

18. Hall, Stevens and Meleis, 'Marginalization', p. 30.

'lying at home [οἰκία] paralyzed, in terrible distress' (v. 6). Synonyms for the vivid descriptor of his suffering, βασανίζω, include 'torture' and 'severe torment'.[19] Evans suggests that readers might assume the man is nearing death.[20] Rather than fulfilling its function as a place of stability and well-being, then, the house or household (intriguingly translated here as 'home' in the NRSV) functions as a spatial barrier preventing the servant's full social and economic participation.[21]

The healing of Peter's mother-in-law also makes reference to a 'house' (οἰκία), this time belonging to Peter. In this case the house fails to properly function according to expected ideals that are embedded within the text's gendered social and cultural texture. Wainwright notes, for example, how the entry of Jesus alone into the presence of a woman lying sick with a fever would appear to breach the construction of private and public space in the first-century cultural mind-set.[22] This wary association of illness with the house/household points toward a subtle disruption of the household's function as a stable home place for both Jesus and his disciples. Taken together, then, these healing narratives, which precede Jesus' lament of homelessness in 8.20, establish the house/household as a site of turmoil and instability, thereby underscoring its potential exploitation as a means of ideological desublimation.

Nowhere to Lay his Head (Matthew 8.20)

Having surveyed Jesus' public activity within Matthew 5–8 and identified some of the ways in which it sets the literary context for 8.18-22, I now turn to Jesus' lament of homelessness in 8.20. This brief pericope features as an interlude to Jesus' healings and deeds of power in the surrounding chapters. It contains two parallel scenes depicting brief exchanges between Jesus and would-be followers. The first involves an eager scribe who approaches Jesus

19. 'βασανίζω', *BAGD*, p. 168.
20. Evans, *Matthew*, p. 187.
21. The centurion's concern for his servant may be insincere and driven by the economic benefit derived from owning a healthy and able servant. If this is the case, then Jesus' commendation of the centurion's faith could perhaps be seen as double-speak. Alternatively, the recent suggestion that the centurion and his servant are in a pederastic relationship means that the commendation by Jesus is also consistent with Jesus' affirmation of outsiders and sexual dissidents. See Theodore W. Jennings and Tat-Siong Benny Liew, 'Mistaken Identities but Model Faith: Rereading the Centurion, the Chap, and the Christ in Matthew 8:5-13', *JBL* 123 (2004), pp. 467-94; D.B. Sadding-ton, 'The Centurion in Matthew 8:5-13: Consideration of the Proposal of Theodore W. Jennings, Jr., and Tat-Siong Benny Liew', *JBL* 125 (2006), pp. 140-42.
22. Elaine M. Wainwright, *Women Healing/Healing Women: The Genderization of Healing in Early Christianity* (BibleWorld; London: Equinox, 2006), p. 144.

and enquires about following him. Jesus' response is rather cryptic and does not directly answer the scribe's question. In the second scene, a man who is already a disciple of Jesus asks if he can first go and bury his dead father before following. This time Jesus' response is more direct although still confusing, 'Follow me, and let the dead bury their own dead'. In this section I analyse the central statement in 8.20, especially the ideological texture of the text, as it relates to the categories of homelessness and displacement. In the next section, I gauge how the surrounding verses function to amplify Jesus' lament of homelessness.

At first sight, Jesus' words in v. 20 appear to evoke a sense of help-lessness or inevitability surrounding his itinerant predicament. The phrase 'nowhere to lay his head' indicates not only his desire to secure rest and ref-uge but also evokes destitution within the text's sensory–aesthetic texture. It casts Jesus' homelessness as an excremental excess, an unsavoury expe-rience of the lowest order. For Moxnes, '[t]his saying presents "the son of man" as a wanderer who "does not have anywhere to lay his head". . . . This is a picture of a man without a house and shelter; we might say a vagabond or a homeless person.'[23] Given this highly evocative texture, Arland D. Jacobson contends that '[t]he structure of the saying does not permit us to think of elective homelessness. The homelessness of the son of man is thrust upon him; it is unnatural, unjust.'[24]

As discussed above, Jesus' comparison of human necessities to God's provision for animals in nature (6.25-34) implies that the economic sys-tem is at fault if people go hungry or thirsty. Jesus asserts that even the birds of the air are provided for, and so the crowds need not worry about securing food, drink or clothing (v. 26). In 8.20, however, the Son of Man has descended in value to below that of the birds. Nolland claims that the contrast with the birds of the air and foxes is a contrast with creatures of minor status in the larger scheme of things.[25] Alternatively, Carter suggests that the mention of foxes might allude to the political elite: 'Suetonius calls the greedy Vespasian a fox. Herod is called a fox in Lk. 13.32, and the birds of the air are Gentiles in [Mt.] 13.32.'[26] If so, Jesus here compares his alternative, marginal existence with the security of the settled elite. In either case, Jesus' 'homelessness is presented as a fact of life that substantiates his existence on the margins of subsistence'.[27] The Roman historian Plutarch, writing in the first century CE, similarly compares homeless wandering to

23. Moxnes, *Putting Jesus in his Place*, pp. 49-50.

24. Arland D. Jacobson, *The First Gospel: An Introduction to Q* (Sonoma, CA: Polebridge Press, 1992), p. 135.

25. Nolland, *Matthew*, p. 366.

26. Carter, *Margins*, p. 207.

27. Brawley, 'Homeless in Galilee'.

animals: 'The wild beasts grazing in Italy have dens [φωλεός], and for each of them a lair and a hiding place; but those fighting and dying for Italy have no share in such things, only air and light, and they are forced to wander unsettled with their wives and children' (*Ti. C. Gracch.* 9.5). Plutarch's encouragement of sympathy for those fighting for Italy by comparing them to the wild beasts appears to correspond to Jesus' lament in Mt. 8.20, which seeks to elicit sympathy for his own forced predicament.

Jesus' lament of homelessness also alludes to his perceived uprooting from normalized society. In discussing the contrast Jesus makes between the Son of Man and the foxes and birds, Moxnes writes:

> [The comparison] seems to revolve not around a point about nature, but about civilization and what it was that characterized civilized, that is, human, life. The images used of the foxes and the birds and the terminology used of their dwellings indicate that they have permanent dwellings, something that was the sign of human society, a mark of civilization. In light of that, the dislocation of "the son of man" takes on an ominous meaning. This person is not only dislocated from a more to a less privileged position in society. He is simply dislocated from civilized society, with its characteristics of permanent human dwellings; he is made less than the foxes and the birds.[28]

An exploration of the desperation and destitution encoded within Jesus' lament of homelessness can be further enhanced by looking to the text's strategic use of language.

The verb κλίνω, translated in the NRSV as 'lay', is multitextured and signifies the action of bending, sloping, turning and/or reclining. *BAGD* has as its definition, 'to cause something to incline or bend'.[29] It does not appear elsewhere in the Matthean text. Exploring intertextually, the verb occasionally appears in connection with the end of the day (Lk. 9.12; 24.29; LXX Judg. 19.9, 11; Jer. 6.4). Most striking, however, is its connection to episodes of death. For example, the epistle of Jeremiah uses the verb to refer to bending in the context of the death of gods, 'because, if any of these gods falls to the ground, they themselves must pick it up. If anyone sets it upright, it cannot move itself; and if it is tipped over [κλιθῇ], it cannot straighten itself. Gifts are placed before them just as before the dead' (1.27). The verb also appears in other Gospel texts in connection with the death and resurrection of their Jesus simulacra. John, for example, employs κλίνω to describe his Jesus simulacrum's action of bowing his head at the moment of his death, 'When Jesus had received the wine, he said, "It is finished." Then he bowed his head [κλίνας τὴν κεφαλὴν] and gave up his spirit' (Jn 19.30). Luke uses the term to describe the action accompanying the terror of the women visiting

---

28. Moxnes, *Putting Jesus in his Place*, p. 50.
29. 'κλίνω', *BAGD*, p. 549.

Jesus' tomb when they find it empty, 'The women were terrified and bowed their faces to the ground' [κλινουσῶν τὰ πρόσωπα εἰς τὴν γῆν] (Lk. 24.5).

The object that cannot get any rest or 'lay' (κλίνη) is the Son of Man's 'head' (κεφαλήν). In biblical literature, κεφαλή is used to designate both the literal head of an animal (i.e. the part of the body that contains the brain), but also, like its English equivalent, a being of high social status.[30] Within the Matthean text, the term κεφαλή is predominantly clustered around episodes of death and displacement. In Mt. 14.1-12, for example, the forerunner of Jesus, John the Baptist, is beheaded (14.8, 11), prompting Jesus to withdraw (ἀναχωρέω) to 'a deserted place by himself' (v. 13). Additionally, the term appears repeatedly during the passion narrative (chaps. 26–28): first, a woman pours ointment over Jesus' head (26.7), directly after the chief priests, elders and the high priest conspire to arrest and kill him (26.3); second, a crown of thorns is placed on Jesus' head by Roman soldiers to mock him (27.29-30); third, the sign 'This is Jesus, the King of the Jews' is placed above Jesus' head at the crucifixion (27.37); and finally, passers-by of the crucified Jesus deride him by shaking their heads (27.39).

Echoes of death and displacement, then, are intratextually and intertextually infused within Jesus' lament about his homeless predicament. Such associations are not entirely unexpected. In his extensive study of sleep in the OT, for example, Thomas H. McAlpine observes a significant lexical relationship between sleep and death across a number of ancient texts. For example, one speaks not simply of death in terms of sleep but also of 'spreading out one's bed in Sheol' (Ezek. 32.25; Ps. 139.8; Job 17.13; and perhaps Isa. 57.2), and also of 'rising from death' in terms of waking up (2 Kgs 4.32; Isa. 26.19; Jer. 51.39, 57; Job 14.12; Dan. 12.2).[31] The association between Jesus' experience of homelessness and death is made once again in the request of the second would-be disciple in 8.21-22.

The subject of Jesus' lament is the elusive 'Son of Man' (υἱὸς τοῦ ἀνθρώπου). This peculiar expression continues to receive a lot of scholarly attention.[32] Within the Matthean text, the phrase is always used by Jesus and not by others about him. It likely contains a Hebrew or Aramaic background, and is possibly multilayered in its meaning, conveying both theological and political connotations. While typically understood as self-referential, that is, to substitute for the personal pronoun 'I', the expression might also stand

---

30. 'κεφαλή', *BAGD*, pp. 541-42.

31. Thomas H. McAlpine, *Sleep, Divine and Human, in the Old Testament* (JSOTSup, 38; Sheffield: Sheffield Academic Press, 1987), p. 144.

32. See, for instance, the following recent collection: Larry Hurtado and Paul Owen (eds.), *Who Is This Son of Man? The Latest Scholarship on a Puzzling Expression of the Historical Jesus* (London: Continuum, 2011); cf. Maurice Casey, *The Solution to the 'Son of Man' Problem* (LNTS, 343 ; London: T. & T. Clark, 2007).

for humankind generally, or for a particular subset of society ('a person in my situation').[33] It is possible to argue, by reference to *4 Ezra* 13 and the parables in *1 Enoch* 37–71, that the 'Son of Man' was already an established title of messianic significance in the first century CE, denoting an eschatological and supernatural figure of judgment.[34] Moreover, a background in the OT literature is sometimes claimed via the citation of Dan. 7.13-14. Associated with this line of argument is the implication that the historical Jesus might have viewed himself and his mission within this tradition of the coming Son of Man in the clouds of heaven as a victorious figure enthroned by God to rule over all nations.[35]

It is worth noting that Matthew's Jesus simulacrum never explicitly identifies himself as the Son of Man. In many respects, if still assumed to refer to Jesus, this depersonalizes his individual experience—a possible rupture that connects his suffering to the objective violence of the wider ideological–political order. Luz, however, suggests that Matthew's Jesus speaks about the Son of Man when referring to his experience as 'the one who is homeless, rejected, blasphemed, the one with power over sins, the one who is handed over, killed, risen and who comes for judgment'.[36] Accordingly, the expression's appearance in Mt. 8.20 probably functions in a titular sense; 'the saying contains much irony. The one without a home is the majestic judge of mankind. Hence we have the ultimate illustration of the first being last.'[37] In other words, the state of earthly deprivation in 8.20 is a stark contrast to the heavenly glory of Dan. 7.13-14.

Given this ambiguous and paradoxical usage of the phrase 'Son of Man', the comparison to animals in nature, and the associations between laying down, a head, death and displacement, Jesus' lament in Mt. 8.20 is richly layered with an assortment of inner and intertextual meaning and reality effects. These associations cumulatively accentuate the evocative disposition of the saying and intensify the desperation and chronic destitution that accompany Jesus' homeless existence. Consequently, Jesus' lament gestures toward the desublimation of homelessness in the text's ideological

---

33. Vermes argues that the underlying Aramaic idiom *bar nāšāʾ*, was used in Galilean Aramaic as a substitute for the personal pronoun and was used especially in contexts alluding to danger or death. See Geza Vermes, *Jesus the Jew: A Historian's Reading of the Gospels* (London: SCM, 1983), pp. 160-91.

34. W.D. Davies and Dale C. Allison, *The Gospel according to Saint Matthew 8–18*, vol. 2 (ICC; Edinburgh: T. & T. Clark, 1991), pp. 43-52.

35. Morna D. Hooker, 'Is the Son of Man Problem Really Insoluble?', in *Text and Interpretation* (ed. E. Best and R. McL. Wilson; Cambridge: Cambridge University Press, 1979), pp. 155-68.

36. Ulrich Luz, *Studies in Matthew* (trans. Rosemary Selle; Grand Rapids, MI: Eerdmans, 2005), p. 110.

37. Davies and Allison, *Matthew*, II, p. 52.

texture. The stark reality of having nowhere to lay one's head confronts the reader with the actual excremental experience of homelessness, and so disrupts attempts at its sublime romanticization.

Homeless or Houseless?

Matthew 8.20 is regularly used as a proof text to demonstrate Jesus' supposed homelessness or itinerant 'lifestyle'.[38] Even though, as has been observed, the saying evokes desperation and destitution, homelessness is regularly depicted as an isolated 'choice' made arbitrarily by an individual. This not only reinforces the underlying logics of neoliberal capitalism but transforms Jesus' homelessness into a sublime object through which interpreters organize their surplus enjoyment (*plus de jouissance*). As was discussed in Chapter 1, however, there has been resistance from a minority of commentators to the idea that Matthew's Jesus is even homeless at all. Nolland, for instance, objects that Jesus cannot possibly be homeless because he is connected to a house at various points in the Gospel (a detail unique to Matthew, e.g., 4.13; 9.10, 28; 12.46; 13.1, 36; 17.25) and because Jesus and the disciples expect to be provided with temporary lodging during their travels (10.12-14).[39] Nolland's reasoning assumes that houselessness means the same thing as homelessness, which, as we will see below, is guided by a modern fusion of the concepts of 'house' and 'home'. A similar semantic muddle undergirds an influential article by Jack Dean Kingsbury, who suggests that we should not regard 8.20 as referring to 'literal homelessness' but rather a 'metaphorical homelessness' that shares many of the qualities of not having a home.[40]

While this clarification might at first appear helpful, it is potentially misleading.[41] The distinction feeds from and into the romanticization of Jesus'

38. See, for example, Daniel Caner, *Wandering, Begging Monks: Spiritual Authority and the Promotion of Monasticism in Late Antiquity* (Berkeley, CA: University of California Press, 2002), p. 59; Joel B. Green, Scot McKnight and I. Howard Marshall (eds.), *Dictionary of Jesus and the Gospels* (Downers Grove, IL: InterVarsity, 1992), pp. 44, 777; Keener, *Matthew*, p. 274; Jung Young Lee, *Marginality: The Key to Multicultural Theology* (Minneapolis, MN: Augsburg Fortress Press, 1995), p. 87; Luz, *Studies in Matthew*, p. 107; Ekkehard W. Stegemann and Wolfgang Stegemann, *The Jesus Movement: A Social History of its First Century* (trans. O.C. Dean Jr; Edinburgh: T. & T. Clark, 1999), p. 202.

39. Nolland, *Matthew*, p. 366; cf. Carter, *Margins*, p. 208; France, *The Gospel according to Matthew*, p. 157.

40. Jack Dean Kingsbury, 'On Following Jesus: The "Eager" Scribe and the "Reluctant" Disciple (Matthew 8:18-22)', *NTS* 34 (1988), pp. 45-59.

41. Kingsbury's distinction is problematic not only on ideological grounds but also historical and literary-critical grounds. Casey, for instance, challenges Kingsbury for proceeding with the assumption that the question is whether Jesus ever lived in a

homelessness, for the opposition between the literal and the metaphorical assumes priority for the 'literal', which is considered closer to reality, whereas a 'metaphorical' homelessness is not directly connected to tangible economic and political factors. In fact, the effort to metaphorize homelessness, by reducing it to its symbolic status, could paradoxically disclose an unconscious attempt to escape its disturbing reality in the world before the text. Furthermore, the interpretation that Jesus is not literally homeless is framed by assumptions about what constitutes a 'home' in the first place. Are we talking here about a structure that serves as a place of residence, or do we have in mind a concept related to space and place, with more of an emphasis on social identity and meaningful relationships? Both definitions can be tied to socio-economic factors, and so the literal-versus-metaphorical distinction seems rather unhelpful. Moreover, the statement 'nowhere to lay his head' would seem to indicate an experience of physical deprivation, in that he lacks a bed within which to seek rest and refuge.

It is appropriate at this point to revisit the clarification between a 'house' and a 'home' introduced in Chapter 1. This is because Nolland and Kingsbury unknowingly equate the term 'house', which generally designates a structure used primarily for residential purposes, with 'home', which signifies a more complex and nuanced entity in which a person or group of people are connected to a particular place by a sense of a relational social and spatial identity. While a house will often function as a home, it is possible to speak about home as place without the need for a physical structure, the house.

Within contemporary popular culture, the distinction between 'house' and 'home' is seen to play out in the Australian, low-budget, comedy film *The Castle* (1997), in which a blue-collar family man, Darryl Kerrigan (Michael Caton), is threatened by the compulsory acquisition of his family house for the expansion of the neighbouring Melbourne Airport. Undergirding Kerrigan's motivation to fight the eviction is his strong belief, repeated a number of times through the film, that 'it's not a house, it's a home'. What the film is really about, then, is not so much the David-versus-Goliath subplot that sets simple-man Kerrigan against the systemic violence of the government but rather Darryl's innate fear of the semantic collapse of the terms 'house' and 'home'. From the government's perspective, Darryl could make his home wherever he chooses; they see his house simply as a house. Kerrigan's distinction, however, gestures toward the surplus enjoyment he associates with his house. When a government appraiser inspects the house,

---

house, a question 'which ignores the context of migratory ministry'. Casey's refutation of Kingsbury's argument is partially the result of a clash of methodologies, but nonetheless reveals some of the creative (mis)reading that undergirds Kingsbury's distinction. See Casey, *Solution*, pp. 176-77.

for example, Kerrigan points out all of its faults with pride, believing that they will add value. Although, for him, it is *more than* a house, it is also *less than* a house, which is what effectively makes it a home.

Such a distinction also goes in reverse: one can have a house, but it may *not* function as a home. So while Jesus might be connected to a house in Capernaum, or have precarious accommodations and so on, he does not necessarily have a permanent home, at least not for the entirety of Matthew's Gospel. As was discussed above, the house/household is identified as a site of turmoil and illness directly preceding Jesus' lament of homelessness in 8.20. Furthermore, recall that for Matthew's Jesus, home place was originally Bethlehem (2.1). Kingsbury's interpretation, that Jesus is not 'literally' homeless, is problematic in that it not only ignores the wider literary context of Jesus' ministry as itinerant but also fails to adequately incorporate episodes of forced displacement, such as the flight to Egypt (2.13-23) or Jesus' flight to Capernaum directly after hearing of the arrest of John the Baptist (4.12-13).[42]

As a result, the distinction between 'house' and 'home', as well as the divide between having a 'home' and/or being 'homeless', is fractured by the observation that Matthew's Jesus is both connected in some transitive sense to a house and/or household (οἶκος/οἰκία) but is also at times homeless with nowhere to lay his head. A partially housed, homeless one challenges essentialist definitions of homelessness that reduce the phenomenon to the rather obscure (and Western, capitalist) category of simply 'having a residence'. Jesus' lament of homelessness in 8.20, therefore, traverses any literal-versus-metaphorical distinction.

Would-be Disciples (Matthew 8.18-22)

I now take a step back and inspect the verses surrounding Jesus' lament of homelessness to observe how they amplify Jesus' claim of 'having nowhere to lay his head'. As mentioned above, the pericope begins with Jesus assuming authority over the crowd, ordering them to go to the other side of the lake (v. 18). The setting of the Sea of Galilee recalls the previous call to discipleship narrative in 4.18-22, in which an emphasis on the seaside setting aids the sensory–aesthetic rhetography of the text. The following section is divided into three parts: first, I analyse the exchange between Jesus and the scribe (vv. 19-20); second, I discuss the exchange between Jesus and the man who is already a disciple (vv. 21-22); and third, I consider the agency

42. When engaging these texts, Kingsbury skirts around the issue of displacement. For example, he describes the flight to Egypt as a 'journey' and the constant 'withdrawals' of Jesus as gesturing toward his supposed repudiation of Israel. See Kingsbury, 'On Following Jesus', p. 50.

of these two characters respectively as it is constructed within the social and cultural texture of the text. As will become apparent, the text contrasts these two characters in a way that draws attention to the in/voluntary nature of discipleship, in addition to the symptomatic production of Jesus' homelessness.

An Eager Scribe? No Thanks!

In v. 19 the character of the scribe (γραμματεύς) is introduced. The reader is introduced to the scribe only by his occupation and his desire to follow Jesus 'wherever he goes'. The verb 'to follow' (ἀκαλουθέω) is repeated twice in 8.18-22 and is generally understood as an action of discipleship (cf. 4.20-25; 9.9; 10.38; 16.34).[43] But the text also makes sense in terms of literal travel from one place to another. Jesus' response to the scribe likewise makes sense in terms of travel: it implies that Jesus has no determined point of orientation; his travel is precarious and restless.

With regard to its carefully crafted inner texture, Robbins argues that the unit in 8.19-20 reads like a Cynic chreia, in that it thwarts intentions and overturns presuppositions. He observes:

> Three contrasts or opposites occur. First, whereas the scribe intends to start a joint venture with a teacher, the rejoinder tells him that the person whom he has approached is "the Son of man." Second, while the scribe expects to accompany the teacher to important places, the rejoinder tells him that this person possesses no place. Third, whereas the scribe thinks the person is travelling, the rejoinder tells him that the person cannot lay down his head. This unit frustrates each part of the scribe's statement. It is not clear at the end of the unit whether the scribe should try to accompany Jesus or not. Should the scribe give up his intentions? Should the scribe try a new approach? Only one thing is clear. The prospect of wandering aimlessly around with the Son of man who has no place to relax has replaced the possibility of following a teacher who is travelling toward an established goal.[44]

This condition of 'placelessness' or aimless wandering converges with an understanding of homelessness, as was discussed in Chapter 1. On the one hand, Matthew's Jesus is unable to sink his roots firmly into any geographical region and is socially dislocated from normalized society. On the other

---

43. Kingsbury argues that the presence of two factors, including 'personal commitment' and 'cost' determine whether the verb signifies an action of discipleship. These two factors are evident in the case of 8.18-22. See Jack Dean Kingsbury, 'The Verb *Akolouthein* ("To Follow") as an Index of Matthew's View of his Community', *JBL* 97 (1978), pp. 56-73; cf. Dennis C. Stoutenburg, '"Out of my Sight!", "Get behind Me!", or "Follow after Me!": There Is No Choice in God's kingdom', *JETS* 36.1 (1993), p. 175.

44. Burton L. Mack and Vernon K. Robbins, *Patterns of Persuasion in the Gospels* (Sonoma, CA: Polebridge Press, 1989), p. 71.

hand, the scribe is likely situated at the centre of normalized society; his occupation is principally concerned with upholding the status quo of the ideological–political order that has seen Jesus displaced to the margins.

In his study *Pharisees, Scribes, and Sadducees in Ancient Palestinian Society*, Anthony J. Saldarini outlines the status and typical role of scribes in the ancient world.[45] The figure of the scribe first appears in the OT as a muster officer (Judg. 5.14). Later, the chief scribe at the court in Jerusalem was concerned with finance, policy and administration (2 Kgs 22; Jer. 36.10), and the scribe who recorded Jeremiah's words, Baruch, was a highly educated and influential person who moved in the top government circles.[46] The roles of the scribes during the postexilic period were not that of a single uniform group and often overlapped with the religious functions of priests. By the first century, scribes were heavily involved in the administration of the financial, organizational and jurisdictive procedures of Jewish society.[47] As first-century bureaucrats, then, they were the official upholders of normalcy. Sociologically, they formed part of the *retainer class*: those who had left the peasantry but did not possess an independent place of power in society.[48]

Many characters in the Matthean text are either at the margin of society or at the centre of power and influence. While Jesus and his disciples negotiate their plight from the margins, the scribes are generally grouped together with others from the elite social strata, namely, the elders (Mt. 16.21; 26.57; 27.41), the chief priests (16.21; 20.18; 21.15; 27.41) and those adhering to the dominant Jewish philosophy of the first century, the Pharisees (5.20; 12.38; 15.1; 23.2, 13, 15, 23, 25, 27, 29).[49] On their social standing, Saldarini contends that most scribes

> were middle level officials. They were the agents of the central government and probably served in various bureaucratic posts. Their position gave them some power and influence, but they were subordinate to and dependent on the priests and leading families in Jerusalem and Herod Antipas in Galilee during the time of Jesus.[50]

As colluders with elite political power, the scribes in Matthew's Gospel participate in the systemic violence that methodically functions to exclude

---

45. Saldarini, *Pharisees, Scribes and Sadducees*.
46. Saldarini, *Pharisees, Scribes and Sadducees*, p. 243.
47. Saldarini, *Pharisees, Scribes and Sadducees*, p. 250.
48. Within the Matthean text, the scribes' role as upholders and interpreters of the Torah can be seen in Mt. 5.20; 7.29; 9.3; 17.10.
49. While historically speaking the Pharisees were distinct from the Jerusalem bureaucracy, and many had little political influence or power, the Matthean text does not readily deal with such distinctions.
50. Saldarini, *Pharisees, Scribes and Sadducees*, p. 274.

Jesus, eventually resulting in his extermination on the cross.[51] In 15.1, for instance, they come up to Galilee from Jerusalem to accost Jesus. Earlier in 2.4, Herod brings together 'all the chief priests and scribes of the people' to inquire where the Messiah, Jesus, will be born. It is from this information that Herod enacts his policy of terror, slaughtering the infants in and around Bethlehem (2.16-18). By the end of Matthew's story of Jesus, scribes are central collaborators in the plan to arrest and execute him (20.18; 27.41).

In the case of 8.19-20, Jesus' ambiguous response to the eager scribe perhaps reflects their complicated relationship. Scribes are entirely wrapped up in the violence of the wider socio-political and economic system in which their primary role is to implement and maintain its smooth, uninterrupted functioning. Moreover, because the scribe likely benefits from his social status, as a member of the retainer class, the restlessness of which Jesus speaks is something he cannot fully comprehend, let alone choose to imitate. If someone from an elite social stratum chooses to descend the socio-economic ladder, this does not mean he will necessarily share in the experiences and outlook of those on a lower rung.[52] For a crude analogy we might imagine a charitable celebrity sleeping rough for a weekend as part of a publicity stunt. No matter how well intentioned, his or her experience will never correlate to the psychological impact of knowing that week after week one will be impoverished and disenfranchised. While the scribe seems sincere in his desire to follow Jesus, Jesus' response makes it clear that travel from one destination to the next with no expectation of rest or refuge is best not romanticized.

A Grieving Disciple? Yes, Please!

As was explored above, within the intertexture of Jesus' lament of homelessness there reside echoes of death and displacement. Death is again presented in the second exchange of Mt. 8.21-22 with the introduction of the grieving disciple. The request of the second would-be disciple to go and bury his father evokes meaning on at least two levels. On the one hand, the disciple wants to fulfil his familial duties by returning to his home place and attending to his father's corpse. On the other hand, the disciple seeks to

---

51. Even as upholders of the law, however, scribes have the ability to be trained as disciples for the *basileia*. Bringing to a close his parables in Matthew 13, Jesus opines: 'every scribe who has been trained for the kingdom of heaven is like the master of a household who brings out his treasure of what is new and what is old' (13.52). For more on the scribal ideal and Matthew's Gospel, see David E. Orton, *The Understanding Scribe: Matthew and the Apocalyptic Ideal* (JSNTSup, 25; Sheffield: Sheffield Academic Press, 1989).

52. Compare with the call of Matthew in 9.9 in which a character who might also come from the retainer class does not choose to follow Jesus, but is chosen.

'bury' his remaining ties to his father. Such a request seems initially quite reasonable and in accord with the commandment to honour one's parents in the Decalogue (Exod. 20.12). Moreover, the burial of the dead was regarded as a loving act of kindness in first-century Jewish culture.[53] Jesus' hyperbolic response to 'let the dead bury their own dead', however, implores the primacy and immediacy of following Jesus. It is highly unlikely that dead people would be able to bury other dead people, and so a common interpretation is that Jesus is referring to the spiritually dead.[54] However, a text does not have to make perfect literal sense for it to evoke some kind of meaning. Nolland cautions that '[t]o introduce the idea of a category of spiritually dead people is to add a new thought that has no clear links with the context'.[55] Perhaps there is a perceived danger in returning to home place once these familial ties are severed. Indeed, such a possibility is explored further in the next chapter.[56]

The intertexture of the text recalls an exchange between Elisha and Elijah in 1 Kgs 19.20. Elisha 'left his oxen, ran after Elijah, and said, "Let me kiss my father and my mother, and then I will follow you." Then Elijah said to him, "Go back again; for what have I done to you?"' In this scenario the disciple (Elisha) is granted permission to return home before following (cf. Josephus, *Ant.* 8.354). This contrasts with the exchange in Mt. 8.21-22, in which Jesus denies his disciple the opportunity to attend to pressing matters at home.

Elsewhere in the OT, we find references to prophets refraining from grieving for the dead as witness to God's approaching judgment over Israel. In Ezek. 24.15-24, for instance, Yahweh forbids the prophet from lamenting over the dead and from carrying out the mourning ritual on the occasion of his wife's death. This is intended to infer judgment against the Israelites. Similarly, Yahweh forbids Jeremiah from visiting a house of mourning to take part in lamentations for the dead (Jer. 16.5-7). Combined with other restrictions, such as abstaining from marriage and not taking part in banquets and gatherings (cf. Jer. 16.1-4, 8), this anti-social behaviour is also intended to serve the purpose of testifying to an approaching judgment. The

53. Laurie Brink, '"Let the Dead Bury the Dead": Using Archaeology to Understand the Bible', *TBT* 49.5 (2011), pp. 291-96; Davies and Allison, *Matthew*, II, p. 53.

54. Davies and Allison, *Matthew*, II, p. 56; France, *Matthew*, p. 330; Martin Hengel, *The Charismatic Leader and his Followers* (trans. James C.G. Greig; Edinburgh: T. & T. Clark, 1981), pp. 7-8.

55. Nolland, *Matthew*, p. 368.

56. As a third possibility, Evans suggests that the would-be follower is most like referring to the ossilegium, that is, the Jewish custom of gathering and reburying the bones of the deceased one year after primary burial. See Evans, *Matthew*, p. 194; cf. Byron R. McCane, '"Let the Dead Bury their Own Dead": Secondary Burial and Matt 8:21-22', *HTR* 83 (1990), pp. 31-43.

itinerancy of discipleship, as such, is framed as anti-social behaviour that bears prophetic witness to the objective violence of wider society.

In his classic work *The Charismatic Leader and his Followers*, Martin Hengel undertakes a historical study (using redaction and form criticisms, in addition to *Religionsgeschichte*) of the radical nature of discipleship based on an exegesis of Mt. 8.21-22.[57] He argues that the nature of following Jesus is not akin to the rabbinical practice of a teacher and his pupil living together in the service of the Torah but, in fact, something much more 'radical'. For Hengel, the historical Jesus' instruction to help him in the service of his mission was a new thing and did not fit with customary rabbinic phenomena. Hengel does not incorporate the idea of displacement and the culmination of hostile social forces as potential reasons for Jesus' and the disciples' break from kin and home place, although it would make sense given the connection between discipleship and homelessness made in 8.20. Ultimately, Hengel reasons that the break from family is instead driven by an eschatological conception of the imminent end of the world: 'In the light of its [the *basileia*] urgent proximity, there was no more time to be lost and so he had to be followed without procrastination and to the abandonment of all human considerations and ties'.[58] Such a view complements what is found within the intertextual precedents of Jesus' command in 8.22. It should not, however, detract from an understanding of Jesus' homelessness as an excremental excess. While Jesus' response to the grieving disciple likely points toward eschatological judgment tied up with the approaching *basileia*, it also highlights the necessary hardship of an itinerant existence. Hengel observes that '[t]he saying is incompatible with the old liberal picture of Jesus and with more modern attempts to resuscitate this', for the unique offensiveness of the saying is clearly expressed.[59] One scholar even describes Jesus' response to the disciple as cruel and senseless.[60]

As a result, the combination of the two exchanges within 8.18-22 are typically understood as demonstrating the cost associated with following Jesus. Such a reading is exemplified by Carter, who suggests the pericope emphasizes the theme that 'the hardship and uncompromising cost of discipleship as a marginal and countercultural existence . . . shape the audience's identity and lifestyle as followers of Jesus'.[61] Jesus' response in the second exchange to 'let the dead bury their own dead' indicates that these followers of Jesus are to prioritize their association with him and what has been called

---

57. Hengel, *Charismatic Leader*.

58. Hengel, *Charismatic Leader*, p. 15.

59. Hengel, *Charismatic Leader*, p. 14.

60. Kaufmann Kohler, *The Origins of the Synagogue and the Church* (New York: Macmillan, 1929), p. 212.

61. Carter, *Margins*, p. 207.

Jesus' 'fictive kinship' above the obligations one might have to biological kin or responsibilities within one's original household. Barton, for example, connects this pericope to the call to discipleship text in 4.12-25 (and counterpart texts in Mark) in light of the dissolution of family ties. He observes that the custom of filial piety and association with conventional household structures are subordinated to the greater obligation of discipleship. A link is drawn between the brothers leaving their father and the command to leave the dead to bury the disciple's father in 8.22.[62]

The disciples, and of course Jesus, distance themselves from their respective households, which feeds into their status as deviants. Jesus explicitly states his perceived dislocation from biological kin in 12.46-50 where he redefines the boundaries of his family (his mother and brothers on the outside, contrasted with Jesus and 'those who do the will of the father' on the inside). The reverse takes place in 13.53-58 when Jesus is rejected by the people of his hometown.

Forced Choice

While dominant interpretations stress the hardship of itinerancy, however, an exploitable gap is left open by the framing of this hardship as a chosen attitude or 'lifestyle' advocated by Jesus and arbitrarily adopted by his disciples. As argued throughout this book, dominant interpretations of Jesus' (and others') homelessness facilitate the re-inscription of neoliberal assumptions about individual moral and economic agency. However, as we have seen, such a heightened view of agency is not always supported by the Matthean text, which often encodes social, cultural and political barriers limiting the hypothetical self-determination of its characters.

In a similar vain to the discussion of the first disciples' in/voluntary marginality earlier, it might be useful to theorize the possible agency of the two would-be disciples mentioned in 8.21-22, given their likely social, economic and psychological predispositions. On the one hand, for instance, Jesus' disciples do not always choose to become followers, but rather it is Jesus who chooses them (cf. 4.18-22; 9.9). On the other hand, Jesus does recognize that some disciples have made significant sacrifices in joining him and promises them eschatological reward (cf. 19.16-30).

On the problem of free will, Žižek frequently refers to a 'totalitarian disavowal' in the suspension of ideological belief. Essentially, the more we believe that we operate as independent thinkers and actors, have free choice and so on, the more we blind ourselves to external ideologies that submit us to the wider socio-political order. In liberal Western societies, for example, subjects are encouraged to take a cynical distance from traditional ideologi-

---

62. Barton, *Discipleship and Family Ties*, p. 130.

cal belief, which effectively suggests they are already caught in the system's ideological loop, such as the logic of the free market. While Žižek does not deny the existence of free will, he does emphasize how its very notion functions as a supremely effective ideological formula.[63]

A similar disavowal takes place in the interpretation of this text in the way that the prospective disciples' agency is curiously heightened within conventional interpretations. This projection occurs as a result of both the ambiguity surrounding Jesus' response to the scribe (8.20) and the vacuity of details about the second would-be disciple, his social status or his identity. What we do know about the second man, however, is that his father has recently passed away. Within the Greco-Roman world the father would generally function as the head of the household, looking after its economic affairs and managing the provisions for the wider kin group.[64] If this disciple is the eldest male, it would be his duty to assume responsibility for the affairs of the household, hence his desire to return 'home' and tend to his father's burial (cf. Tob. 4.3; 6.15). What can be deduced from the text, then, is that this disciple's judgments are likely shaped by these emotional and economic pressures. Indeed, the man is divided between his intention to continue to follow Jesus and the social and cultural expectations surrounding the burial of his father. His split identity is challenged by Jesus' hardhitting response that the dead should be left to bury themselves. Social and cultural obligations become secondary when one is already marginalized in the economically and socially desperate situation of itinerancy.

This leads to an anecdote Žižek employs to illustrate his notion of the 'forced choice'. He recalls the story of a Yugoslav student called to regular military service in which, at the beginning of one's service, a certain ritual is performed:

> [E]very new soldier must solemnly swear that he is willing to serve his country and to defend it even if it means losing his life, and so on—the usual patriotic stuff. After the public ceremony, everybody must sign the solemn document. The young soldier simply refused to sign, saying that an oath depends upon free choice, that it is a matter of free decision, and he, from his free choice, did not want to give his signature to the oath. But, he was quick to add, if any of the officers present was prepared to give him a formal order to sign the oath, he would of course be prepared to do so.

63. Žižek writes that '[w]hen a determinist claims that our free choice is "determined," this does not mean that our free will is somehow constrained, that we are forced to act *against* our will—what is "determined" is the very thing that we want to do "freely," that is, without being thwarted by external obstacles'. See Slavoj Žižek, *Less Than Nothing: Hegel and the Shadow of Dialectical Materialism* (London: Verso, 2012), p. 212.

64. Santiago Guijarro, 'The Family in First-Century Galilee', in *Constructing Early Christian Families* (ed. Halvor Moxnes; London: Routledge, 1997), pp. 42-65.

The perplexed officers explained to him that because the oath depended upon his free decision (an oath obtained by force is valueless), they could not give him such an order, but that, on the other hand, if he still refused to give his signature, he would be prosecuted for refusing to do his duty and condemned to prison.[65]

Žižek perceives that

[i]n the subject's relationship to the community to which he belongs, there is always such a paradoxical point of *choix forcé*—at this point, the community is saying to the subject: you have freedom to choose, but on condition that you choose the right thing; you have, for example, the freedom to choose to sign or not to sign the oath, on condition that you choose rightly—that is, to sign it. If you make the wrong choice, you lose freedom of choice itself. And it is by no means accidental that this paradox arises at the level of the subject's relationship to the community to which he belongs: the situation of the forced choice consists in the fact that the subject must freely choose the community to which he belongs, independent of his choice—he must choose what is already given to him.[66]

In the case of Mt. 8.18-22, the scribe is denied his free choice by Jesus. The destitution and desperation that accompany homelessness cannot be shared by someone occupying the privileged status of a scribe within the ideological–political order. The second man, however, is 'already a disciple'. His first choice has already been made. Jesus' command not to return to home place and bury his father is riddled with the pretension and paradox of forced choice: the disciple is given the freedom to choose to bury his (relationship to his) father, but his father is already dead, and so the ties to his father are already buried. In the eyes of wider society, though, he has no option but to choose to fulfil his cultural and familial obligations.

By choosing to ignore these cultural obligations and continuing to follow Jesus, his split from normalized society and its associated stigmatization is exacerbated. But if he chooses to bury his father's corpse, his relationship to Jesus and the community of disciples is strained. Either option results in estrangement from kin, whether biological or fictive. Does it really make sense, then, to speak of his dislocation from home place as a choice? As with Jesus' apparent homelessness, the text provides details that problematize the heightening of agency within a structured environment.

Conclusions

This chapter has probed the connection between Jesus and homelessness within the interpretation of Mt. 8.18-22. The dominant trend to regard Jesus

---

65. Žižek, *Sublime Object*, p. 185.
66. Žižek, *Sublime Object*, p. 186.

and the disciples' apparent homelessness as voluntary is in some ways challenged by this text but in other ways re-inscribed. While Jesus' lament of homelessness in v. 20 appears to discourage the scribe from following, the man who is already a disciple is told in the midst of a family tragedy that he must let remaining familial obligations and responsibilities 'bury themselves'. This emphasis on the dissolution of family ties, combined with the restlessness of itinerancy, provides narrative amplification for the characterization of Matthew's Jesus as the homeless one.

The pericope is situated in the midst of Jesus' public ministry, which includes acts of healing, deeds of power and dissident tutelage. Jesus' lament in 8.20 evokes the desperation and chronic destitution that accompany his homeless predicament. The comparison to animals recalls his earlier discourse in 6.25-34 and ironically twists it so as to emphasize his destitution. Within the intertexture of the Matthean text, there also reside echoes of death and displacement. Such a statement, then, traverses the romanticization of homelessness within the text's ideological texture and functions as a reflexive appropriation of his objective condition.

The abject reality of Jesus' homelessness is heightened by the surrounding verses. In the case of the eager scribe, issues of class and social status are introduced and problematized. The scribe's primary role is to uphold and administer the smooth, uninterrupted functioning of the institutional order that has seen Jesus displaced and marginalized and will eventually see him exterminated. In the case of the grieving disciple, social and cultural obligations are weighed against the primacy of discipleship. Jesus and the community of disciples around him are in many ways maligned by the customs of normalized society, and Jesus' hard-hitting response to the would-be disciple emphasizes the offensiveness of an itinerant existence.

The next chapter further examines Jesus' estrangement from meaningful social bonds during the return to his hometown in 13.53-58. The one without a place to lay his head is perceived as a deviant within the eyes of normalized society, and so is met by his hometown with disdain and rejection. Such a hostile reception only further antagonizes Jesus' social distancing from normalized society, leading eventually to his arrest and execution by the jurisdictive apparatus of the ideological–political order.

5

Rejection

It is true that Jesus' vagabond, footloose condition is a scandal to the more suburban-minded citizens of first-century Palestine. . . . Yet Jesus' homelessness . . . is more an assault on family values than a Bacchic lifestyle. . . . He has come, he declares, as a sword to divide households and set family members at each other's throats. The Real which he signifies disrupts the symbolic order, driving a coach and horses through conventional structures of kinship.

Terry Eagleton[1]

Because of their perceived estrangement, those coming home after a long absence could be legally considered foreigners and deprived of their rights. As late as the fourth century B.C., there were trials in Athens to recognize the rights of those who had spent so much time abroad as to pick up the local accent and to be (in good or bad faith) mistaken for foreigners upon their homecoming. A person who had returned but who was not yet admitted remained a *xenos*.

Silvia Montiglio[2]

The eighth element of Bouma-Prediger and Walsh's phenomenology of home suggests that it should function as a place of affiliation and belonging in which one gains an identity. Home is a place of recognition and acceptance rather than disdain and rejection. They write, 'Home is, minimally, where they have to take us in, like it or not. Ideally, it is where we are loved and cherished even though we are known. Home is where we have a shot at being forgiven.'[3] But, of course, home can also be a place of ambivalence. For much of the homeless population, home has likely degenerated into a 'precarious site of transience, meaninglessness, forgetfulness, fear, violence, disrespect, disorientation, and estrangement'.[4]

1. Terry Eagleton, *Holy Terror* (Oxford: Oxford University Press, 2005), pp. 31-32.
2. Silvia Montiglio, *Wandering in Ancient Greek Culture* (Chicago: University of Chicago Press, 2005), p. 36.
3. Bouma-Prediger and Walsh, *Beyond Homelessness*, p. 66.
4. Bouma-Prediger and Walsh, *Beyond Homelessness*, p. 67.

Because of their perceived deviancy, the homeless population repeatedly faces rejection from both wider society and smaller assemblages (such as one's family, household, church/synagogue or local community) on economic, political and relational/inter-personal levels. The rejection of Jesus by some of these core institutions should alert us to the relational and social dysfunction incurred by Jesus as he comes ever closer to the point of his final rejection, that is, his crucifixion. A useful means of understanding *rejection* is through the lens of 'social exclusion'.[5] While the phrase is somewhat contentious, it generally refers to the 'dynamic process of being shut out, fully or partially, from any of the social, economic, political, or cultural systems which determine the social integration of a person in society'.[6] This implies that social exclusion can occur on both macro and micro levels: in the smaller community or family as well as in the systems and structures of wider society.

Often neglected in its Matthean form, dominant interpretations of Jesus' rejection by his hometown (Mt. 13.53-58) appear superficial and dependent on meaning extracted from parallel texts (Mk 6.1-6//Lk. 4.16-30). The reader's gaze is directed away from the degenerative social and political effects of rejection and instead obsesses over Matthew's redaction of Mark.[7] Careful analysis of the text, however, reveals how this episode further advances Jesus' alienation from some of the core ideological and social institutions of first-century Palestinian society, such as the kinship structure that lies at the heart of an agrarian based political economy. Jesus' rejection, as such, adds another dimension with which to disrupt the sublimation of his homelessness in the text's ideological texture.

This chapter begins by tracing the seeds of familial breakdown within the Matthean text, which eventually lead to a breaking point in Mt. 13.53-58. After this, Jesus' hometown rejection is probed with a hermeneutic of radical desublimation. Two important observations emerge: first, an examination of the narrative elements of structure, setting, conflict and characterization reveals how the institutionalization of power within Jesus' hometown

---

5. Nicholas Pleace, 'Single Homelessness as Social Exclusion: The Unique and the Extreme', *Social Policy and Administration* 32.1 (1998), pp. 46-59.

6. David Byrne, *Social Exclusion* (Maidenhead: Open University Press, 2nd edn, 2005), p. 2.

7. For a comprehensive study of the redaction of this pericope from its Markan source, see Boris Repschinski, *The Controversy Stories in the Gospel of Matthew: Their Redaction, Form and Relevance for the Relationship between the Matthean Community and Formative Judaism* (Göttingen: Vandenhoeck & Ruprecht, 2000), pp. 146-54. Repschinski claims that Matthew's version presents a clearer focus on the teaching of Jesus with the Markan interest in miracles reduced, the text is also restructured into a chiasm in order to infuse the townsfolk's opposition with irony, and the redaction of v. 58 reveals Matthew's concern for a higher Christology.

produces his exclusion; second, the text's social and cultural texture, as it encodes ancient Mediterranean models of kinship and honour and shame, underscores the derisive impact of his rejection and gestures toward his approaching extermination. Through this analysis, intertextual echoes both contained within the language of the text and pertaining to the theme of rejection are raised as necessary. Such a reading further rounds off the presentation of Matthew's Jesus simulacrum as a homeless outsider, rejected from normalized society as an excremental remainder to the reigning ideological–political order of first-century Palestine.

Itinerancy and Familial Breakdown

Although Jesus' hometown rejection is often viewed as a standalone event, the narrative threads that lead to the current episode and follow on beyond it are integral to understanding its function within the overall Matthean text. The episode builds primarily upon the mission discourse in Matthew 10 and Jesus' previous encounter with his family in 12.46-50. In this section I address the pericope's immediate literary context before turning to some key component texts.

Matthew 13.53-58 principally concerns the reception of Jesus and his message within his hometown. It signposts the mounting concern with which his perceived behaviour as a deviant outsider is met and underscores the divisive outcome stemming from his proclamation of the *basileia* of the heavens. The pericope follows the day of parables (13.1-52), in which Jesus teaches about the *basileia* and is able to rationalize why some people reject him and his message. In his explanation of the parable of the sower (13.10-16), for example, Jesus constructs an 'insider' and 'outsider' dichotomy; the insider community around Jesus are set in opposition to those who see but do not perceive. Harrington observes that this theme of rejection is made concrete in Jesus' return to his hometown.[8] Ironically, however, the dichotomy is now reversed with Jesus as the 'outsider' and his former community functioning as exclusive 'insiders'.

Furthermore, Nolland claims that Jesus' hometown rejection functions as a theme-setting piece, after which a subtheme of rejection continues through the death of John the Baptist (14.1-12) and various other conflicts over tradition and authority between Jesus and the Pharisees (15.1-20; 16.1-20).[9] The text demonstrates how Jesus' interactions with those around him will eventually culminate in his crucifixion by the ruling powers. The Baptist's execution, for instance, foreshadows the eventual fate of deviant out-

---

8. Harrington, *Matthew*, p. 212.

9. Nolland, *Matthew*, 573; cf. Frederick Dale Bruner, *The Churchbook: Matthew 13–28*, vol. 2 (Grand Rapids, MI: Eerdmans, 1990), pp. 60-61.

siders. The Pharisees have already conspired to eliminate Jesus (12.14) and his continued conflict with both them and other prominent social subgroups prompts them to take further offense (15.12).

Most crucially, 13.53-58 functions to traverse the romanticization of Jesus' homelessness by once again demonstrating some of its abject properties. As was discussed in Chapter 3, Jesus encourages certain men to in/voluntarily withdraw from some of the governing ideological institutions of their socio-economic context and to come follow him. This results in a deviant subject position for both Jesus and the disciples. Before getting to an analysis of Jesus' hometown rejection, then, it is prudent to examine this deviant subject position in more detail. The properties of rejection and offensiveness, for example, are emphasized during the missionary discourse in Matthew 10, in what functions as Jesus' first major teaching block since the Sermon on the Mount (chaps. 5–7).

The Mission Discourse (Matthew 10.1-42)
Within Matthew 10, Jesus' missionary discourse elaborates on what the disciples' itinerancy means for their interaction with wider society. How does their subjective experience of in/voluntary homelessness relate to the objective processes of social reality? After summoning his twelve disciples in 10.1-4, Jesus sends them out with instructions to extend his activity of subversive preaching, healing and exorcism. Verses 5-10 detail their expanded set of mission directives: first, they are to target the 'lost sheep of the house of Israel' (v. 6) and proclaim (κηρύσσετε) the good news of the *basileia*; second, they are instructed to '[t]ake no gold, or silver, or copper in your belts, no bag for your journey, or two tunics, or sandals, or a staff; for labourers deserve their food' (vv. 9-10).[10]

The reason for doing so is not immediately evident from the text. Carter suggests that the disciples are expected to 'embrace the margins of poverty

---

10. This second directive has received an intriguing amount of attention from scholars. On the one hand, the pericope is sometimes seen as echoing a connection to the Greek philosophical school of Cynicism. Deutsch, for instance, argues that 'Matthew imposes upon his wandering preachers a lifestyle more radical even than that of the Cynics'. See Celia M. Deutsch, *Lady Wisdom, Jesus, and the Sages: Metaphor and Social Context in Matthew's Gospel* (Harrisburg, PA: Trinity Press International, 1996), pp. 115-16. On the other hand, historical-critical scholarship has often attended to the disharmony between this text and its Markan counterpart, particularly in terms of the staff. For some examples of possible harmonies, see Edmond Power, 'The Staff of the Apostles: A Problem in Gospel Harmony', *Biblica* 4.3 (1923), pp. 241-66; Barnabas M. Ahern, 'Staff or No Staff?', *CBQ* 5 (1943), pp. 332-37; Tjitze Baarda, '"A Staff Only, Not a Stick": Disharmony of the Gospels and the Harmony of Tatian (Matthew 10,9f; Mark 6,8f; Luke 9,3 and 10,4)', in *The New Testament in Early Christianity* (ed. Jean-Marie Sevrin ; Louvain: Leuven University Press, 1989), pp. 311-33.

and powerlessness'.[11] But what does such an activity achieve besides underscoring poverty as a *chosen* lifestyle? This gap in the text facilitates another gesture of ideological sublimation in the world before the text. France, for example, supposes the essence of this instruction is to travel light by not making special provision for their material needs. This provides the opportunity to exercise a practical trust in God's provision.[12] Nolland similarly explains that 'travelling in an impoverished state . . . will make visible a trust in God, and God alone, for . . . [their] needs'.[13] Such an interpretation, however, re-inscribes the neoliberal logic of homelessness as a chosen lifestyle. The positive framing of poverty, moreover, functions to extract the destitution and loss of autonomy that the act entails.

Rather than providing an opportunity to exercise trust in God's provision, Jesus' directive might function as a visible externalization of their internal struggle, and, as such, bestow a prophetic indictment on the wider ideological–political order. Homelessness tends not to be taken seriously when it is invisible. (Those who experience secondary and tertiary forms of homelessness are usually not counted in the homeless statistics and their struggles are invalidated.) With the exception of his explicit statement in 8.20, Jesus' homelessness has, for the most part, occurred off the radar. The directive in 10.9-10, however, externalizes the disciples' subjective experience of homelessness. A lack of provisions alludes to an absence of power; it renders visible their social and political exploitation in a form that others will instantly recognize.

Given this deliberate externalization of their inner turmoil, Jesus expects that some towns will not welcome them with the level of hospitality customary to their first-century cultural context.[14] The fault of rejection, however, lies not with the disciples themselves but with the inhabitants of each town. Jesus teaches that hospitality toward his disciples is expected (10.40-42). Those who welcome a prophet such as himself or the disciples are deemed worthy, for they also welcome God. The disciples are advised, 'If the house is worthy, let your peace come upon it; but if it is not worthy, let your peace return to you. If anyone will not welcome you or listen to your words, shake off the dust from your feet as you leave that house or

11. Carter, *Margins*, p. 235.
12. France, *Matthew*, p. 384.
13. Nolland, *Matthew*, p. 417.
14. Within Greco-Roman society there was a well-developed notion of hospitality and its obligations. So too was the case for the ancient Hebrews. The Torah explicitly prohibits the abuse or exploitation of aliens, the poor, widows, and orphans (Exod. 22.21; 23.9; Deut. 24.14-15). For more on hospitality in early Christianity, see Amy G. Oden (ed.), *And You Welcomed Me: A Sourcebook on Hospitality in Early Christianity* (Nashville, TN: Abingdon Press, 2001).

town' (10.13-14). Shaking a garment invokes judgment (Neh. 5.13) and discharges the disciples of personal responsibility (cf. Acts 13.51; 18.6).[15] Jesus then warns that the towns who fail to receive the disciples will reap a fate worse than that of Sodom and Gomorrah on the Day of Judgment (Mt. 10.15).[16] The intertext to Genesis 18–19 intensifies the warning by connecting inhospitality toward Jesus and the disciples with that which is directly opposed to God's purposes.

The next segment (Mt. 10.16-23) also elaborates on the hardship of mission, and connects rejection specifically to the leaders of the synagogue, governors and kings (note that Jesus' hometown rejection occurs in the synagogue). Again, Jesus encourages perseverance, 'You will be hated by all because of my name. But the one who endures to the end will be saved. When they persecute you in one town, flee to the next; for truly I tell you, you will not have gone through all the towns of Israel before the Son of Man comes' (vv. 22-23). The action of being exiled from one town to the next represents the success of accusations and persecution against Jesus and his disciples (cf. 5.11-12). Nolland suggests the immediate imagery is of 'wandering refugees' persecuted and finding no place of permanent welcome. He adds that because of the mission context we must also include the image of persecuted itinerant messengers.[17] The verse recalls the trials that the Matthean Jesus has already experienced in his interaction with the wielders of political power such as Herod (2.13-23; cf. 14.1-12; 24.16), and foreshadows the hostility that he will encounter upon returning to his hometown.[18]

In 10.34-39 the breakdown of family associated with the call to discipleship is once again made explicit. Jesus proclaims he has come not to bring peace but division, 'For I have come to set a man against his father, and a daughter against her mother, and a daughter-in-law against her mother-in-law; and one's foes will be members of one's own household' (vv. 35-36). Dominant interpretations often seek to soften the radical and violent thrust of this passage.[19] In response, Luz points out that the saying creates a feel-

15. Carter, *Margins*, p. 236.

16. Within early Jewish tradition, Sodom and Gomorrah became the epitome of social injustice, including especially the treatment of those without provisions. See *Gen. Rab.* 49.4-6, 50.7; *m. Sanh.* 10.3.

17. Nolland, *Matthew*, p. 426.

18. Jesus expects his disciples to encounter similar hostility and rejection. Weaver, for example, highlights the parallel between the situation of the disciples in these verses and the experience of Jesus himself. See Dorothy Jean Weaver, *Matthew's Missionary Discourse: A Literary Critical Analysis* (JSNTSup, 38; Sheffield: Sheffield Academic Press, 1990), pp. 101-102.

19. Sim observes that the Gospel of Matthew presents two versions of Jesus that often stand in tension: a violent Jesus and a pacifist Jesus. He argues that the reason for

ing of estrangement. He writes, 'Jesus did not come simply to bring about an inner struggle in people'.[20] Rather, conversion to the new group splits families and sets members against one another. It is precisely this kind of deviancy that will lead to his targeting and public execution; the judicial apparatus of the ideological–political order must exterminate lingering dissent in order that society can return to its smooth, uninterrupted functioning. Becoming a member of the new Jesus faction produces new boundaries: people are forced to cross borders and shift allegiances. In doing so, they also become outsiders and disturb the sensibilities of the reactionary propertied classes.

The True Kindred of Jesus (Matthew 12.46-50)
When Jesus encounters members of his own kin in 12.46-50, he puts his previous claims about the family into action. While speaking to the crowds, Jesus is informed that his mother and brothers are standing outside and wish to speak with him. 'Outside' (ἔξω) evokes for the reader the impression of distance between Jesus and his relatives. While Jesus' mother, Mary, appeared earlier in the infancy narratives (Matthew 1–2), we know nothing of his brothers.[21] The family do not sympathize with Jesus or his work and merely seek to interrogate him. Instead of going to speak with them, Jesus claims that his disciples and those who do the will of God are his real family. He rejects his biological kin in favour of the disciples, who constitute a new family or fictive kinship. This redefinition of the family disrupts the traditional kinship structure central to the dominant mode of economic and social organization and further cements Jesus' outsider status in the eyes of the normalized population.

The heavy use of repetition is immediately striking: the phrase 'mother' (μήτηρ) and 'brother/s' (ἀδελφοί) appears five times. Luz observes that its repetition has a *ritardando* effect and increases the tension.[22] Intriguingly, however, Jesus' mother and brothers' only action is to stand on the outside, (ἔξω) and their interaction is possible only through the proxy of a nameless someone (τις) who alerts Jesus to their presence and intention to speak with him. Instead of heeding his relatives' wishes, Jesus responds with a

the violent portrayal of Jesus can be explained sociologically; the Matthean community was undergoing conflict and persecution, and the image of a violent (and eschatological) Jesus functioned as a coping mechanism. See David C. Sim, 'The Pacifist Jesus and the Violent Jesus in the Gospel of Matthew', *HvTSt* 67.1 (2011): http://www.hts.org.za/index.php/HTS/article/view/860.

20. Ulrich Luz, *Matthew 8–20* (trans. James E. Crouch; Hermeneia; Minneapolis, MN: Fortress Press, 2001), p. 115.

21. The absence of Joseph might imply his prior death although the Matthean text gives no details.

22. Luz, *Matthew 8–20*, pp. 225-26.

question, 'Who is my mother and my brother?' Pointing to his disciples he proclaims, 'Here are my mother and my brothers!' The physical gesture of stretching out his hand emphasizes his reversal of inclusion/exclusion.[23] Jesus' family is constituted not by blood but by whoever does the will of his heavenly Father.[24] Jesus becomes the householder of a new household entity that imitates conventional household structures but is not based on traditional familial connections. On this alternative community of disciples, Carter writes that

> Jesus challenges the conventional patriarchal household based on kinship and centred on the husband/father/master. He redefines the household as centred on him and committed to God's will. The new household is not based on birth, ethnicity, or gender; it is open to anyone who commits to Jesus and obeys his teaching of God's will.[25]

The challenge to the centre, however, only further alienates Jesus from normalized society. As discussed below, Jesus' detachment from traditional kinship structures is cause for real concern not only for the people of his hometown but also for his biological family who are dependent upon Jesus for their own honour, and economic and social stability. Having considered this tentative redefinition of kinship, I now turn to Jesus' hometown rejection in which the narrative events discussed above reach yet another breaking point.

The Structuring of Jesus' Hometown Rejection (Matthew 13.53-58)

The account of Jesus' hometown rejection is episodic and begins by means of a movement in geography, 'When Jesus had finished these parables, he left that place' (13.53). Jesus arrives in his hometown to teach the people (v. 54). They react, however, with hostility and suspicion (vv. 54-57). After a heated interrogation by the townsfolk, Jesus laments his increasing estrangement from home place and household, recognizes his loss of honour and performs few deeds of power there (vv. 57-58).

---

23. The phrasing here echoes the language of Jesus' various acts of healing and so the gesture evokes for the reader the inclusive and restorative nature of Jesus' mission (cf. 8.3; 9.25; 12.13; 14.31). For more on the meaning and meaning effects of gestures during this period, see Gregory S. Aldrete, *Gestures and Acclamations in Ancient Rome* (Ancient Society and History; Baltimore, MD: Johns Hopkins University Press, 1999), esp. pp. 5-8.

24. Doing 'the will of God' is different from the Matthean discipleship theme of righteousness (δικαιοσύνη), see Przybylski, *Righteousness*, pp. 288-93.

25. Carter, *Margins*, p. 279. The redefined household is, of course, still based on a patriarchal structure.

Although the pericope has much in common with its parallel texts in Mk 6.1-6 and Lk. 4.16-30, Matthew's version appears reworked into a chiastic structure:

I. Jesus comes to his hometown (πατρίς) and teaches in the synagogue (vv. 53-54a)
II. The townsfolk respond (vv. 54b-57a)
    A. They are amazed (v. 54b)
    B. They ask 'From where did this man . . . ' (v. 54c)
    C. 'Is this not (οὐχ) . . .' (v. 55a)
    D. 'Is not (οὐχ) his mother . . .' (v. 55b)
    E. 'And his sisters, are they not (οὐχὶ) . . .' (v. 56a)
    F. 'From where then did this man . . .' (v. 56b)
    G. The townsfolk are scandalized (v. 57a)
III. Jesus responds, mentions his hometown (πατρίς) and performs few miracles (vv. 57b-58)[26]

This chiastic structure draws the reader's attention to the main rhetorical concepts of the pericope: first, the settings of Jesus' hometown and the synagogue; and second, the perception that Jesus no longer belongs to this place. The second point is underscored by questions of his origin and reinforced by questions about his kin and/or household. The resultant effect is that Jesus is shut out from his previous place of belonging. He experiences yet another abject dimension of homelessness that disrupts the romanticization of homelessness in the text's ideological texture.

The Narrative Setting of Jesus' Rejection

Elements of setting within 13.53-58 provide an important backdrop for the events that unfold within the text's inner texture. The pericope is staged not only within the geographical setting of Jesus' hometown (πατρίς) but also within the socio-religious arena of the local synagogue (συναγωγή). These details suggest that this is no ordinary rejection like those forewarned in Matthew 10.

The Hometown or Πατρίς
First, the setting of the πατρίς—fatherland or hometown—is reiterated twice in 13.53-58 and frames the episode. Its root derives from πατήρ (father), signalling an association with the patriarchal household structure of the ancient Greco-Roman world that Jesus has previously disrupted (cf. 10.34-38; 12.46-50). The term, which does not appear elsewhere in the Matthean

26. Adapted from Davies and Allison, *Matthew*, II, p. 451.

text, establishes both a geographical and ideological setting that charges the pericope with emotional and political overtones.

Πατρίς and its more common form πατρίδα barely register across the NT corpus. Apart from an appearance in the corresponding rejection pericopes (Mk 6.4//Lk. 4.24//Jn 4.44),[27] the term features only once, namely, in the epistle to the Hebrews following a lengthy discussion of the faith of Israel's primordial and patriarchal heroes. The author writes,

> All of these died in faith without having received the promises, but from a distance they saw and greeted them. They confessed that they were strangers and foreigners on the earth, for people who speak in this way make it clear they are seeking a homeland [πατρίδα ἐπιζητοῦσιν]. If they had been thinking of the land that they had left behind, they would have had opportunity to return. But as it is, they desire a better country, that is, a heavenly one. Therefore God is not ashamed to be called their God; indeed, he has prepared a city for them (Heb. 11.13-16).

This passage is often used in conjunction with others (e.g. the ascension in Acts 1.9) to supplement the romanticization of Jesus' homelessness in the popular imagination. It is reasoned that Jesus appears to be homeless on earth only because his real home is in heaven with his heavenly Father. A fundamentalist Christian tract entitled 'Jesus: Homeless on Purpose', for example, maintains that the proclaimed Jesus (that is the glorified, post-Easter Jesus) is no longer homeless because after his crucifixion and resurrection he 'returned to his glorious home with His Father', and so his true home (and by extension the home of all true Christians) is in heaven.[28] This sublimation of Jesus' homelessness sustains the capitalist fantasy that homelessness is a private, subjective experience and not symptomatic of structural failure and/or objective violence. It should be noted that in the case of Mt. 13.53-58, the setting of the πατρίς is very much grounded in the concrete reality of everyday village life; the Matthean text firmly identifies the 'true home' of Jesus on earth in a first-century Palestinian village and not in heaven. It is from this place that he is rejected, and the *mythos* and conflation of later tradition only work to de-emphasize the significance of his rejection on the mundane level of socio-political interactions.

Exploring intertextually through the LXX, πατρίς is predominantly employed to translate the Hebrew noun מוֹלֶדֶת which means the native land or original place to which one belongs and/or where one's relatives live

---

27. On the usage of the term across the Synoptics and its possible historical origin in the mouth of Jesus, see Richard L. Sturch, 'The πατρίς of Jesus', *JTS* 28 (1977), pp. 94-96. For more on the use of πατρίς and the relationship between the Synoptics and John, see John W. Pryor, 'John 4:44 and the Patris of Jesus', *CBQ* 49 (1987), pp. 254-63.

28. See an online version of the tract here: http://www.printmytract.com/store/tract-library/standard-tracts/jesus-homeless-on-purpose-nkjv.html.

(e.g. Jer. 22.10; 46.16; Ezek. 23.15).²⁹ In certain instances, however, מוֹלֶדֶת signifies more specifically one's kindred (Esth. 2.10, 20; 8.6). Interestingly, the LXX uses πατρίς once to translate the noun מִשְׁפָּחָה (usually rendered φυλαῖς), denoting an extended family, clan or group in which the blood relationship is still felt.³⁰ The residual meaning of home as place can still be garnered from the context of the Levitical passage, which concerns itself with the jubilee celebration and echoes a return to one's home place after exile, 'And you shall hallow the fiftieth year and you shall proclaim liberty throughout the land to all its inhabitants. It shall be a jubilee for you: you shall return, every one of you, to your property, and every one of you to your family [מִשְׁפָּחָה/πατρίς]' (Lev. 25.10). These examples demonstrate how the πατρίς can signify not only a geographical area but also an imagined space of belonging and return.

The intertextual associations between πατρίς and kinship similarly load the term with sentimental significance. This more emotive nuance suggests that the πατρίς functions as an integral part of one's identity. For example, the ancient Greek logographer Andocides, himself formally exiled from home place (Athens), reflects sentimentally, 'I would never consent to a life abroad which cut me off from my country [πατρίδος]' (*Andocides* 1.5). The English word *patriot*, and its relatives *patriotism* and *patriotic,* derives its etymology from the Greek term, and carries through notions of loyalty and passion for one's home country. In addressing the emperor, the Jewish philosopher Philo, for example, insists that

> [i]n all men, O emperor! a love of their country [πατρίδος] is innate, and an eagerness for their national customs and laws. And concerning these matters there is no need that I should give you information, since you have a heart-felt love of your own country [πατρίδα], and a deeply-seated respect for your national customs. And what belongs to themselves appears beautiful to every one, even if it is not so in reality; for they judge of these things not more by reason than by the feelings of affection (Philo, *Leg. Gai.* 277).

The subordinate clause of the first sentence is a rather clumsy translation of the Greek construction οἰκείων νόμων ἀποδοχή, which more accurately communicates the notion of wanting to receive approval or acceptance (ἀποδοχή) among one's own kin or household (οἰκείων, lit. 'belonging to the house')³¹ according to their customs or laws (νόμων). The term πατρίς thus carries connotations of place that innately commands an enduring love or fondness (ἔρως) and benevolent affection (στέργω) from its inhabitants.

---

29. 'מוֹלֶדֶת', *HALOT,* II, p. 556.
30. 'מִשְׁפָּחָה', *HALOT,* II, p. 651.
31. 'οἰκεῖος', *BAGD,* p. 694.

From Philo we also learn that the πατρίς can function as a storied place integral to one's history, identity and theological worldview. He writes,

> And I am, as you know, a Jew; and Jerusalem is my country [πατρίδος], in which there is erected the holy temple of the most high God. And I have kings for my grandfathers and for my ancestors, the greater part of whom have been called high priests, looking upon their royal power as inferior to their office as priests; and thinking that the high priesthood is as much superior to the power of a king, as God is superior to man; for that the one is occupied in rendering service to God, and the other has only the case of governing them (Philo, *Leg. Gai.* 278).

Philo's excursus on the πατρίς echoes the multidimensional concept of home: it provides a point of orientation around which we structure our worldview and in which we root our identity.[32]

Does the πατρίς of Jesus function in a similar sense as a point of orientation and identity? Having explored Jesus' multiple displacements from home place since his infancy, the strategic deployment of πατρίς in 13.53-58 might indicate that Jesus is entering nothing more than a precarious site of transience. In fact, it is difficult to determine where the πατρίς of Matthew's Jesus simulacrum is located. Nowhere in the Matthean text is Jesus' πατρίς identified as the small village of Nazareth in Galilee.[33] Capernaum and Nazareth, or perhaps even Bethlehem, are all possible contenders. On the one hand, Nolland asserts that for Matthew the πατρίς of Jesus is more likely in Capernaum. He observes that the geographical setting would allow the present episode to stand in continuity with the condemnation of and threat against the town in 11.23-24. Moreover, it 'allows the "from there" in 14.13 to refer to the seaside Capernaum rather than the land-locked Nazareth, and thus fits the departure by boat of that verse'.[34] On the other hand, Carter, among others, settles on Nazareth, given the link to Jesus' family in

---

32. This also echoes Heidegger's conception of home as being: this imagined vision of home place is a construction, but it also constructs. See Heidegger, 'Building Dwelling Thinking', pp. 143-61.

33. In the Lukan text, the parallel pericope begins with the unambiguous 'when he came to Nazareth . . .' (Lk. 4.16). The πατρίς could refer to either a relatively large geographical area associated with one's familial connections and personal life or to a relatively restricted area as the locale of one's immediate family and ancestry. While the term can denote a wider area, as in 'country' or 'fatherland', the term also functions in a precise and narrow sense, to refer to one's place of belonging and/or to a specific village or city. See 'πατρίς', *BAGD*, pp. 788-89.

34. Nolland, *Matthew*, p. 574; cf. J. Spencer Kennard, 'Was Capernaum the Home of Jesus?', *JBL* 65 (1946), pp. 131-41.

13.55-56.[35] It is assumed that his family remained in Nazareth when Jesus withdrew to Capernaum in 4.13.

Perhaps the omission of any explicit geographical setting is itself indicative of the cautious approach we should take; this rupture reminds the reader of some of the excremental properties of Jesus' homelessness.[36] By using the term πατρίς instead of naming a specific village, the text alludes to Jesus' emotional involvement with the setting, and so prepares the reader for the conflict that is about to unfold.

The Synagogue

While the setting of the πατρίς provides the wider backdrop for the pericope, other indicators of setting emphasize Jesus' outsider identity. The episode begins 'in *their* synagogue', that is, the synagogue belonging to the people of Jesus' hometown. Redaction critics point out that the fracture between Jesus and his former townsfolk is underscored by Matthew's peculiar addition of αὐτῶν after Mark's original rendering ἐν τῇ συναγωγῇ (Mk 6.2). This subtle shift in language differentiates Jesus from his former community.[37]

Furthermore, from a narrative standpoint the Matthean text constructs the synagogue as a highly dysfunctional setting. Prior to this episode it has been associated with hypocrites (Mt. 6.2, 5), and Jesus warns his followers about the people found in synagogues (10.17).[38] After 13.53-58, Jesus will never again enter the synagogue. He later remarks that prophets will be 'flogged [μαστιγώσετε from μαστιγόω, lit. "to beat with a whip"] in synagogues and pursued/persecuted [διώξετε] from town to town' (23.34). This dysfunction of the synagogue has led some scholars to develop a hypothetical relationship between the Matthean community and first-century Judaism.[39] Beare, for example, suggests that the distancing from the synagogue

35. Carter, *Margins*, p. 298; cf. Beare, *Matthew*, p. 319; Davies and Allison, *Matthew*, II, p. 454; Evans, *Matthew*, p. 289; France, *Matthew*, p. 549; Harrington, *Matthew*, p. 212; Keener, *Matthew*, p. 395.

36. It could also be argued that the absence of any definite place implies that πατρίς should be understood in a general sense. Writing from a Jewish-sensitive perspective, however, Harrington warns that efforts to interpret πατρίς as Israel in general go much too far. See Harrington, *Matthew*, p. 210.

37. Beare, *Matthew*, p. 318; Davies and Allison, *Matthew*, I, pp. 413-14; France, *Matthew*, p. 549.

38. The synagogue does, in fact, feature positively in 4.23 as a place where Jesus proclaims the *basileia*, although it is still distanced by the addition of αὐτῶν.

39. See, for example, Saldarini, *Matthew's Christian-Jewish Community*. An important debate in recent decades has involved locating the composition of Matthew to sometime during the crucial transition phase of Judaism and early Christianity. Davies, for example, situates the Gospel in the wider context of Judaism and the early

'reflects Matthew's sense of the alienation between synagogue and church; probably among Jewish Christians their own local meeting-place was also called a synagogue'.[40]

More recently, this theory has been challenged on the basis that in the first century synagogues were not overly concerned with doctrinal matters. Moreover, the term συναγωγή in the Gospels refers not to a specific building but to assemblies within the local village.[41] Moxnes, for example, writes that

> most synagogue buildings excavated in Galilee are much later than first century CE, and that the influence of Pharisees and rabbis was also a later phenomenon. Our perceptions of the synagogues mentioned in the gospel narratives have been colored by later traditions. In Galilee at the time of Jesus, synagogues most likely were gathering places for the village, covering a broad range of communal affairs and dominated by local community leaders.[42]

It is difficult to determine, therefore, whether Jesus' hometown rejection is narratively set in a building or another setting like the town centre or a

church and contends that the Gospel is formulated in direct confrontation with Pharisaic Judaism (which was the strongest leadership group within first-century Judaism, particularly after the destruction of Jerusalem and the temple in 70 CE). Building on this hypothesis, Overman argues that given the complex diversity and fracturing of Judaism, especially after 70 CE, many sects or factions were each claiming to be faithfully Jewish and considered their opponents and the established authority as corrupt. The Jewish Christians in Matthew's community believed that by following the teaching of Jesus the Messiah they constituted authentic Judaism. However, this community viewpoint was marginal, and the Pharisaic perspective was gaining dominance over 'formative Judaism'. While there has been some debate as to whether the Matthean community had actually broken with Judaism to become a Christian community, many scholars suggest that conflict and tension between factions are evident within the Gospel. See W.D. Davies, *The Setting of the Sermon on the Mount* (Cambridge: Cambridge University Press, 1964); Overman, *Matthew's Gospel and Formative Judaism*; Donald Senior, *What Are They Saying about Matthew?* (Mahwah, NJ: Paulist Press, 1996), pp. 10-15.

40. Beare, *Matthew*, p. 319.

41. Richard A. Horsley, 'Synagogues in Galilee and the Gospels', in *Evolution of the Synagogue: Problems and Progress* (ed. Howard Clark Kee and Lynn H. Cohick; Harrisburg, PA: Trinity Press International, 1999), p. 64.

42. Moxnes, *Putting Jesus in his Place*, pp. 152-53. Archaeologically speaking, we know of relatively few synagogue buildings from the pre-70 period: Gamla, Masada and Herodium in Palestine. However, from late antiquity onward the number rises to more than one hundred. This suggests that while some synagogues probably existed in Galilee during the first century, Moxnes is correct in asserting that they were not widespread.

prominent person's house. The term does, however, evoke a strong socio-religious function, as explored below.

Συναγωγή and its cognate verb συνάγω appear more than two hundred times in the LXX to translate eighteen different Hebrew words for 'gathering'. Only in Num. 16.24 and Sus 28 does it refer to a building. In addition to groups of people, the objects gathered include waters (Gen. 1.9; Lev. 11.36), stones (Job 8.17) and even the dead (Prov. 21.16).[43] Josephus invariably uses the term to denote either a synagogue building or a meeting, although his preference is for the latter. In his autobiography, for instance, he writes about a town meeting in Tiberias in which everyone comes together (συνάγονται ἅπαντες) in a large οἴκημα, that is, a dwelling or storehouse (*Life* 277). The central feature, of course, is the gathering itself and not the facility where it occurs (cf. *Ant.* 19.299-307).[44]

The importance of the 'synagogue' (συναγωγή) as the setting of Jesus' hometown rejection becomes more evident once we observe its socio-religious function in the everyday lives of first-century Jews. Carsten Claussen, for instance, argues that ancient synagogues are best understood as Jewish community centres, and it is impossible to make a clear distinction between their religious and communal functions.[45] Similarly, in his study on the ancient synagogue, Lee I. Levine asserts that by the first century CE the synagogue was playing a central role within the Jewish communities of Judea and the diaspora. He writes,

> The synagogue was created by the local Jewish community in response to its need for a central institution which would provide it with a range of services. As a result, the synagogue became firmly rooted in Jewish communities of late antiquity as their communal institution par excellence. . . . The synagogue was referred to as a *bet 'am* ('house of people'), and it functioned in this capacity.[46]

Horsley also points out that because local communities in the ancient Mediterranean and other traditional agrarian societies were not admin-

---

43. Claussen observes that during the period of the first and second centuries CE the term was undergoing a transition from an original meaning of 'meeting' or 'community' to the more specific designation of a Jewish synagogue building. See Carsten Claussen, 'Meeting, Community, Synagogue: Different Frameworks of Ancient Jewish Congregations in the Diaspora', in *The Ancient Synagogue: From its Origins until 200 CE* (ed. Birger Olsson and Magnus Zetterholm; Stockholm: Almqvist & Wiksell International, 2003), p. 152.

44. See also Howard Clark Kee, 'Defining the First-Century CE Synagogue: Problems and Progress', *NTS* 41 (1995), p. 487.

45. Claussen, 'Synagogue', p. 152.

46. Lee I. Levine, *The Ancient Synagogue: The First Thousand Years* (New Haven, CT: Yale University Press, 2000), p. 357.

istered by central or regional governments, villages and towns remained
semi-autonomous local communities with relatively continuous membership over the generations, communal relations and responsibilities, traditional social forms, and traditional ways and customs. The synagogue
was the central governing institution that administered local communal
affairs. Rulers such as the Herodians interfered very little in the day-to-
day business of local villages except to collect taxes.[47] The synagogue was
thus integral to the smooth functioning of village life, and it symbolized
the identity and autonomy of the local community.[48] In this respect, the
synagogue also institutionalized dominant arrangements of power within
the community. Because of its centrality, with a leadership structure likely
appointed by influential members of the πατρίς, it would function in a
way that legitimated the values and beliefs of its dominant members,
while merely tolerating or excluding those it deemed outside the scope of
acceptable conduct.

Against this backdrop, the ironic phrase 'in *their* synagogue' is especially
potent: while the term συναγωγή literally denotes the 'gathering together'
of the townsfolk, Jesus is immediately thrust to the outside. The synagogue
enacts the power of the collective to formally exclude and subordinate those
it deems deviant. As such, the setting carries additional undertones of institutional estrangement that should help to underscore our interpretation of
the interaction between characters.

Characterization and Conflict

Jesus' return to home place evokes within the text's intertexture the common biblical theme of return from exile. This motif became integral to the
collective memory of the Jewish nation after the experience of exile during
the Babylonian occupation of Palestine during 586–538 BCE and is encoded
throughout much of the OT. Matthew 13.53 marks Jesus' return from exile,
his homecoming, as it were. Upon arriving in his hometown Jesus begins to
teach the people (13.54). Filson writes that any Jewish man might speak at
the synagogue when invited.[49] The disciples, whom Jesus now regards as his

47. Horsley, 'Synagogues', p. 56.
48. Levine contends that there is some element of uniqueness to be found in the
synagogue's communal dimension, which perhaps rests in its highly concentrated centrality. Although many similar functions were being carried out in pagan temples and,
later on, by Christian churches, neither of these institutions appears to have combined
so many communal and administrative activities within the one arena. For an exploration of the specific institutional functions of the ancient synagogue, see Levine, *Synagogue*, pp. 367-86.
49. Floyd V. Filson, *A Commentary on the Gospel according to St Matthew* (London: Adam & Charles Black, 1960), p. 166.

fictive kin, are absent from this episode. The people of the synagogue presumably consist of various members of the πατρίς, including its local leaders. The text gives no indication that Jesus' audience consists of his usual
antagonists, the Pharisees.[50] Rather, these townsfolk are walk-ons—faceless
and nameless characters who are not fully delineated and individualized but
rather amplify the hostile environment. They also have an important narrative role to play by functioning as a barrier that Jesus must overcome in his
struggle as a displaced outsider.

The townsfolk's wariness toward Jesus is evident through their actions
and dialogue. Upon hearing Jesus' teaching, they react with astonishment
(ἐκπλήσσεσθαι). While Harrington claims that this initial reaction is at least
neutral or perhaps even positive, this seems dubious.[51] The passive construction of the verb ἐκπλήσσω communicates their shock or even fear of
Jesus (cf. 7.28; 19.25; 22.33).[52] Given the unsympathetic interrogation that
follows, a more hostile rendering seems plausible; the townsfolk identify a
perceived dangerousness in Jesus that must be quelled immediately.

Their strategy is to pursue a series of rhetorical questions: an unrestrained
bout of cross-examination that highlights not only their aggressive intent
but also an attempt to displace Jesus' authority and identity. The conflict
appears to proceed much like a courtroom drama and enables the narrator
to externally develop and elaborate the values, beliefs and norms against
which Jesus' identity is contrasted. Questions are framed by the interroga-
tive adverb πόθεν, 'from where, from which, whence?' does Jesus get his
wisdom and power (13.54) and 'all these things [ταῦτα πάντα]' (13.56)?
His ability to influence the behaviour of others is challenged on the basis
of his familial credentials. In seeking to establish the disarray of his household, the townsfolk repeat the objective negative adverb (οὐ) three times,
rhetorically adding force to their inquest. All questions concern Jesus, his
claim to wisdom, deeds of power, and his relationship to others, yet none
are directed toward Jesus and so preclude him from any right of reply. In

50. With the exception of 12.9-14, the Matthean text never invokes an explicit link
between the synagogue and the Pharisees, and so the reader should not be too hasty in
assuming the conflict is necessarily over the interpretation of the Torah. In a typical
village setting, the synagogue would likely consist of Jews holding a variety of opin-
ions on how to live as a Jew, the Pharisees being only one part of this. See Malina and
Neyrey, *Calling Jesus Names*, p. 60. Horsley also refutes the idea that the Pharisees
were leaders in local synagogues by asserting that leaders were usually drawn from the
local community membership, and there is no evidence that Pharisees predominantly
assumed power. See Horsley, 'Synagogues', pp. 60-62; cf. Martin Goodman, *State and
Society in Roman Galilee, A.D. 132–212* (Totowa, NJ: Rowan & Allanheld, 1983), pp.
104, 23-24.

51. Harrington, *Matthew*, p. 211.

52. 'ἐκπλήσσω', *BAGD*, p. 308.

fact, the protagonist appears powerless and constrained by their one-sided interrogation; the institutionalizing power of the synagogue means that the gathering speaks with one voice. The repeated question, 'Where then did this man get all this?', highlights Jesus' lack of stable foundation—an objectionable property of his homeless existence—thus causing an effect of desublimation in the text's ideological texture. The townsfolk conclude by 'taking offence' (ἐσκανδαλίζοντο) at Jesus (13.57) which re-emphasizes his status as a deviant outsider.

Jesus' response is expressed by a sharp riposte in proverbial form, 'Prophets are not without honour [ἄτιμος] except in their own country [πατρίδι] and in their own house [οἰκίᾳ]' (13.57). The text takes the evaluative point of view of God to suggest that, although Jesus has been thoroughly dishonoured by his former community and household, his prophetic mandate means he remains in good stead with regard to God's values and purposes.[53] The maxim reconfigures the rejection of prophets' words and actions that features as a reoccurring theme in the OT (e.g. 2 Chron. 24.19; 36.16; Neh. 9.26, 30; Jer. 35.15; Ezek. 2.5; Hos. 9.7; Dan. 9.6, 10). Jeremiah, for example, was opposed by people from Anathoth, his hometown (Jer. 1.1; 11.21; cf. 12.6). Likewise, in the LXX translation of Isa. 53.3 the suffering servant is said to be 'without honour' (ἄτιμος) and rejected by his people. The label 'prophet' also recalls the Baptist's arrest in Mt. 4.12 and anticipates his death in 14.1-12.[54]

As discussed above in the analysis of Matthew 10, Jesus expects himself and his disciples to be received hospitably; failure to do so results in judgment on the community. Matthew 10.41 enshrines this expectation while also foreshadowing Jesus' response to his rejection in 13.57, 'Whoever welcomes a prophet in the name of a prophet will receive a prophet's reward; and whoever welcomes a righteous person in the name of a righteous person will receive the reward of the righteous'. A prophet is an envoy of God's message and so acts on behalf of God in relation to the human community. As such, the rejection of a prophet is more or less analogous to the rejection

---

53. Keener points out that in a small town or village where virtually everyone knew Jesus, the inhabitants would not expect him to be a great prophet for he seemed 'too ordinary' (especially as a carpenter's son) to claim such as status. Moreover, they would not expect the kingdom to come in such a hidden way or as close to them as it does. See Keener, *Matthew*, pp. 395-96.

54. The narrative further develops this theme in the parable of the tenants (21.33-41), in which the landowner's servants (God's prophets), followed by the landowner's son (Jesus), are beaten and stoned to death by the irresponsible tenants (the political and religious elite). An allegorical reading is but one interpretive possibility, however. See Klyne Snodgrass, *The Parable of the Wicked Tenants* (Tübingen: Mohr, 1983). For a socio-rhetorical reading, see James D. Hester, 'Socio-Rheotorical Criticism and the Parable of the Tenants', *JSNT* 14 (1992), pp. 27-56.

of God.[55] Jesus' self-identification with the prophetic tradition is a means of directly relating his subjective experience of isolation and estrangement to the social processes of objective reality: the townsfolk reject Jesus, and so they reject God.

Intertextual echoes within Mt. 13.53-58 also illustrate the difficulty with which an itinerant such as Jesus could expect to return home with his honour still intact. In her book on wandering in Greco-Roman culture, Silvia Montiglio argues that an itinerant wanderer could never return to his hometown and simply expect to recover his previous position in the community. All prestige and power he previously held would be lost and could probably never be recovered. While these sources predominantly reflect the perspectives of elite society, they are still useful for comparison. She cites the ancient Greek poet Theognis of Megara and observes that he 'is firmly convinced that an exile cannot be fully reintegrated into his community: "Never make friends with an exile if you nurture hopes, Cyrnos. Even if he returns home, he no longer becomes the same man."'[56] She argues that the wording here suggests an objective rather than a subjective interpretation: 'It is not stated that the exile who comes home is no longer the same but that he does not become (γίνεται) the same again'.[57] In other words, there is a great risk associated in returning to one's hometown, for restoration of previous benefaction, with its associations of honour and status, is highly improbable.

The cynic philosopher Dio Chrysostom, writing toward the end of the first century CE about his own experiences of exile and homecoming, compares his situation to the critical condition of Odysseus (*Or.* 45.11), who feared that upon returning home after a long absence he would not be recognized and reintegrated into his community. Moreover, Dio Chrysostom suspected some of his compatriots of being ill-disposed toward him as they might toward a 'foreigner' and an 'extravagant' (*Or.* 40.1-2). Jesus' epithet in v. 57 intertextually echoes these ideas about re-integrative and restorative difficulty from the wandering cultural tradition of Greco-Roman society. Like Dio Chrysostom, Jesus recognizes the liminal space he now occupies between his home community and the outside world; he is now an outsider, not much different from a foreigner who has no claim to honour or worth in this place.

Matthew 13.53-58 concludes with an indication that Jesus 'did not do many deeds of power there, because of their unbelief' (v. 58). Commentators usually attribute the redaction from Mark's 'could not' to Matthew's

55. In 1 Sam. 8.7, for example, Samuel is reassured by God that the people have not rejected him, but indeed have rejected God from being king over them (cf. Exod. 16.8).
56. Montiglio, *Wandering*, p. 36.
57. Montiglio, *Wandering*, p. 36.

'did not' to Matthew's heightened Christology; Mark's primitive version hints at a lack of agency, and Matthew, so it is claimed, intends to restore Jesus' divine ability to perform 'deeds of power' regardless of others' belief in him.[58] A cautious reading of the text, however, suggests that the assumptions lying behind this dominant approach are flawed. This is because Jesus is shown to lack agency on many occasions in the Matthean text, and this lack of agency is often presented in fulfilment of Jesus' divine destiny rather than precluding him from it. From a socio-rhetorical perspective, Jesus' refusal to perform deeds of power amplifies the rebuke of his former community. He withdraws from their judgmental gaze to avoid further hostility.[59]

Furthermore, the meaning effect evoked by the noun ἀπιστίαν (rendered by the NRSV as 'unbelief') should not be understood in purely dogmatic terms, as is often read by the dominant confessional Christian hermeneutic (e.g. they did not believe that Jesus was the Messiah). Rather, the verb signals 'a lack of commitment to a relationship',[60] as in, the people of his hometown have cut Jesus out of their lives.[61] Their unbelief collapses into the socio-religious function of the synagogue, in its institutionalization of the rejection of Jesus.

---

58. See Beare, *Matthew*, p. 320; Bruner, *The Churchbook*, II, p. 62; Davies and Allison, *Matthew*, II, p. 460, cf. Davies and Allison, *Matthew*, I, pp. 104-105; France, *Matthew*, p. 550; Keener, *Matthew*, p. 396; Meier, *Matthew*, p. 159; Nolland, *Matthew*, p. 577; Eduard Schweizer, *The Good News according to Matthew* (trans. David E. Green; London: SPCK, 1975), p. 316. Some commentators slightly nuance the dominant perspective or give other plausible reasons for Matthew's redaction. Schnackenburg, for example, contends that although Matthew softens Mark, he brings out the reason more strongly ('. . . because of their unbelief'); nevertheless, Jesus' healing power still presupposes believing trust (cf. Mt. 9.22). See Rudolf Schnackenburg, *The Gospel of Matthew* (trans. Robert R. Barr; Grand Rapids, MI: Eerdmans, 2002), p. 138. Harrington notes that while it is not improbable that Matthew softens Mark, v. 58 can simply be taken as an economical version of the long and awkward sentence in Mk 6.5. See Harrington, *Matthew*, p. 211.

59. Carter seems to agree with this when he writes that '[t]he town's "no-faith" contrasts with the disciples' little faith (6.30; 8.26; cf. 14.31; 16.8). Its rejection does not stop him working miracles. Rather he refuses to do so because of its opposition.' See Carter, *Margins*, p. 300.

60. 'ἀπιστία', *BAGD*, p. 103.

61. Verseput points out that 'belief' is a developing subtheme through the midpart of the Gospel (13.53–16.20) and that its meaning should become clearer through narrative analysis. Unfortunately, however, he still appears to focus narrowly on the religious connotations of the term. He argues that in 13.58, the unbelief of the townsfolk lies with their refusal to recognize the true origin of Jesus' wisdom and power as arising from his filial relationship to his heavenly Father. See Donald J. Verseput, 'The Faith of the Reader and the Narrative of Matthew 13.53–16.20', *JSNT* 46 (1992), pp. 3-24.

While ἀπιστία barely registers across Matthew, its antonym πίστις (belief) occurs frequently. The Matthean text often employs the noun πίστις to describe an admirable trait or quality of characters who respond positively to Jesus. The term is linked predominantly to healing episodes, and is some-times used of characters that show extraordinary diligence toward those in their care. For example, Jesus commends the incredible faith (πίστιν) of the centurion who requested that Jesus heal his servant (8.10). Moreover, in 9.2, a small group of walk-on characters show their care for a paralyzed man by carrying him around on a bed. The men risk contamination accord-ing to the purity customs that are embedded in the text's social and cultural texture, and so when Jesus sees their (not the paralytic's) faith (πίστιν), he forgives/discharges (ἀφίενται) the sins of the paralytic before healing him. In another well-known example, the Canaanite woman demonstrates remarkable devotion to her daughter when she kneels (προσεκύνει) before Jesus and begs him to heal her (15.21-28). Jesus is impressed by her faith (πίστις) and heals the daughter instantly (v. 27). Similarly, when Jesus heals an epileptic boy with a demon (17.14-20), the father kneels (γονυπετῶν) before Jesus and asks for mercy upon his son. This time, however, the man recounts how he already brought the boy to the disciples but they could not heal him. Before healing the boy, Jesus abruptly remarks, 'You faithless [ἄπιστος] and perverse generation, how much longer must I be with you? How much longer must I put up with you?' (v. 17). When the disciples ask Jesus privately why they could not heal the boy, they are told it is because of their little faith (ὀλιγοπιστίαν). In other words, they did not possess enough concern and compassion for the boy necessary to heal him.

These examples illustrate the more relational meaning effects of the term πίστις that are infused narratively within the Matthean text. Its antonym ἀπιστία thus designates the townsfolk's lack of commitment to and care for Jesus. He no longer has a recognized place in their community and is divorced from both his hometown and his household. As a result, Jesus' refusal to perform deeds of power both externalizes his internal experience of exploitation and bestows a prophetic indictment against this community in their failure to receive him.

Further Social and Cultural Dimensions (Matthew 13.53-58)

In seeking to gain a deeper understanding of the motives behind Jesus' hostile reception, the reader must look beyond the narrative texture of the episode to the level of social and cultural interactions. What is it about Jesus, his actions and teaching that is deemed so offensive by his hometown? Domi-nant interpretations are prone to spiritualizing the text, whereby the rejec-tion of Jesus is blamed purely on the townsfolk's lack of faith and religious commitment or understanding.[62] Such an interpretation reveals an exploitable ideological remnant, for the reality of social exclusion is sublimated into the fantasmatic realm to foster both the surplus enjoyment (*plus de jouissance*) of Christian exclusivity and the related desire for supersessionist readings of the Gospel. Take, as a pre-Holocaust example, Alfred Plummer, who connects the rejection of Jesus by his hometown to the rejection of the Messiah by the Jewish people, 'The Evangelist probably regarded the rejection of Jesus by His own people at Nazareth as a prophetic intimation of His rejection by the whole nation at Jerusalem'.[63] Such a statement requires careful clarification in terms of the power differentiation among groups that allow dominant people to act upon those in a subordinate position.

Within Mt. 13.53-58, for example, a conflict is present between the people of the synagogue who, through the cohesive nature of the institution, adopt the prevailing cultural norms and values of their surrounding social context, and Jesus' liminal social location, which exists at the outer edge of identity and seems incapable of negotiating a clear identification within the dominant culture. Harrington notes that 'even if Matthew's readers lived in a big city like Antioch, they would have known the dynamics of village life in the ancient Near East', and so we expect these dynamics to be encoded within the social and cultural textures of the text.[64] In order to better understand the conflict between Jesus and the townsfolk, I will now inspect two specific social and cultural features: first, the tension between individual and collective personality structures; and second, the likely employment status of Jesus as an itinerant outsider.

---

62. Although this spiritualizing tendency is widespread within scholarship, it manifests itself at varying levels. It often comes across subtly in purely historical-critical work. Davies and Allison, for instance, write that '13:52-8 illustrates that the failure to understand leads not to indifference but to hostility. Those who do not grasp the secrets of the kingdom of Heaven necessarily find Jesus offensive.' See Davies and Allison, *Matthew*, II, p. 453. Also intriguing is the title that Bruner gives this pericope, 'Nazareth's Mental Rejection'. See Bruner, *The Churchbook*, II, p. 58. By emphasizing the 'mental rejection' of the townsfolk, interpreters might neglect the social and cultural implications of rejection and social exclusion. For other examples, see Fenton, *Matthew*, pp. 237-39; Hagner, *Matthew*, I, pp. 406-407; Senior, *Matthew*, p. 163. Less subtle examples are cited below.

63. Alfred Plummer, *An Exegetical Commentary on the Gospel according to St Matthew* (London: Robert Scott, 1909), p. 199. More recently, Meier suggests that because within this pericope 'the name of "his own country" is not mentioned; the reference may be purposely vague and so paradigmatic of all Israel'. Meier, *Matthew*, p. 158. Likewise, France observes that it is significant that the incident occurs in the synagogue, for after this episode Jesus is 'seen increasingly outside the structures of traditional Judaism'. See France, *Matthew*, p. 547.

64. Harrington, *Matthew*, p. 213.

Personal Responsibility?

The neoliberal framing of homelessness as an individual choice appears more coherent in Western societies than in non-Western societies. This is because non-Western societies are often thought to construct the self as a more interdependent unity. The emphasis on homelessness as an individual choice provides an anchor for neoliberal ideology to naturalize itself within the modern Western psyche as a hegemonic mode of discourse.[65] As was discussed above, the questions put to Jesus by the townsfolk concern his relationship to the members of his immediate kin and insinuate that he is an outsider who has distanced himself from his family members. In doing so, the narrative encodes ancient Mediterranean understandings of kinship structures. Because in the ancient world personal identity was ascribed more than acquired, identity functioned not as a matter of self-discovery but rather a function of group membership and belonging.[66]

Collectivism and individualism are, according to Malina, somewhat technical terms to describe in general how people conceive of themselves and others. On the one hand, 'collectivistic persons think of themselves primarily as part of a group'.[67] Their initial judgments prioritize the needs and concerns of group members. Groups are seen to be unique and distinctive, rather than individualistic. On the other hand, individualism, the primary self-psychological profile of the modern Western world, means that people see themselves as distinct from other people. Although they might reside within groups, they conceive of themselves as separate entities who think for themselves and make their own choices alone.[68] Malina claims that the Mediterranean selves we read about in the Bible could not be individualists but rather were group-oriented selves, sharing the viewpoints of the group members whose fate they shared. He writes,

> The unique and distinct groups to which persons belong through no choice of their own are groups into which a person is born and socialized: parents and family by birth, place by location of the kin group, gender by patriarchal gender roles. Genealogy, geography, and gender serve to define single groups as unique and distinct. It is group features that then define single group members.[69]

65. See, for example, Harvey, *Neoliberalism*, pp. 175-82.

66. Margaret Y. MacDonald, 'Kinship and Family in the New Testament World', in *Understanding the Social World of the New Testament* (ed. Dietmar Neufeld and Richard E. DeMaris; London: Routledge, 2010), pp. 29-43.

67. Bruce J. Malina, 'Collectivism in Mediterranean Culture', in *Understanding the Social World of the New Testament* (ed. Dietmar Neufeld and Richard E. DeMaris; London: Routledge, 2010), p. 17.

68. Malina, 'Collectivism in Mediterranean Culture', p. 18.

69. Malina, 'Collectivism in Mediterranean Culture', p. 19.

Malina does allow for some exceptions to these two broad categories. He contends that even in collectivistic societies there were persons who had some individualistic traits. These 'pseudo-individualists' emerged from situations of social dissonance; extremely hierarchical societies with rigid social stratification 'tend to produce pockets of individualistic-like behavior in otherwise collectivistic situations at the extremes of the societal hierarchy: the extremely wealthy and the extremely downtrodden'.[70] The Jesus simulacrum of Matthew's Gospel would appear to fit into this pseudo-individualist category as he becomes further alienated from his biological kin group and associates with his new fictive kin. Within 13.53-58, Jesus is accused by those in his hometown of distancing himself from his biological kin group. In other words, Jesus is acting as a pseudo-individual in a collectivist culture. Because the family and wider household function as an embedded collective within which an individual not only gains an identity but also worth and respect by virtue of association, Jesus is thrust into 'no-place'; without connection to the other members of his collective he has no legitimate claim to identity.

There is, however, an intriguing parallel between the construction of the Western individual self, as articulated by Malina, and the individualist definition of homelessness. On the one hand, the neoliberal individual is conceptualized as a free-roaming moral agent who is accountable for his or her own actions. On the other hand, the collectivist model places the subject within a much more structured and complex web of interpersonal relationships. One of the effects of this binary model is that Jesus, constructed as a so-called pseudo-individual, is potentially made more Western (and less Mediterranean and/or Jewish) as he comes into conflict with ancient Mediterranean social norms.[71] Moreover, the model fixates on what Jesus has done or has not done to become different from his contemporaries, inadvertently ascribing a level of agency that might not be realistic.

This sublimation of Jesus' outsider status, however, potentially fractures once we observe that his 'pseudo-individualist behaviour' is, in part, a product of the townsfolk's imagination. Jesus returns to his hometown with the intention of participating in the synagogue. His deviant status emerges only as a remnant to the breakdown in relations between himself and the community. For instance, in v. 54 the people are shocked (ἐκπλήσσεσθαι) by Jesus and attempt to limit his ability and authority. Further, the townsfolk attempt to keep their inner-circle pure from Jesus' deviance through the process of boundary-making; Malina and Neyrey write that '[s]hould pollution

---

70. Malina, 'Collectivism in Mediterranean Culture', p. 23.
71. This has ideological repercussions on a number of levels, including the harbouring of both anti-Arab and anti-Jewish sentiments. For an extensive exploration, see Crossley, *Jesus in an Age of Terror*, pp. 110-35; Crossley, *Neoliberalism*, pp. 175-84.

be found within the group, then the rite appropriate to this condition is the expulsion of the contaminating member'.[72] Being excluded from the collective, without his father, mother, brothers and sisters, Jesus has no platform from which to speak (vv. 55-56). The townsfolk's refusal to recognize his wisdom and deeds of power means that Jesus no longer has a basis of sociability for him to contribute positively on an interpersonal level.

The townsfolk's unwillingness to reach out to Jesus and believe in him is presented as the reason for his eventual reluctance to perform deeds of power. As discussed above, the Matthean text constructs a normative ideological point of view that vindicates Jesus and highlights the complicity of the townsfolk to meaningfully recognize that Jesus has a legitimate claim to their community.[73] The text insinuates that they, as participants and upholders of dominant arrangements of power in society, are ultimately responsible for his social exclusion.[74]

An Unemployed Artisan Dishonoured

The ancient Mediterranean value system of honour and shame is explicitly invoked by Jesus in v. 57. The self-imposed label ἄτιμος signifies Jesus' recognition of his deviant status within the community. According to Neyrey, honour in the ancient Mediterranean refers to 'the value of an object, namely, its price or worth, as well as to the public role and status which individuals enjoy. Honor basically has to do with evaluation and social perception: What do people think of this person?'[75] One environment where honour was often determined was within the village context and particularly in a public space such as the synagogue. Neyrey writes that 'people in villages and neighborhoods strive to estimate accurately the worth of a family and its reputation, so as to calculate its social standing'.[76]

Neyrey's model of honour and shame adds another dimension to how the experience of rejection from his hometown has left Jesus thoroughly dishonoured (ἄτιμος) within the village context. Jesus' itinerancy has resulted in his dishonouring not only within his πατρίς (hometown) but also within the household. While the term ἄτιμος appears just once in the Matthean

72. Malina and Neyrey, *Calling Jesus Names*, pp. 13-14.

73. See Carter, *Margins*, p. 299.

74. In this sense, then, the text ascribes a subjective responsibility to underlying objective violence.

75. Neyrey, *Honor and Shame*, p. 5. Lawrence criticizes Neyrey for assuming that the Gospel's composition depends on the forms laid out by rhetorical handbooks. However, apart from the obvious limitation to one genre, the sources come from the literate elite stratum and therefore only reflect a narrow perspective. She cautions that Matthew's Gospel contains information about individuals and groups from numerous social strata. See Lawrence, *Ethnography*, pp. 20, 244-46.

76. Neyrey, *Honor and Shame*, p. 21.

text, the verb τιμάω (to honour) appears five times (15.4, 6, 8; 19.19; 27.9), and, with one exception (27.9), is always connected to honouring one's parents and/or the tradition of one's elders. It features three times in Jesus' conflict with a delegation of Pharisees and scribes from Jerusalem over tradition and authority in 15.1-20. As a microcosm of wider society, the household functioned as an ideological apparatus, prescribing ideal roles and duties for each of its members. As Moxnes observes, to be denied honour from the household was to be marginalized and displaced. The male role in the household was 'identified with that of the householder as overseer, father, husband, supplier of resources, person responsible for his house and its inhabitants'.[77]

Jesus' personal failure to enact this role with regard to his biological kin is identified as a seditious threat to the smooth, continued functioning of the ideological–political order. From the townsfolk's perspective, Jesus' dishonour is *achieved* based on his public, overt action.[78] For instance, the question 'Is this not the carpenter's son?' alludes to Jesus' unemployment. Instead of following in his father's trade, Jesus wanders about preaching the counter-cultural imaginary of the *basileia*.[79] Moreover, his shaming extends to those dependent on him for their reputation and survival. The naming of his mother, his four brothers and his sisters further stresses that Jesus has not lived up to his household responsibilities and/or social obligations.

The narrative's inclusion of Jesus' family trade, however, exposes another potential means of desublimation within the text's ideological texture. From a symptomatic understanding of homelessness, for example, Jesus' unemployment highlights the destitution and desperation that is intrinsic to his social experience. As a carpenter's son, Jesus would likely have witnessed the struggle of his father who, as a landless artisan, would have to work for wages where and when work could be found. Carter, for instance, suggests that the occupation (τέκτον) signifies the family's lowly status and Jesus' lowly origins.[80] Because land constituted the primary measure of wealth in the ancient world, and artisans had none, they were completely reliant on the demand of the 'market' for work. Brawley also suggests that τέκτον likely places Jesus among peasants who lost their land and had to resort to serving other peasants.[81] Carpenters were, in fact, underemployed and

---

77. Moxnes, *Putting Jesus in his Place*, pp. 95-96.

78. For more on this see Malina and Neyrey, *Calling Jesus Names*, p. 62.

79. The text does not disclose whether Joseph is still alive at this point. Jesus, if the eldest son (it is only implied by the infancy narrative), has the responsibility of providing for and managing his household's affairs in the absence of Joseph.

80. Carter, *Margins*, p. 299.

81. He writes that 'as an artisan, Jesus was likely an example of downward mobility from the peasant class to a status where he served other peasants. If Jesus' homeless-

regularly struggled to make ends meet.[82] It was, therefore, quite possible for an artisan to descend the social ladder into the expendable class—that strata reserved primarily for those excluded from the dominant cycles of economic production.

Despite the harsh accusations of the townsfolk and the denigrated remains of his social and economic standing, Jesus still attempts to defend his honour. Malina and Neyrey suggest that a person accused of deviancy can engage in many strategies: they might flee and begin anew elsewhere or simply acquiesce in a deviant label. If they adopt the label they can choose to deny responsibility by suggesting that their actions were due to forces beyond their control, or they might appeal to higher loyalties such as God.[83] In 13.53-58, the townsfolk, focusing on Jesus' biological kin, employ conventional cultural categories to define him. Jesus attempts to circumvent conventional notions of honour by indicating that the source of his honour comes not from his biological family but rather from his Father in heaven.

This reclamation of honour has already been hinted at previously in the Gospel as the Matthean text retroactively seeks to make the deviant Jesus prominent. According to Neyrey, Jesus, during the Sermon on Mount (chaps. 5–7), changes the way the honour game is played by redefining the source of honour, namely, acknowledgement by God, not by neighbour.[84] So too in the case of his hometown rejection, Jesus is honoured through his experience of dishonour. By aligning himself with the prophetic tradition, he is relocated to an alternative site of cultural recognition. Rejection serves as a touchstone of authenticity for Jesus as it exposes the vacuity of home place as a space of meaningful and unconditional acceptance within the Matthean text's ideological point of view.

Conclusions

In this chapter I have explored how Jesus' identity as a displaced outsider of the expendable class is reified during the return to his hometown. If home-

ness was voluntary, it could easily symbolise the abandonment of security grounded in possessions. On the other hand, if it were a sheer social reality, it would more readily reflect the need under imperial systems for equitable access to the resources of the land.' See Brawley, 'Homeless in Galilee'.

82. Oakman, for instance, cautions us from crediting too much opportunity to marginal artisans, reminding us by way of a citation from Xenophon, 'In small towns the same man makes couches, doors, ploughs, and tables, and still he is thankful if only he can find enough work to support himself' (Xenophon, *Cyr.* 8.2.5). See Douglas E. Oakman, *Jesus and the Economic Questions of his Day* (Lewiston, NY: E. Mellen, 1986), p. 178.

83. Malina and Neyrey, *Calling Jesus Names*, pp. 62-65.

84. Neyrey, *Honor and Shame*, pp. 164-65.

lessness is defined as not just a lack of physical dwelling, but rather a condition of exclusion and uprootedness from society, then within Mt. 13.53-58 Jesus is constructed narratively as experiencing yet another dimension of homelessness. Social exclusion occurs gradually as a process of denial and rejection, and Jesus is systematically denied a space in both his home village and local synagogue. Ironically, Jesus is rendered homeless by his own hometown. The synagogue institutionalizes and consolidates the power of the community to exclude Jesus, placing him on the outside of social normalcy.

This process of exclusion, then, causes another effect of desublimation in the text's ideological texture. Jesus' expendable status emerges not as an idyllic manifestation of his agency but as an excremental excess to the regulating processes of the synagogue and first-century social and cultural norms. His rebellious redefinition of the dominant kinship model disrupts the sensibilities of the townsfolk, who subsequently latch on to this aspect as a means of discrediting and dishonouring him.

Rather than diminishing the threat to dominant arrangements of power, however, Jesus' exclusion makes him appear even more dangerous to his contemporaries. Detachment from the household means that he has no foundation on which to stand; he acts not as part of the collective and so has no legitimate claim to identity. These threads of rejection and displacement resound in the background of the Matthean narrative until they once again resurge in the arrest and execution of Jesus. As will be advanced in the next chapter, Jesus' status as an expendable and displaced outsider is, in part, responsible for his targeting and extermination by the judicial apparatus of the ideological–political order. It is to this final stage in Matthew's narrative that I now turn.

6

EXTERMINATION

The closure of society that is the aim of securing the public requires that a public place for the homeless body be denied. The resultant contradiction between a material body that most certainly occupies space and the denial of any place for such a body cannot be resolved: nonetheless, an attempt at such resolution is continually enacted through violent processes of containment, constriction, and compression that seek not simply to exclude or control the homeless but rather to efface their presence altogether.

Samira Kawash[1]

We arrive at the end of Matthew's story of Jesus to find the various narrative threads we have been examining reach their anticipated climax. The protagonist has experienced a number of episodes of displacement and alienation right from the beginning of his life, and these are recalled once again in the moments surrounding his death. As a result, this study's central ideological categories of homelessness and displacement have important implications for an interpretation of the passion narrative. During the arrest and execution of Jesus, the fear of otherness—its associations with deviancy, alienation and exteriority—is put to death. Like a pest, Jesus is exterminated in order that society can return to its smooth, uninterrupted functioning.

It is common and expected that conventional readings of the passion will focus on the theology of cross. What does Jesus' death mean for Christians and the Christian life? While this is a worthy enough pursuit, this question does not concern me here. Rather, the following analysis is focused on the relationship between the arrest and punishment of Jesus in the context of the Judean and Roman imperial jurisdictive apparatus. It is not too much of a stretch to suggest that the crucifixion has become tamed; its radical and tortuous nature is frequently subsumed by a grander narrative of resurrection and atonement. Perhaps all the effort to sanitize Jesus' crucifixion is nothing more than an attempt to escape and/or domesticate the terrifying impact of the Thing, by reducing it to its symbolic status for believing Christians.

---

1. Samira Kawash, 'The Homeless Body', *Public Culture* 10 (1997), p. 330.

The traumatic reality of the cross is precisely what gets extracted within ideology. Such a strategy of containment enables readers to organize their *jouissance* around the victory of the cross in its role as a mediator of eternal (surplus) life. At the material level, however, crucifixion functions as an instrument of torture and as part of a broader politics of extermination. It combines a method of elimination with the spectacle of stigmatic degradation to generate social order and cohesion.

In this chapter I advance my discussion of the nexus between Jesus and homelessness by examining how it plays out in two specific pericopes of Matthew's passion narrative. While the entire passion is notable for its systematic arbitration of Jesus' fate, this chapter will focus on his arrest (26.47-56) and moment of execution (27.38-50). The stress on these two texts, in particular, provides a suitable exploration of the punitive measures that a society will enact in its negotiation of deviant behaviour. The chapter begins, however, by considering the social and cultural reasons for Jesus' death as they are encoded within the wider text. Following this, Jesus' arrest can be re-read in a way that foregrounds the diffusion of power and violence among characters and institutions. Finally, I discuss Jesus' final moments on the cross, drawing particular attention to the social function of crucifixion within its wider context as a politics of extermination. Matthew's story of Jesus does not finish with his death, however, and so a brief section is included about the resurrection. What is the meaning effect of an exterminated homeless body that has, against all expectations of normalcy, risen and conquered death?

The Reasons for Jesus' Death

Explanations for the execution of the various Jesus simulacra abound, although it is difficult to establish an exact cause.[2] Justin Meggitt notes that '[i]t did not take much to end up on a cross in the empire, if you were a non-citizen and of low status'.[3] He observes via a quote from the Roman poet Juvenal how the power to crucify someone was applied casually to those who had little or no social standing:

> 'Crucify that slave', says the wife. 'But what crime worthy of death has he committed?' asks the husband. 'Where are the witnesses? Who informed against him? Give him a hearing at least. No delay can be too long when a man's life is stake.' What a fool you are! Do you call a slave a man? Do

---

2. In fact, one of the criteria used to establish historical Jesus material is that which provides an adequate explanation for his death. See John P. Meier, *A Marginal Jew: Rethinking the Historical Jesus*, vol. 1 (New York: Doubleday, 1991), p. 177.

3. Justin J. Meggitt, 'The Madness of King Jesus: Why Was Jesus Put to Death, but his Followers Were Not?', *JSNT* 29 (2007), p. 380.

you say he has done no wrong? This is my will and my command. Take it
as authority for the deed' (Juvenal, *Sat.* 6.219ff.).

In the case of Matthew's Jesus, a combination of theological and historical explanations is usually provided. Carter suggests that Matthew's Jesus
is condemned as a blasphemer by the religious elite, and then crucified by
Rome as a treasonous insurrectionist. He writes that 'Jesus' crucifixion in
Jerusalem primarily results from proclaiming and embodying God's reign
or empire. The life-giving and just power of God's empire conflicts with
and challenges the hierarchical, exploitative, and oppressive practices of
Rome's empire and the allied religious elite.'[4] Irrespective of this, Jesus
is in all likelihood considered a nonentity by the higher social strata. His
extermination could be used 'to intimidate others who might be inspired by
what he did. He was crucified as a warning to others: this is what happens
to people who might be tempted to think as he dared to think.'[5] Of course,
Jesus is punished not merely for what he thought, but for his status as a
deviant outsider, that is, as an expendable surplus to the needs of economic
production and social stability.

France adds that the most direct explanation for the events that unfold
during the passion are given by the character of Jesus himself at the Last
Supper (Mt. 26.17-30), where, 'in the redemptive context of the Passover
festival, and using the OT language of covenant, he speaks of his blood
shed for many for the forgiveness of sins (26.28)'.[6] Accordingly, France
sees the theological transaction of Jesus' death as a source of life for others
(and linking back to the initial declaration of Jesus' mission in 1.21) as the
primary lens through which to understand the passion narrative.[7]

As has been observed in the analysis of previous texts, however, such
an emphasis sometimes features as a fantasmatic barrier, obscuring the
reader's view from significant social and political textures encoded within
the Matthean text. For example, just as conventional interpretations frame
Jesus' homelessness as a choice in life, thereby emphasizing the role of
the individual and downplaying structural factors that cause and construct
homelessness, we find a similar framing of Jesus' supposed 'choice' to die.

---

4. Carter, *Margins*, 498; cf. Harrington, *Matthew*, p. 364.

5. Stephen J. Patterson, *Beyond the Passion: Rethinking the Death and Life of
Jesus* (Minneapolis, MN: Fortress Press, 2004), p. 9.

6. France, *Matthew*, p. 969; cf. Robert J. Daly, 'The Eucharist and Redemption: The
Last Supper and Jesus' Understanding of his Death', *BTB* 11 (1981), pp. 21-27.

7. See also Adela Yarbro Collins, 'Finding Meaning in the Death of Jesus', *JR* 78.2
(1998), pp. 175-96; W.D. Davies and Dale C. Allison, *The Gospel according to Saint
Matthew 19–28*, vol. 3 (ICC; Edinburgh: T. & T. Clark, 1997), p. 440; Fenton, *Matthew*,
p. 408; John P. Galvin, 'Jesus' Approach to Death: An Examination of Some Recent
Studies', *TS* 41 (1980), pp. 713-44; Meier, *Matthew*, pp. 307-308.

In his study of *The Passion of Jesus in the Gospel of Matthew*, for instance, Donald Senior writes,

> The crucifixion was no surprise, falling on Jesus like a tile off a roof. The Gospels make it clear that the hostility against Jesus was a result of Jesus' own mission. Because of his unyielding commitment, his 'passion': Jesus put himself on a collision course with certain powerful forces in society. From this perspective Jesus' death was the outcome of his life; he 'chose' death. In the language of the Gospel, he 'took up the cross.'[8]

While Senior is correct to emphasize the conflict between Jesus and the ruling elite as a primary cause leading to his death, this conflict is not merely the product of an arbitrary choice (or succession of choices) by Jesus. Rather, as has been consistently argued, Jesus' outsider status is produced through a complex combination of structural determinants, social and geographical displacements, and reactions. His homelessness, in fact, emerges as a symptom of the reigning ideological–political order. These external realities are occasionally expressed as internal initiatives. While some parts of the Matthean text do emphasize Jesus' agency, the theological idea that Jesus 'chooses' to die is, in fact, much stronger in the Gospel of John than it is in the Synoptic Gospels in general or in Matthew in particular.[9]

The recent work of Justin Meggitt draws attention to alternative reasons for why Jesus is put to death. Focusing on the historical Jesus (as opposed to the Jesus simulacra of the Gospels) he argues that the dominant idea that Jesus was put to death by the Roman authorities because they believed him to be a royal pretender fails to satisfactorily explain why only he was killed and his followers were not. Meggitt demonstrates how this was an unusual procedure if the Romans feared that Jesus was the leader of a political insurgency. As a hypothetical solution, Meggitt suggests that the Romans thought Jesus was a 'deranged and deluded lunatic'.[10] In some respects, this proposal complements the desublimation of Jesus' homelessness, and adds an additional heuristic lens through which to interpret Matthew's passion. Aside from the more obvious connections that can be made between the

---

8. Senior, *Passion*, p. 8.

9. Senior's analysis focuses on Matthew's theological perspective(s) of the passion, which he sees as running through the Gospel and finding their 'resolution and most eloquent expression in the dramatic events of Jesus' arrest and resurrection'. See Senior, *Passion*, p. 11.

10. Meggitt, 'Madness', pp. 379-413. Marcus's response to Meggitt's proposal praises the re-opening of the conundrum of why Jesus was put to death but points out that his solution, that Jesus was a lunatic, is not conclusively supported. See Joel Marcus, 'Meggitt on the Madness and Kingship of Jesus', *JSNT* 29 (2007), pp. 421-24; cf. Paula Fredriksen, 'Why Was Jesus Crucified, but his Followers Were Not?', *JSNT* 29 (2007), pp. 415-19.

prevalence of mental illness among the homeless population in contemporary society,[11] Meggitt's argument brings into focus the need for more socially and politically comprehensible reasons for Jesus' execution. Rather than wanting to remove a political agitator, the authorities were motivated by *policing*; the arrest and execution—or extermination—of Jesus can be seen as a pragmatic solution to the disturbance of deviancy within his local socio-political context.[12]

In recent decades, many Western societies have implemented 'get-tough' policies that attack the symptoms of homelessness without addressing its deeper social and economic roots. Within this cultural matrix, a new trend toward the criminalization of homelessness has emerged, in which governments turn to the criminal justice system for solutions, manifested by restrictions on the use of public space for sleeping and/or sitting, outlawing begging, and police sweeps of 'problem' areas.[13] The strategy of physically removing homeless people from the streets serves a perceived social role of protecting society from the embodied threat of deviant behaviour. So too, while Jesus, within the logic of Roman imperial society, is not a credible threat, he is nonetheless *perceived* as a threat to its smooth, uninterrupted functioning. Accordingly, criminalization of the poor undergirds the rationale for Jesus' extermination. It is with this in mind that I turn to Jesus' arrest sequence in the garden of Gethsemane.

The Arrest of Jesus (Matthew 26.47-56)

The account of Jesus' arrest contains three smaller scenes: the first concerns Judas (vv. 47-50); the second involves the cutting off of the ear of the high priest's servant (vv. 51-54); and the third concerns Jesus' speech against the crowd and his abandonment by his disciples (vv. 55-56).[14] Leroy Huizenga observes that scholars generally interpret the Matthean Gethsemane and

---

11. Talbot, 'Social Exclusion and Homelessness', p. 15.

12. This does, of course, leave unanswered the question of why Jesus was put to death and his followers were not. Perhaps Jesus' experience of homelessness is more chronic than his followers (cf. 8.18-22) and so he is perceived of as more of a threat to the smooth functioning of society.

13. For more on this trend, and how it potentially interferes with the 'human rights' of the homeless population, see Maria Foscarinis, Kelly Cunningham-Bowers and Kristen E. Brown, 'Out of Sight–Out of Mind?: The Continuing Trend toward the Criminalization of Homelessness', *Georgetown Journal on Poverty Law and Policy* 6.2 (1999), pp. 145-64; Randall Amster, 'Patterns of Exclusion: Sanitizing Space, Criminalizing Homelessness', *Social Justice* 30.1 (2003), pp. 195-221; Maria Foscarinis, 'Downward Spiral: Homelessness and its Criminalization', *Yale Law and Policy Review* 14 (1996), pp. 1-64.

14. Davies and Allison, *Matthew*, III, p. 505.

arrest sequence in one of three ways: first, the sequence emphasizes Jesus' commitment to continue to the cross; second, it features as a narrative of nonviolence (serving a paradigmatic function);[15] and/or third, it demonstrates a 'negative apologetic' in the way that Jesus refuses the physical defence of his disciples as well as any angelic assistance, such that it refutes the idea he was a brigand or magician.[16] As with other texts, redaction criticism remains the dominant methodological approach to this text.[17] The following analysis, however, focuses predominantly on the narrative features of the text's inner texture in tandem with social intertexture that encodes social roles and relationships. In doing so, it draws out the distribution of power across the various characters, and the institutions of power that support them. This section begins by analysing the setting of the text. As with 13.53-58, Jesus' arrest is set within an emotionally charged environment that intensifies the drama of the episode.

Setting

Matthew 26.47-56 takes place in the garden of Gethsemane, an olive orchard located on the Mount of Olives just outside of the city of Jerusalem. Keener describes the mountain as having three summits parallel to Jerusalem for about two and a half miles on the east, and rising higher than the Temple Mount, 'The narrative may refer specifically to the central summit, for which the title was often used'.[18] He also notes that '[i]f the press originally belonged to an individual estate rather than a local village, the estate must have been sizeable'.[19] The spatial setting of the 'Mount of Olives' (26.30) recalls the prophetic sermon Jesus preached 'up the mountain' (5.1) at the beginning of his ministry, the two occasions Jesus spent alone up the mountain (14.23; 15.29), and the transfiguration before Peter, James and John (17.1, 9). Harrington notes that during the Passover pilgrimage, the Mount of Olives would have been crowded, which is why the officials had to have a pre-arranged signal 'in order to arrest the right man as quickly and smoothly as possible'.[20]

The temporal setting at night intratextually reminds the reader of the flight to Egypt, which also took place under the cover of darkness (2.13-23).

---

15. Davies and Allison, *Matthew*, III, p. 512.

16. Harrington, *Matthew*, p. 377; Leroy Andrew Huizenga, 'Obedience unto Death: The Matthean Gethsemane and Arrest Sequence and the Aqedah', *CBQ* 71 (2009), p. 507.

17. See especially Raymond E. Brown, *The Death of the Messiah: A Commentary on the Passion Narratives in the Four Gospels*, vol. 1 (New York: Doubleday, 1994).

18. Keener, *Matthew*, p. 634.

19. Keener, *Matthew*, p. 634.

20. Harrington, *Matthew*, p. 374.

While the precise term for night, νυκτός, does not appear in Matthew 26, the arrest occurs shortly after the disciples repeatedly fall asleep while attempting to keep vigil in the garden of Gethsemane (26.40, 43, 45). Davies and Allison suggest that the 'setting at night matches the intention of the Jewish leaders to take Jesus "by stealth" and avoid a riot' (cf. 26.4, 16).[21] The setting signifies a time of trouble or turmoil, and gestures toward the approaching danger that is about to find Jesus.

By constantly alluding to the immanent arrest of Jesus, the text also sets the scene for the conflict that is about to unfold. In v. 45, Jesus announces that 'the hour is at hand, and the Son of Man is betrayed into the hands of sinners', thus alluding back to the homelessness of the Son of Man in 8.20. Indeed, the text gives no indication that Jesus and his immediate group of followers have a place to reside in Jerusalem during the festival. Rather, Jesus stays in Bethany (21.17), outside of Jerusalem, perhaps in the house of Simon the leper (cf. 26.6).

Diffusion of Power and Violence
Other elements of inner texture point to the manifestation of systemic violence that makes the efficient arrest of Jesus possible.[22] The system of power differentiations that has produced the protagonist's expendable status resurface once again in the actions and dialogue of the various characters.

The Crowds. Aside from acknowledging the presence of the high priests and elders, the text does not provide further details about the crowds (οἱ ὄχλοι). The identification of the crowds in Matthew's Gospel, including their characterization and function, has gained little consensus in recent scholarly opinion.[23] In his major study on *The Crowds in the Gospel of Matthew*, J.R.C. Cousland contends that the crowds are not a minor character but rather are emblematic of the people of Israel as distinct from their lead-

21. Davies and Allison, *Matthew*, III, p. 506.
22. Siker observes three layers of violence within this pericope: first, the violence of betrayal; second, the physical violence of the crowds; and third, violence in the act of desertion. See Judy Yates Siker, 'Matthew 26:47-56', *Interpretation* 58 (2004), pp. 386-89.
23. Kingsbury, for instance, claims that the crowds function as a single 'flat' character, devoid of conflicting traits, except toward the end of the Gospel when they appear with Judas to arrest Jesus. See Kingsbury, *Matthew as Story*, p. 24. In contrast, Saldarini describes the crowds as 'anonymous, shifting, unstructured, and are thus contrasted with Jesus' disciples who are a constant group, committed to Jesus, and given special instruction. The [Galilean] crowds are portrayed as fundamentally friendly, but also unreliable.' See Saldarini, *Matthew's Christian-Jewish Community*, p. 37.

ers.[24] He observes that the crowds can be readily interpreted both positively and negatively. While on the one hand they frequently appear predisposed toward Jesus, for example by exhibiting astonishment at his words and deeds (7.28; 9.33; 12.23; 15.31; 22.33) or when following him (4.25; 8.1; 12.15; 14.13; 19.2; 20.29; 21.9), they are, on the other hand, described as being devoid of understanding (13.10-17), and, more crucially, play a significant role in Jesus' arrest (26.47) and taking responsibility for his death (27.24-25).[25]

Within 26.47-56, the large crowd's hostile intentions are signalled by their weaponry. Reference to swords (μάχαιρα) is made six times, and there are two references to clubs (ξύλον). According to *BAGD*, μάχαιρα refers to a relatively short sword or dagger. As well as signifying the instrument itself, the noun stands as a symbol of violent death and the power of authorities to punish evildoers (cf. Rom. 8.35).[26] The term ξύλον refers to an object made of wood, a club or cudgel, and possibly also alludes to the wooden structure that will be used for the cross upon which Jesus is eventually crucified (cf. Acts 5.30; 10.39).[27]

Accordingly, Evans describes the protractors of elite enforcement who arrest Jesus as 'thugs' and reasons, via Josephus, that such collusion is attested to in the turmoil of Jerusalem of the mid-first century.[28] Similarly, France writes that a 'force sent out by the "chief priests and the elders of the people" sounds like an official posse recruited by or on behalf of the Sanhedrin . . . and so would probably have consisted of some of the temple guards, perhaps augmented by less formal recruits or volunteers'.[29] Brown, however, cautions that the impression of an armed rabble that has come with Judas needs to be modified by the indication within Matthew that the crowd has a delegation 'from' (ἀπό) the Jewish authorities who make up the Sanhedrin, 'No vigilantism or lynch mentality is implied then; and there is no suggestion that the arrest at night is illegal'.[30] The label 'chief priests and elders' (cf. Mt. 26.3-5, 14-16) signifies members of the governing class, and allies with Herod (2.4) and Pilate (27.62-66), 'beneficiaries and protectors of the status quo and its unjust hierarchical practices. . . . They value

24. J.R.C. Cousland, *The Crowds in the Gospel of Matthew* (NovTSup 102; Leiden: Brill, 2002).

25. Cousland, *Crowds in the Gospel of Matthew*, pp. 7-8.

26. 'μάχαιρα', *BAGD*, p. 622.

27. 'ξύλον', *BAGD*, p. 685.

28. Evans, *Matthew*, pp. 436-37. According to Josephus, 'Such was the shamelessness and effrontery which possessed the ruling priests that they actually were so brazen as to send slaves to the threshing floors to receive the tithes that were due to the priests, with the result that the poorer priests starved to death' (*Ant.* 20.181).

29. France, *Matthew*, pp. 1011-12.

30. Brown, *Death of the Messiah*, I, p. 247.

their privileged role legitimated by birth, gender, wealth, social position, tradition, and political alliance',[31] and so deem Jesus a threat to their continued stability and leadership.[32] Given both their numbers and weaponry, the crowds visibly possess power over other characters within this pericope.

Judas. The character of Judas is introduced in 10.4 as both a disciple and the one who will betray Jesus. While in Jerusalem, Judas turns Jesus over to the chief priests for thirty pieces of silver (26.14-16). After the antagonists are introduced by the narrator in v. 47, and Judas approaches Jesus, he kisses him. The kiss is a pre-arranged signal to identify Jesus to the arresting party. While the violence of the crowds is underscored by the frequent reference to their weaponry, Judas's arsenal consists simply of his lips.

On a subjective level, Judas's actions are characterized as morally repulsive. The crowd's complicity in the arrest is thus diluted by Judas's excessive act of betrayal. Brown suggests that the address by Jesus to Judas as 'friend' is ironic, in that Jesus already perceives that Judas will betray him.[33] John Suggit argues for the translation of ἑταῖρος as 'comrade', motioning its political overtones.[34] The term ἑταῖρος appears just three times in the NT, all of which occur in Matthew (cf. 20.13; 22.12), and in every case appears in the vocative to address a person who is in the wrong. While Judas and Jesus are supposed to be reacting against the same oppression, Judas's actions are directly opposite to those of a true comrade. This use of irony is continued through the entire episode of Jesus' arrest and execution. The kiss itself is a gesture of affection and inclusion. It suggests familiarity, closeness and intimacy. And yet, in this case it results in an act of betrayal, the arrest of his comrade (ἑταῖρος).

While Christian tradition has predominantly characterized Judas as the scapegoat,[35] conventional interpretations fail to acknowledge the extent to which he is preyed upon by the elite chief priests and elders. He is the weak link within Jesus' group and merely an instrument of Jesus' opponents, and the text identifies him embarrassingly as 'the betrayer' (26.48). Harrington suggests that the betrayal, usually viewed as a treacherous failure of friendship, is puzzling. He observes that '[t]he emphasis of these interpreters

31. Carter, *Margins*, p. 500.
32. Cf. Josephus, *War* 2.410-14.
33. Brown, *Death of the Messiah*, I, p. 256. The foreknowledge thesis dominant in conventional readings (see below) is disrupted by Jesus' question in v. 50, 'Friend, why are you here?'
34. John Suggit, 'Comrade Judas: Matthew 26:50', *JTSA* 63 (1988), pp. 56-58.
35. Ulrich Luz, *Matthew 21–28* (trans. James E. Crouch; Hermeneia; Minneapolis, MN: Fortress Press, 2005), pp. 412-14.

is psychological, individualistic, and romantic'.[36] In actual fact, the verb παραδίδωμι denotes the mechanical task of 'handing over' or 'delivering' Jesus to the authorities.[37] It signals the limited role of Judas within the jurisdictive machinery of the wider ideological–political order (cf. 17.22; 20.18-19; 26.2, 25, 46; 27.3). The use of παραδίδωμι also recalls the 'handing over' of John the Baptist during his arrest in 4.12, the event that pre-empted Jesus' withdrawal from Nazareth to Capernaum. The mechanical language evokes for the reader the indiscriminate production of deviancy and its necessitated extermination. Upon realizing his naive complicity with the elite establishment, Judas internalizes the guilt, returns the money he received and takes his own life (27.3-5).[38]

The Disciples. Having explored the diffusion of power and violence among the crowds and the role of Judas in the arrest of Jesus, I now turn to the actions of the disciples. As noted in previous chapters, Jesus' disciples share in the itinerancy of his mission (8.18-22; 10.5-15). They also function as his fictive kin, a surrogate home place for the one with nowhere to lay his head.

The moment of Jesus' arrest is described by the physical actions of the arresting party: they 'lay their hands on him' [ἐπέβαλον τὰς χεῖρας]—a phrase repeated twice within 26.47-56. Carter observes that '[w]hereas here hands denote betrayal, hostility, and violence (as they have in 26.23, 45, 51), Jesus has used his hands to heal (8.3, 15; 9.18, 25), to define his community/family (12.49), to save (14.31), and to bless (19.13, 15)'.[39] The soldiers who come to arrest Jesus are armed as if Jesus were a λῃστής, which means 'robber', or in some cases 'revolutionary'.

Not surprisingly, Jesus' disciples react negatively to the arrest. When the armed authorities approach Jesus, one disciple draws his sword and strikes 'the slave of the high priest, cutting off his ear' (v. 51). But Jesus orders him to sheath his sword with the epithet 'all who take to the sword will perish by the sword' (v. 52). Brown remarks that the concise command is bolstered by the poetic chiastic assertion.[40] Such a statement appears to contradict the violent sentiments of Jesus earlier in the Gospel (10.34-36) and confuses the

36. Harrington, *Matthew*, p. 377.

37. 'παραδίδωμι', *BAGD*, pp. 761-62. In an effort to rehabilitate the historical Judas, Klassen argues that παραδίδωμι only means 'hand over' and not 'betray'. William Klassen, *Judas: Betrayer or Friend of Jesus?* (Minneapolis, MN: Fortress Press, 2004).

38. Reed argues that Judas's act of suicide is a noble attempt to reclaim his lost honour, and the guilt of responsibility rests with the chief priests. See David A. Reed, '"Saving Judas"—A Social Scientific Approach to Judas's Suicide in Matthew 27:3-10', *BTB* 35 (2005), pp. 51-59.

39. Carter, *Margins*, p. 513.

40. Brown, *Death of the Messiah*, I, p. 275.

noble but misguided attempt to argue for a nonviolent Jesus, as there is no clear unadulterated message on the use of violent action.[41] It is also complicated by the fact that at least one of those in Jesus' immediate company is brandishing arms, and is therefore set up for violent action.[42]

Furthermore, Jesus' next statement—that he could appeal to his Father in heaven to send more than 'twelve legions of angels' (v. 53)—reveals that Jesus believes not in a universal ethic of nonviolence but rather in (the threat of) divine violence. The text's inner logic suggests that this disciple's violent actions are not intrinsically wrong in any moral sense; it is rather that they are not violent enough! Any attempt to subjectivize violence, such as in the case of this disciple, is a means of distracting from the systemic violence that undergirds Jesus' arrest.

The appeal to divine violence, moreover, affirms that Jesus' attitude is entrenched in brutal forms and violent imagery (and in continuity with the prophetic tradition). Evans notes that in the Judaism and Christianity of late antiquity, angels were thought of as warriors, in addition to their function as messengers and worshippers of God.[43] Davies and Allison suggest that the 'reference to an enormous host of supernatural warriors, which reference reveals Jesus' majesty and control, mocks the far from mortal sword thrust of the sole unnamed disciple'.[44] Evans reasons that the '[r]eference to "twelve legions" is probably meant to parallel the twelve disciples, who offer ineffectual resistance'.[45] A legion (a Latin loanword) comprised about six thousand soldiers. Accordingly, Jesus could potentially call on seventy-two thousand angels, 'more than enough to overwhelm the crowd with its

41. For an example of a pacifist reading, see Robert R. Beck, *Banished Messiah: Violence and Nonviolence in Matthew's Story of Jesus* (Eugene, OR: Wipf & Stock, 2010). Through a selective reading of the Gospel, Beck argues that Jesus is 'determinedly nonviolent' and that the conflict surrounding Matthew's story of Jesus is resolved via the motif of the banished and returning prince. On this particular text, Carter suggests that Jesus chooses the inevitable road to death as a testament to an ethic of nonviolence. See Carter, *Margins*, p. 514. France wrongly identifies a 'contrast between the Jerusalem establishment, which depends on stealth and physical force' and Jesus' nonviolent approach. See France, *Matthew*, p. 1014; cf. Stephen J. Binz, *The Passion and Resurrection Narratives of Jesus: A Commentary* (Collegeville, MN: Liturgical Press, 1989), p. 51; T.R. Hobbs, 'Soldiers in the Gospels: A Neglected Agent', in *Social Scientific Models for Interpreting the Bible* (ed. John J. Pilch; Leiden: Brill, 2001), p. 347; Pennington, *Heaven and Earth*, p. 324; Sim, 'Pacifist and Violent'.

42. Desjardins argues that the NT is suffused with violence, and that Jesus and his followers can be found accepting, condoning and even inciting physical violence. See Michel Desjardins, *Peace, Violence and the New Testament* (Biblical Seminar, 46; Sheffield: Sheffield Academic Press, 1997).

43. Evans, *Matthew*, p. 439; cf. 1QS 7.6; 13.10.

44. Davies and Allison, *Matthew*, III, p. 513.

45. Evans, *Matthew*, p. 439.

swords and clubs, and more than enough to deal with the whole of the local Roman military!'[46] Angelic assistance is often available to help God's people in need as envisaged in military terms by the OT phrase 'the host [army] of heaven' (1 Kgs 22.19) and the angelic armies in Dan. 10.13, 20-21; 12.1; and Rev. 12.7.[47] Jesus' apparent refusal to rely on divine intervention in this instance, however, mirrors an earlier refusal during his cycle of homelessness in the wilderness (Mt. 4.6-7).

The disciples are hopelessly ineffectual in their support of Jesus, and their abandonment features as another point of desublimation in the text's ideological texture. In fact, Judy Yates Siker regards the desertion itself as a violent act: cowardice and fear override any sense of obligation or loyalty.[48] Apart from the text's naming of Judas and the mention of 'one of those who was with Jesus' drawing his sword, the disciples are conspicuously absent from the arrest sequence until they desert him in v. 56.[49] Jesus' abandonment by his fictive kin is amplified by the two verbs employed to describe their actions. First, the verb φεύγω, 'to flee', is the same action taken by Joseph, Mary and Jesus in 2.13 and also the instruction from Jesus to the disciples in the mission discourse of Matthew 10, 'When they persecute you in one town, flee to the next, for truly I tell you, you will not have gone through all the towns of Israel before the Son of Man comes' (10.23; cf. 24.16). Although the text does not indicate that the disciples are themselves subject to arrest, they likely have a legitimate fear of the authorities, given their association with an accused criminal now held in custody.[50] Second, the verb ἀφίημι, 'to desert', within 26.56 marks a striking reversal from its use in the call of the first disciples of Jesus, during which they 'deserted' their fishing nets, livelihoods and family ties (4.20). The total abandonment of Jesus is indicated by the adjective πᾶς ('each/all/every'), stressing that *all* the disciples (οἱ μαθηταὶ πάντες) flee from the scene.

The repeated denial of Jesus by Peter (26.69-75), which becomes a fixture of the trial narrative, further emphasizes the desertion of Jesus' closest comrades. Peter promised that he would never leave Jesus in 26.33. As pre-

46. Carter, *Margins*, p. 514.
47. France, *Matthew*, p. 1014.
48. Siker, 'Matthew 26:47-56', p. 388.
49. This is prefaced by the phrase 'all this has taken place, so that the scriptures of the prophets may be fulfilled', recalling the marginal identity formed during Jesus' infancy and his role as a liberated liberator.
50. Davies and Allison ask why '[t]he disciples' flight does not come when Jesus is seized but only after he speaks'. To answer, they refer to John Chrysostom, who writes, 'Thenceforth they saw that escape was no longer possible, when he was giving himself up to them voluntarily, and saying, that this was done according to the Scriptures' (*Hom. Mt.* 84.2). In witnessing Jesus' refusal to stay and fight, they flee the scene. See Davies and Allison, *Matthew*, III, p. 516.

dicted by Jesus at the Last Supper, however, Peter denies Jesus three times before the cock crows (26.31-35). In his time of need, Jesus is forsaken and left alone. The arrest of their leader, combined with the fear of punishment, fractures the community and disrupts its capacity as a surrogate home place of fictive kinship. The expendable Jesus is rendered completely homeless with nowhere to lay his head and nobody to call his kin.

Jesus' Passivity and the Reclamation of Honour

The passive role of Jesus in Matthew's passion narrative has aided all kinds of theological speculation. Within 26.47-56, for example, Jesus does not appear to resist the arrest by the hostile crowd, and commands his disciple to re-sheath his sword and not fight back (v. 52). Jesus supposes that although he could call upon his Father for heavenly backup, this would hinder the fulfilment of scripture and the prophets (vv. 53-56).[51] Jesus' passivity is also in accord with his own passion predictions in 16.21, 17.22, and 20.17-19.[52]

Even though Jesus does not actively resist the arresting party, a number of interpreters suggest, somewhat incongruously, that this in fact counts as a *demonstration* of his agency. Senior, for example, asserts that the text 'highlights the prophetic knowledge and majestic power of Jesus even when he seems to be the victim of his foes. . . . At the very moment he is arrested, Jesus declares his absolute freedom to carry out his messianic mission in accordance with God's will.'[53] France also suggests that Jesus' words make it clear that it is not that he *cannot* resist the arresting party, but that he *will not*, in accordance with his Father's will. Jesus is taken by the Jerusalem authorities not because he has no choice, but because he accepts it as his messianic calling. France reasons that

> while Jesus now has no chance of escape, the narrative nonetheless reads as if he is in charge of the situation. . . . The Jesus whom Judas and his posse meet is now resolute, calm, and authoritative. He himself makes no attempt to resist arrest, and when one of his disciples tries to defend him, it is Jesus himself, not the arresting party, who puts an end to the attempt. He speaks of the supernatural resources available to him, and declares that it is his choice not to call on them, because his purpose is that the Scriptures should be fulfilled.[54]

51. Huizenga argues that the text's narrative dynamics evoke the Aqedah within the intertexture of the text, presenting Jesus as a new Isaac who willingly faces his sacrifice with unflinching courage. See Huizenga, 'Obedience unto Death', pp. 507-26.

52. For more on how the Matthean text links the passion prophecies to the story of the passion, see Eugene LaVerdiere, 'The Passion Story as Prophecy', *Emmanuel* 93 (1987), pp. 85-90.

53. Senior, *Passion*, p. 84.

54. France, *Matthew*, p. 1011.

The ascription of a heightened capacity for agency here features as a blind spot in the text's ideological texture. In addition to sustaining a neoliberal emphasis on individual responsibility, a focus on the divinely ordained fate of Jesus effectively fetishizes him as the object-cause of theological desire. Jesus' extermination is no longer deemed a symptom of the reigning ideo-logical–political order, but instead is sublimated into an instrument of God's redemptive outworking (Jesus must die in order that we can be saved). In a somewhat ironic twist, the culpability of those arresting Jesus is negated, for they are simply following what has already been set in motion by the big Other.[55]

This potential for the text to facilitate the sublimation of Jesus' *chosen* death calls for a careful reading against the grain of the text: the reader should first attend to the conflict between human characters and violent insti-tutions of power. A more judicious understanding of Jesus' apparent passiv-ity within the Matthean passion, for example, can be found by deferring to the social-scientific topic of honour and shame as it is encoded within the social and cultural texture of the text. I have already mentioned how honour and shame were pivotal values within ancient Mediterranean society, and that the Matthean text is at pains to negotiate these widely shared cultural values in its characterization of Jesus. The mention of 'prophet' in 26.56 evokes intratextually Jesus' rejection from his hometown (13.53-58) during which a similar struggle for honour recognition took place. Within 26.47-56, Jesus likely realizes that the arresting party is too overpowering to sim-ply fight off. As a result, he refuses to engage in violent resistance. Instead, Jesus' threat of divine violence asserts a capacity for supreme power over and above that possessed by his arresters and executioners. His motioning toward the big Other suggests that his death will not be the final meas-ure, and the prerogative to a higher honour is eventually achieved through his resurrection, which functions, in part, as the overcoming of the unjust power structures of this world.

In their book *Calling Jesus Names*, Malina and Neyrey similarly con-tend that Jesus' passion ought to be read through the prism of a prominence model. The Matthean text intends to redefine Jesus' deviant status as an outsider in an affirmative light.[56] They write that a 'prominent person is a person perceived to be out of place to such an extent or in such a way as to

---

55. In Lacanian theory, the 'big Other', as the symbolic substance of being, refers not necessarily to God but to the unwritten, implicit rules in a society that regulate etiquette and social conversation.

56. Malina and Neyrey reason that a deviancy model explains why Jesus' oppo-nents rise against him and engineer his execution. It also gives weight to the various degradation rituals that accompany his crucifixion given the aim of discrediting and rejecting his honour. See Malina and Neyrey, *Calling Jesus Names*, pp. 81-91.

be redefined in a new, positive place'.[57] Within such a framework, the tension between Jesus' honour and shameful arrest and execution is retrospectively played out within the Matthean text: on the one hand, the text does not want to underemphasize the degrading experience of being arrested by force; but, on the other hand, the text attests to Jesus' surplus of heavenly honour that will be revealed in its fullness during the resurrection. In such a scenario, Jesus' passivity does not downplay the strategic collusion of institutions of power that target and exterminate deviant outsiders, nor does it enhance his capacity for agency. Rather, passivity functions as a means of honour acquisition and reclamation as it is encoded within the text's social and cultural texture.

The Death of Jesus (Matthew 27.38-50)

Following the arrest of Jesus, a trial ensues. The accused is taken before Caiaphas, the high priest, and tried by the Sanhedrin, the ruling Jewish council in Jerusalem made up of various scribes and elders (26.57-68). Jesus then appears before Pilate, the Roman governor, who orders his execution by crucifixion (27.1-26). The soldiers of the governor take Jesus, strip him and dress him in royal garb in order to mock him (27.27-31). After spitting and deriding him they take him away to be crucified. Senior remarks that the crucifixion, which takes place *outside* of Jerusalem, captures the abject rejection of the Messiah that has commanded the attention of much of the second half of the Gospel.[58] Indeed, the crucifixion can also be regarded as Jesus' final rejection from home place. Not only is Jesus afforded social and political indignity, he is removed from Jerusalem, which ideally functions as a spiritual and cultural point of orientation for Jews, especially during the Passover festival. In this section, I argue that the method of crucifixion combined with the taunting from onlookers engineers a spectacle of deviancy that creates social order and cohesion in its extermination of a perceived irritant.

The Method of Crucifixion

Matthew 27.38-50 depicts Jesus' death by means of violent crucifixion: the extermination of a deviant outsider who managed to offend the ruling elite of Judea. The tortuous method of Jesus' execution is entwined in the text's cultural intertexture in a number of ways. Josephus describes crucifixion as 'the most wretched of deaths' (*War* 7.203). It was a common punishment within the Hellenistic world and was often used by the Romans as a method of execution intended for traitors of the empire. Brown notes that '[i]t was

---

57. Malina and Neyrey, *Calling Jesus Names*, p. 40.
58. Senior, *Passion*, p. 126.

primarily a punishment applied to the lower classes, slaves, and foreigners'.[59] Tacitus, for example, describes it as a 'slave-type' punishment (*Hist.* 2.172.1-2), and Cicero expresses disgust at the thought of possibly crucifying a Roman citizen (*Verr.* 2.5.63, 66).[60] Crucifixion of Jews became a matter of policy as Roman armies began to interfere in the administration of Judea. Brown cites as an example the Roman governor of Syria, who crucified two thousand Jews in 4 BCE (cf. Josephus, *Ant.* 17.295).[61] In his study on the practice of crucifixion in the ancient world, Martin Hengel similarly notes that crucifixion was an obscene and 'utterly offensive affair'. He writes, 'A crucified messiah, son of God or God must have seemed a contradiction in terms to anyone, Jew, Greek, Roman or barbarian, asked to believe such a claim, and it will certainly have been thought offensive and foolish'.[62]

In the case of Jesus, the utilization of a hill as the place of crucifixion, as in the case of Golgotha (which means the Place of a Skull), would serve the Roman goal of engineering the punishment as a public warning (cf. *3 Macc.* 5.12-14). Golgotha was situated outside the walls of the city and along a popular route making the public humiliation aspect even stronger.[63] The intent of dishonouring Jesus is indicated by the charge placed above his head on the cross, 'This is Jesus, the King of the Jews' (Mt. 27.37). The official charge against Jesus is his claim to be a messianic pretender; of course, in the eyes of his accusers his crimes are not limited to what can be pursued within the constraints of law.[64] As explored above, Jesus is targeted because of his status as a deviant outsider. He is surplus to the demands of labour and so, as an expendable burden on the economic system, he is exterminated in order that society can return to its smooth, uninterrupted functioning.

59. Brown, *Death of the Messiah,* II, pp. 945-46.

60. Roman citizens were occasionally subject to crucifixion. Generally speaking, however, the Romans would spare the upper classes and nobility from this form of punishment. See Martin Hengel, *Crucifixion in the Ancient World and the Folly of the Message of the Cross* (Philadelphia, PA: Fortress Press, 1977), pp. 39-40.

61. Brown, *Death of the Messiah,* II, p. 946.

62. Hengel, *Crucifixion,* p. 10.

63. For more on the meaning of Golgotha and its possible site in Jerusalem, see Brown, *Death of the Messiah,* II, pp. 936-40; cf. Davies and Allison, *Matthew,* III, p. 617. For a discussion of Golgotha within early Christian writings see Jerome Murphy-O'Connor, *Keys to Jerusalem: Collected Essays* (Oxford: Oxford University Press, 2012), pp. 174-80.

64. O'Neill suggests that irrespective of the social and political reasons for Jesus' extermination, it was imperative to find Jesus guilty of a technical legal charge under Jewish law. This necessity saw Jesus charged (probably falsely) with blasphemy. See J.C. O'Neill, 'The Charge of Blasphemy at Jesus' Trial before the Sanhedrin', in *The Trial of Jesus* (ed. Ernst Bammel; London: SCM, 1970), pp. 72-77.

Considering the social function of crucifixion as part of the Roman expertise at public showmanship, Anthony J. Marshall writes,

> The horrifying cruelty of this Phoenician importation should not blind us to the fact that the Romans employed it for a calculated deterrent purpose because of its high visibility and publicity. The location on raised ground near roads or trouble-spots and the drawn-out suffering were the features of the punishment ideally suited to impress the typical criminal subject to it—violent and illiterate malcontents of the lowest social orders.[65]

So while the punishment no doubt serves as a form of retributive justice, the deterrent aspect of crucifixion draws the reader's attention to the spectacle of crucifixion as a regulating mechanism of social control. As Marshall goes on to claim, 'it was a standardized, public "production" with an effect based on calculated exhibition'.[66] The symbolic violence entwined with crucifixion simultaneously points to Roman power over subject peoples, in addition to being a symbol of the triumphant, proud empire for those emotionally attached to imperial rule. Hengel suggests that because the primary targets of Roman crucifixion were typically those who had few if any rights, their 'development had to be suppressed by all possible means to safeguard law and order in the state'.[67] He continues, 'Because large strata of the population welcomed the security and the world-wide peace which the empire brought with it, the crucified victim was defamed both socially and ethically in popular awareness, and this impression was heightened still further by the religious elements involved'.[68] As we will see below, drawing attention to the public humiliation and dishonouring of Jesus is a frequent rhetorical strategy within Matthew's crucifixion scene, and, as such, underscores the abject rejection of Jesus from home place in all its totality.

Taunting the Criminal
Rather than focusing on the gruesome details of the physical torment involved in Jesus' suffering, the Matthean text emphasizes the social and political abjection associated with the spectacle of crucifixion. Directly before his death, while Jesus hangs publicly on the cross, a number of walk-on characters begin to taunt him (27.39-44).[69] These characters fill the void left by the desertion of Jesus' fictive kin, and further cement his

65. Anthony J. Marshall, 'Symbols and Showmanship in Roman Public Life: The Fasces', *Phoenix* 38.2 (1984), p. 127; cf. Hengel, *Crucifixion*, pp. 31-38.
66. Marshall, 'Symbols and Showmanship', p. 127.
67. Hengel, *Crucifixion*, p. 88.
68. Hengel, *Crucifixion*, p. 88.
69. For a narrative analysis of Mt. 27.39-44, see Terence L. Donaldson, 'The Mockers and the Son of God (Matthew 27.37-44): Two Characters in Matthew's Story of Jesus', *JSNT* 41 (1991), pp. 3-18.

abandonment and alienation from normalized society. The taunting on the cross is the last human indignity Jesus faces before his death. Nolland suggests the three groups of mockers echo the material surrounding Jesus' trial (cf. 26.57–27.26).[70] A number of terms are used to describe the reactions of different groups, forming a rich assortment of insults and negative gestures. The collective act of mocking functions to engrave on Jesus' broken body the charges of blasphemy and heresy. It also reasserts the honour of the privileged elite who benefit from both the status quo, and the deviancy of Jesus as a marker of difference. The spectacle of crucifixion engineers social order and cohesion among the bystanders in their condemnation of Jesus' outsider status.[71]

First, passers-by 'deride him, shaking their heads' before mocking Jesus for not being able to save himself (vv. 39-40). Extending beyond its immediate religious connotations, the verb βλασφημέω refers to demeaning through speech. As *BAGD* puts it, 'to speak in a disrespectful way that demeans, denigrates, maligns'. In relation to the transcendent or associated entities, however, it denotes 'slander, revile, defame, [to] speak disrespectfully of or about'.[72] This externalization of public humiliation is akin to the hostile crowds who called for the release of Barabbas and the crucifixion of Jesus in 27.15-26. The shaking of heads externalizes their disapproval.

Such public actions are particularly penetrating in an honour-and-shame-oriented society. Insulting the accused was common practice at a crucifixion. Nolland suggests that the random selection of the Jerusalem population 'marks the Jerusalem leadership's control over public opinion about Jesus as having spread rapidly beyond the crowds gathered before Pilate to

---

70. Nolland, *Matthew*, p. 1196.

71. The supercessionist tendencies noted in the analysis of Mt. 13.53-58 return in some interpretations of Jesus' rejection on the cross. Framed by the title 'Jesus Mocked by Fellow Jews', France insists that the 'combination of representatives of the Jewish people at several different levels (Sanhedrin members, ordinary passersby, and failed insurrectionists) provides a poignant picture of the rejection of Jesus by his own people'. There is, however, no indication that those engaging in mocking Jesus are 'representative' of others. Moreover, while it is probably safe to posit that the passers-by are, in fact, Jewish, given the vicinity close to Jerusalem, the text does not make this explicit and does not draw attention to the racial-religious identity of those mocking Jesus. See France, *Matthew*, p. 1069; cf. the criticism of France in Davies and Allison, *Matthew*, III, p. 621. France also mistakenly cites Brown when he says '[t]he mocking bystanders, who represent ordinary Jews . . . ' (France, *Matthew*, p. 1070). Brown only goes as far as to suggest that the passers-by are probably Jewish, but there is no indication within Brown or the Matthean text that they 'represent' anybody but themselves. See Brown, *Death of the Messiah*, II, pp. 986-87.

72. 'βλασφημέω', *BAGD*, p. 178.

ask for Barabbas'.[73] The normalizing function of imperial power persuades passers-by to uncritically focus on the 'absurd' claims of a homeless criminal, effectively obscuring their view from the real ideological–political and economic forces that produced this situation in the first place. Some commentators note that the mocking of Jesus by passers-by fulfils Ps. 22.7, 'All who see me mock me, they make mouths at me, they wag their heads' (cf. Lam. 2.15; Job 16.4; Sir. 13.7).[74] The text's intertexture further supplements a narrative of death.

Second, the chief priests, scribes and elders join in the taunting of Jesus. While they partake in 'the same way' (ὁμοίως) as the passers-by, a different verb is used to describe their action, namely, ἐμπαίζω, which means 'to jeer, deride, ridicule, or mock'.[75] Responsible for sending out the arresting party, and as representatives of the Sanhedrin, they opine, 'He saved others; he cannot save himself. He is the King of Israel; let him come down from the cross now, and we will believe in him. He trusts in God; let God deliver him now, if he wants to; for he said, "I am God's Son"' (27.42-43). The accusation of Jesus' claim to be God's son (repeated as a question in v. 40, 'if you are the Son of God . . . ') recalls Caiaphas's probing as to his identity during the trial (26.61-63) and also alludes to the testing story during Jesus' cycle of homelessness in the wilderness (4.1-11). Their collective taunting highlights his lack of agency and potency; while they are in control of whether he lives or dies, they deflect their responsibility onto the (seemingly) powerless Jesus.[76]

Finally, the bandits introduced in v. 38 also join in the taunting of Jesus. It appears that even they, as victims of the same jurisdictive apparatus, succumb to the belief that Jesus' punishment is deserved and fitting. The reader has not encountered these characters prior to the crucifixion scene,[77] but their introduction is not unusual, given that historically speaking it was common for multiple crucifixions to occur at any one time. The description of them being crucified 'one on his left and one on his right' alludes to the preference of the mother of James and John for her sons to be at his left and right side in God's kingdom (20.20-23). Their characterization as 'bandits'

73. Nolland, *Matthew*, p. 1196.

74. Harrington, *Matthew*, p. 396; Carter, *Margins*, pp. 532-33. Nolland observes that '[t]he shaking of the head is a stock OT image either of condemnation or of mock sympathy'. See Nolland, *Matthew*, p. 1196.

75. 'ἐμπαίζω', *BAGD*, p. 322.

76. A similar ironic form of taunting is echoed in contemporary neoliberal discourse when the disenfranchised homeless population are patronizingly assured that only they can save themselves. Such elite-centred discourse is an effective rhetorical strategy for deflecting undesirable attention away from inequitable social and political structures.

77. Nothing is said of any relationship to Barabbas.

(ληστής), however, has sparked some uncertainty among commentators. Are these men common criminals, or are they popular leaders viewed as a political threat? Moreover, how might their inclusion relate to the exclusion of Jesus?

The Greek noun ληστής (coming from the verb ληΐζομαι, which means 'to plunder') can refer to either (1) robbers, highwaymen and/or bandits; or (2) revolutionaries, insurrectionists and/or guerrillas.[78] Harrington, for instance, opts for the translation 'revolutionaries' (although he admits that it might go too far) and suggests that 'the traditional rendering "thieves" does not go far enough in bringing out the probably "political" dimension connected with the term. Their presence with Jesus brings to fulfillment what was said about the Servant: "he was numbered with the transgressors" (Isa. 53.12).'[79] Irrespective of their own criminal offense(s), Carter insightfully points out that '[i]f a "true" king has a court of elite worthies and notables, this one has a court of sinners and sociopolitical rejects'.[80] In addition to their presence compounding Jesus' indignity (within the mechanics of the jurisdictive apparatus, there is no distinction between Jesus and those among whom he is crucified), there is little or no distinction between common criminals, political revolutionaries or homeless deviants.

The bandits, of course, are also expendable within the eyes of wider society: subjects that disrupt the status quo and so are dealt with punitively. Even so, there is no comradery in death. Jesus suffers alone, disconnected from even those he identifies with the most. This time the verb ὀνειδίζω is employed, which means 'to taunt, defame, or reproach'. It previously featured in one of the beatitudes during Jesus' sermon, 'Blessed are you when people revile [ὀνειδίσωσιν] you and persecute you and utter all kinds of evil against you falsely on my account' (Mt. 5.11; cf. 11.20). The reader is reminded to identify with Jesus, who is righteous, rather than the other characters, which the text constructs as unrighteous.

Darkness and Death

The narrative sets the mood for the last moments of Jesus' life by drawing attention to an all-encompassing darkness that lasts for three hours, 'From noon on, darkness [σκότος] came over the whole land until three in the afternoon' (Mt. 27.45). *BAGD* defines σκότος as darkness or gloom, but it can also refer to a state of spiritual or moral darkness (as in 4.16).[81] While

---

78. 'ληστής', *BAGD*, p. 593.

79. Harrington, *Matthew*, p. 395. Davies and Allison note that under Roman law theft was not a capital offence, and so an association with insurrection is more likely. See Davies and Allison, *Matthew*, III, p. 616.

80. Carter, *Margins*, p. 532.

81. 'σκότος', *BAGD*, p. 932.

there is a temptation to establish the historical veracity of the event,[82] it is more fruitful to focus on the symbolism of this detail of setting which intensifies the drama of the episode. The darkness might allude to the arrest of Jesus and to other episodes that refer to the dark and signifies the danger and/or the threat of impending death. Nolland draws a connection between this text and 'the people who sat in darkness' in 4.16. If correct, this would again reawaken the theme of homelessness and displacement.[83] Intertextually speaking, Davies and Allison observe how such narrative stillness, signified by the darkness and the slowing of time, is a common literary device that appears frequently in the apocryphal Gospels (e.g. *Prot. Jas.* 18). Its rhetorical effect is to isolate and magnify the episode.[84]

The focus on darkness also accentuates certain theological themes that are prominent within Matthew. Carter detects a diverse range of themes, including 'the chaos before creation, oppression and imperial tyranny, exile, injustice, and judgment'.[85] Similarly, Meier contends that the darkness 'is a prophetic and apocalyptic motif, expressing God's wrath on his great day of judgment (cf. Amos 8.9)'.[86] He also detects an allusion to the plague of darkness 'over the whole land of Egypt' (Exod. 10.22). If Meier is correct, this would strengthen the association with the flight to Egypt in 2.13-23, which, as I discussed in Chapter 2, is supplemented by intertextual allusions to the Exodus narrative. Another possibility, according to Nolland, is to view the symbolic significance of darkness as pointing to the activity of Satan or more generally pointing to a period of triumph over evil. Nolland writes that '[t]he darkness marks the frown of God's displeasure'.[87] This refers to the apparent abandonment of Jesus by God.

What common theme might thread these various symbolisms of darkness together? There are, in fact, traces of homelessness and displacement interwoven through Matthew's crucifixion scene. The emphasis on darkness, for instance, links the fear and danger of death intratextually to homelessness, alienation and dislocation from meaningful social bonds. As was mentioned above, the collective mocking of Jesus' disfigured body illustrates in a dramatic way Jesus' alienation from normalized society. He is exiled to the outside of the holy city of Jerusalem, and, most significantly, is crucified

82. See, for instance, Davies and Allison, *Matthew*, III, p. 623.

83. Nolland, *Matthew*, p. 1205.

84. Davies and Allison, *Matthew*, III, pp. 622-23.

85. Carter, *Margins*, p. 534. For more on the symbolism of darkness, see Greg Forbes, 'Darkness over All the Land: Theological Imagery in the Crucifixion Scene', *RTR* 66.2 (2007), pp. 83-96.

86. Meier, *Matthew*, p. 349; cf. Evans, *Matthew*, p. 463. For more on the apocalyptic symbolism of Jesus' cry on the cross see André LaCocque, 'Le grand cri de Jésus dans Matthieu 27/50', *ETR* 75.2 (2000), pp. 161-87.

87. Nolland, *Matthew*, pp. 1203-1205.

as a deviant outsider without home or hearth. Rather than detracting from
the trauma of crucifixion, such components amplify the pain and suffering
associated with his death and abandonment.

Psalm 22. After three hours of darkness, Jesus cries out with a loud voice
in a mix of Hebrew and Aramaic, "'Eli, Eli, lema sabachthani?,'" that is,
"My God, my God, why have you forsaken me?'" (v. 46). The bystanders
misunderstand 'My God' and instead hear 'Elijah'. This becomes an opportunity to mock Jesus yet again; the joke is that the prophet Elijah will come
to Jesus' personal aid, or perhaps set eschatological events in motion. Jesus'
words are in fact an Aramaic re-contextualization of Ps. 22.1 and conjure
up the rest of the memorable Psalm within the text's intertextual resonance.
In her study of Jesus' cry from the cross in Mark's gospel, Holly Carey
argues for a reading of the intertexture that embraces the wider context of
the Psalm beyond just the first verse.[88] Her argument is strengthened by the
Matthean text's inclusion of several additional allusions to Psalm 22, for
instance, the allusion to the casting of lots for clothing (22.19), which in
Matthew is attributed to the enemies of Jesus (Mt. 27.35).[89] The Psalmist
is also taunted and mocked by his enemies, including their insinuation that
God is absent, and so the psalmist is therefore condemned. Carey notes
that by bringing attention to these portions of the Psalm, the Matthean text
emphasizes the ironic misconception of the relationship between Jesus and
God made by those who surround him, 'Like the enemies of the psalmist,
they interpret Jesus' predicament and the "silence" from God as a reflection
of his own delusion, in this case, that he is God's son'.[90]

The use of ἀνεβόησεν ('cry out') combined with φωνῇ μεγάλῃ ('a loud
voice') denotes the acclamation or shout of a crowd, and a desperate cry for
help. Brown suggests that the combination of this loud cry and Jesus' letting
go of his spirit in 27.50 constitutes an apocalyptic sign similar to the other
eschatological themes that surround the text (darkness, torn sanctuary veil,
earthquake and the rising of dead saints).[91] Since not to abandon his people
is one of the promises of God's covenant (Deut. 4.31), an occasion in which
an Israelite finds himself or herself abandoned must raise questions and

88. Holly J. Carey, *Jesus' Cry from the Cross: Towards a First-Century Under-
standing of the Intertextual Relationship between Psalm 22 and the Narrative of
Mark's Gospel* (LNTS, 398; London: T. & T. Clark, 2009); cf. R.E.O. White, 'That
"Cry of Dereliction" . . . ?', *ExpTim* 113.6 (2002), pp. 188-89.

89. Carey, *Jesus' Cry*, p. 180.

90. Carey, *Jesus' Cry*, p. 181.

91. Brown, *Death of the Messiah*, II, pp. 1044-45.

doubts about oneself and God.[92] Jesus' lament is a response to the silence and darkness that envelops him. Somewhat disturbingly for the reader, his question is not audibly or visibly answered.

As was discussed in Chapter 2, an abundance of oral–scribal intertexture within Mt. 2.13-23 intensifies a narrative of displacement. Similarly, this text re-contextualizes Psalm 22, the Psalm of the righteous sufferer, to supplement the darkness surrounding Jesus' crucifixion. It is probably the greatest lament within the Psalter, akin to the book of Job, and, more than in most other Psalms, the sense of personal experience and grief floods through it. Within Jewish tradition the Psalm was read as a reflection of the experience of Queen Esther, who is likened to the 'Deer of the Dawn' in its title. It moves from cries of anguish and desolation in the first half (22.1-21) to a triumphant vindication of faith and trust in God in the second half (22.22-31). The repetition of various animals in 22.12-21 (dogs, a lion and wild oxen) refers to the Psalmist's enemies. The dogs encircle him, stare and gloat over him, 'they divide my clothes among themselves, and for my clothing they cast lots' (22.18).

Davies and Allison note that having been brought up in a pious Jewish household, Jesus would have regularly recited the Psalms, the main part of the Jewish prayer book.[93] They also caution that its inclusion is not to dull the impact of the verse, which, as they see it, is the culmination of a Matthean theme; 'Jesus is first abandoned by his own country (Mt. 13.53-58), then by his disciples (26.56, 69-75), then by the crowds (27.15-26). The climax of this progressing desertion is the experience, following three hours of divine darkness and silence, of felt abandonment of God himself (who is here no longer addressed as "Father").'[94] This complete and utter abandonment by the divine at Jesus' moment of need reflects the absolute climax of his abject homeless existence. His displacement from meaningful social bonds extends beyond human relationships to that of his heavenly Father.

Sympathy before Death; or, a Final Taunt. Upon hearing Jesus' cry of lament, one of the bystanders gets a sponge, fills it with sour wine, puts it on a stick and holds it up for Jesus to drink (v. 48). This alludes intertextually to Ps. 69.22, which describes how the just one is mocked by his enemies:

---

92. Nolland points out that the normal answer to the question of why God has forsaken his people is that they have failed to keep the terms of the covenant (e.g. Jer. 7.29; cf. 12.7-8). However, he admits that Ps. 22 'is an example of a far more puzzling form of abandonment: the situation where the righteous are at the mercy of their enemies with no help in sight'. See Nolland, *Matthew*, p. 1207.
93. Davies and Allison, *Matthew*, III, p. 625.
94. Davies and Allison, *Matthew*, III, p. 625.

> And they gave for my bread gall, and for my thirst they gave me to drink vinegar.[95]

The noun ὄξος refers to a sour wine or wine vinegar and holds connotations of low class or status. *BAGD* states that 'it relieved thirst more effectively than water and, being cheaper than regular wine, it was a favourite beverage of the lower ranks of society and of those in moderate circumstances'.[96] This is in contrast to the wine of high quality (οἶνος) in Jn 2.23.[97] According to Nolland, '[i]t is wine of poor quality, but it would probably have been quite bracing. We should compare the traditional practice of giving brandy to revive someone in need of an immediate "stimulant"'.[98]

It is difficult to determine whether the offer of wine is intended as an act of sympathy or as something more sinister. Davies and Allison note that an apparent act of kindness does not fit the wider context of unremitting hostility and suggest that the intent of their 'charity' could be to prolong his life so as to protract his pain.[99] Nolland, however, cautions that 'idle curiosity' might be closer to the mark.[100] In either case, however, the 'charity' of the bystander draws attention to Jesus' alienation from normalized society.

On the one hand, if the giving of wine is intended as an act of kindness, it is surely a vain response. Would not the true act of kindness consist of letting Jesus down from the cross (or at least to kill him quickly)? A useful comparison can be made to contemporary obsessions with charity: donating money to the homeless allows us to 'buy out' of our greater responsibility to their actual needs, that is, an actual shift in societal arrangements of power. By pandering to their immediate condition, we relieve our own uneasiness with their situation but at the same time effectively avoid engaging with the real problem. In fact, rather than alleviating their suffering, their suffering is potentially prolonged.[101]

---

95. Translation from Brown, *Death of the Messiah*, II, p. 1059.

96. 'ὄξος', *BAGD*, p. 715.

97. Brown admits that it is unclear whether ὄξος in Mt. 27.34 refers to 'vinegar' or 'wine'. The choice depends primarily on whether to draw attention to mockery or the drink. In Ps. 69.22 he uses 'vinegar' because mockery is the main theme, but because of the ambiguity in the Gospel narratives he employs 'vinegary wine' throughout. See Brown, *Death of the Messiah*, II, p. 1059.

98. Nolland also writes that a 'soaked sponge is likely to be an effective way of giving a small drink to an expiring person'. See Nolland, *Matthew*, p. 1208.

99. Davies and Allison, *Matthew*, III, pp. 626-27. Harrington is also unsure of whether the offer of wine is regarded as an act of compassion or as an insult. See Harrington, *Matthew*, p. 400.

100. Nolland, *Matthew*, p. 1209.

101. Oscar Wilde once wrote, '[People] find themselves surrounded by hideous poverty, by hideous ugliness, by hideous starvation. It is inevitable that they should be strongly moved by all this. . . . Accordingly, with admirable, though misdirected

On the other hand, if the giving of wine is intended as an insult, that is, in harmony with the tone of hostility that frames the overall context of the passage, then one meaning effect worth exploring is the action of taunting Jesus with one of his supposed follies, that is, alcohol. The Son of Man was accused of being a drunkard and a glutton in Mt. 11.19. As mentioned above, the type of wine used in 27.49 holds certain class connotations that link it to the lower social strata. Could not the offer of vinegary wine to Jesus be with the intent of taunting a drunkard? Indeed, 11.19 holds a similar irony to the taunting in the crucifixion scene. While the accusations of gluttony and drunkenness would indicate that of a stubborn and rebellious son (Deut. 21.18-21), from God's point of view Jesus is an obedient son with whom God is well pleased (Mt. 2.15; 3.17; 17.5). Bystanders add to the stigmatization of Jesus by insinuating stereotypes (for instance, all homeless people and/or deviants have alcohol problems for which they should take personal responsibility). Such a reading also squares with the offer of alcohol directly before his crucifixion, 'they offered him wine to drink, mixed with gall; but when he tasted it, he would not drink it' (27.34).

The taunting that surrounds Jesus' death is excessive and draws attention to the mundane, abject reality of crucifixion. It features not only as a mechanism of slow and tortuous death but as an effective means of social cohesion through the production and extermination of a rejected body.

The Homeless One Exterminated. Jesus' death is described plainly as follows, 'Then Jesus cried again with a loud voice and breathed his last' (v. 50). The repetition of Jesus crying out draws attention once more to the intertexture of Psalm 22. Jesus' death is accompanied by events of eschatological significance, including the tearing of the temple curtain, an earthquake and the resurrection of dead saints (Mt. 27.51-53).[102]

While the drawn-out tempo of the trial and crucifixion scene has added to the drama of the narrative, the actual moment of Jesus' death is stated very briefly. The focus has been on the stigmatization surrounding his death

---

intentions, they very seriously and very sentimentally set themselves to the task of remedying the evils that they see. But their remedies do not cure the disease: they merely prolong it. Indeed, their remedies are part of the disease. They try to solve the problem of poverty, for instance, by keeping the poor alive; or, in the case of a very advanced school, by amusing the poor. But this is not a solution: it is an aggravation of the difficulty. The proper aim is to try and reconstruct society on such a basis that poverty will be impossible.' See Oscar Wilde, *The Soul of the Man under Socialism* (New York: Max N. Maisel, 1915), pp. 3-4; cf. Slavoj Žižek, *Living in the End Times* (London: Verso, 2010), pp. 117-19.

102. For a survey of the history of interpretation of these briefly stated but enigmatic verses, see Daniel M. Gurtner, *The Torn Veil: Matthew's Exposition of the Death of Jesus* (SNTSMS, 139; Cambridge: Cambridge University Press, 2007).

and the reaction of those around him. This magnifies the social distancing that accompanies Jesus' homeless predicament. Carter surmises that 'Jesus' death at the hands of the political and religious elite is the final form of societal dismissal and marginalization. The elite have accomplished their goal.'[103] Indeed, this goal can be traced back to Herod's own attempts to have Jesus executed in Matthew 2. As the Matthean Jesus' subsequent ministry to the poor and disenfranchised grew with notoriety (4.24), he was perceived as a threat to normalized society. This was played out at an interpersonal level, in particular, within Jesus' lament for his homeless existence (8.18-22) and rejection in his hometown (13.53-58). With Jesus' extermination, the balance of power, honour and sovereignty of the wider ideological–political system is restored and asserted in order that society can return to its smooth, uninterrupted functioning.

After his death, Jesus' mutilated body is afforded charity by a 'rich man' named Joseph of Arimathea who offers a tomb for burial (Mt. 27.57-60). Once again, charity serves the interests of the elite: such an act not only shows Joseph to be a pious Jew (cf. Tob. 1.16-20; Josephus, *War* 4.317) but is, in fact, only possible because of his high socio-economic status. This highlights with dramatic contrast the gap between Jesus and Joseph, and also the inequitable economic system that saw Jesus' expendable social status produced, targeted and exterminated. With permission from the Roman governor, Pilate, Jesus' corpse is wrapped in linen cloth and laid in a rock tomb.[104]

The Resurrection of the Expendable Jesus

Jesus has been crucified. Within any normal understanding and expectation he has been defeated and dishonoured by the exclusionary efficiency of the Roman imperial jurisdictive apparatus. A homeless deviant has met his expected fate, that of fatal rejection. However, Matthew's story of Jesus continues beyond this to include his triumph over death. While the focus of this chapter, in accordance with this project's ideological parameters, has been on the arrest and execution of Matthew's Jesus simulacrum, it is worth briefly addressing the meaning and meaning effects of the resurrection as it pertains to the categories of homelessness and displacement.

---

103. Carter, *Margins*, p. 535.

104. The text also indicates that some of the women followers were there, sitting opposite the tomb (Mt. 27.61), and had been watching the crucifixion from a distance (27.55-56). Their unusual inclusion might point to their faithful discipleship and draws attention to the desertion of Jesus' male followers. See Love, *Marginal Women*, pp. 186-219; Carolyn Osiek, 'The Women at the Tomb: What Are They Doing There?', *HvTSt* 53.1-2 (1997), pp. 103-18; Wainwright, *Shall We Look*, pp. 108-10.

Resurrection refers not to a resuscitation or reanimation but to a rising from a state of death to eternal (surplus) life. With the exception of the Sadducees, the Jews of the first century expected a general resurrection at the end of human history as part of God's kingdom (Dan. 12.1-3; 2 Maccabees 7). Resurrection was understood as eschatological and corporate.[105] Thematically, it functions within the Matthean text as a totalizing negation to the displacement, exile and isolation that Jesus has experienced throughout his life and culminating especially in his tortuous death. The resurrection also features as a reversal to the supposed triumph of the allied religious and political elite and '[t]he opposition to Jesus that coursed through the Gospel and climaxed in the Passion story has proved futile'.[106] The resurrection of Matthew's Jesus simulacrum can be regarded as God's extraordinary vindication of his faithful son over his rejection by the ideological–political machinery of normalized society.

While the resurrection potentially obscures Jesus' suffering, by negating its totalizing impact, the text can be read in an alternative way that interrupts the fantasmatic desire for redemptive sublimation. If the crucifixion projected the guilt of deviancy onto the individual body of Jesus, then the resurrection of his body opens a new symbolic space from which the Real of the ideological constellation is drastically undermined. The perceived impossibility of the resurrection counteracts the impossibility of the Real to fully symbolize itself. It similarly evokes the revolutionary potential of the *basileia*, proclaimed by Jesus throughout the Gospel. On a subjective level, the resurrection signifies God's vindication of Jesus as the homeless one. While the arrangements of power within normalized society excluded and rejected Jesus, the resurrection points to his overcoming of their prejudice and shortcomings.

After an appearance to the women who visited his tomb on the first day of the week (Mt. 28.9-10), and after his command that they 'go to Galilee' (cf. 26.32) and inform his 'brothers', Jesus is reunited with eleven of his disciples (Judas having committed suicide in 27.5) on a mountain in Galilee (28.16-20). After his displacement as an infant in 2.13, Joseph took Mary and Jesus to Nazareth, in Galilee. The region was also the initial location of

---

105. What would the resurrected body look like? While it is hard to know exactly, resurrection expert N.T. Wright helpfully postulates, 'Assuming that a [video] camera would pick up what most human eyes would have seen . . . my best guess is that cameras would sometimes have seen [the resurrected] Jesus and sometimes not'. This evokes intertextually the case of vampirism, another mythical condition, in which the subject's image cannot be captured by any sort of film, camera, or mirror. See N.T. Wright and Marcus J. Borg, *The Meaning of Jesus: Two Visions* (New York: Harper-Collins, 1999), p. 125.

106. Senior, *Matthew*, p. 349.

Jesus' ministry, and of the disciples' call to discipleship (4.12-22; 10.1-4). Carter suggests that 'the meeting will not take place in the center of power, Jerusalem, but, typically, in what that center regards as a less significant and marginal area, yet an area that is central to God's purposes (cf. 2.5-6; 4.15-16)'.[107] The disciples encounter the risen Jesus on the mountain. Reconciled to his fictive kin, Jesus commands his disciples to bring others into the fold, 'teaching them to obey everything that I have commanded you' (v. 20).

Conclusions

In this chapter I have argued that the execution of Jesus via the method of crucifixion amounts to the extermination of a social and political pest. The Matthean Jesus' death on the cross is, in fact, the expected culmination of his repeated exclusion, isolation, displacement, and being labelled as deviant within his wider social and cultural environment. Yet, the extermination of an expendable excess to the normal functioning of the economic order fails to account for its own complicity in producing those who fall outside of the system. A criminal-justice approach to homelessness, for example, while failing to recognize that homelessness is symptomatic of dominant arrangements of power in society, effectively enables us to organize our *jouissance* around this symptom, attributing a heightened sense of responsibility to the individual affected.

Given the importance that the death and resurrection of Jesus have for the theological tradition, it is necessary to revert our gaze back to its abhorrent, tortuous components as they are encoded within the Matthean text. The theology of the cross can occasionally act as a fantasmatic barrier, obscuring the ways in which the text underscores the capacity for power and responsibility of various characters and institutions. In the case of the arrest of Jesus, the power of arrest is dispersed among a number of armed enforcers—crowds, temple police, chief priests and scribes—their collective responsibility is complex and easily confused. Contrary to the emphasis on personal responsibility, this text presents Jesus as blameless and willing to die. Responsibility for his targeting and execution rests with the wider ideological–political system and its repressive judicial apparatus.

The execution of Matthew's Jesus focuses predominantly on the attitudes of those surrounding him at the cross. Their negative predisposition toward Jesus drives their scorn and contempt. Three groups partake in the mocking and taunting: passers-by; the chief priests, scribes and elders; and finally, the two criminals who are crucified either side of Jesus. In addition to the verbal insults thrown at him, certain stereotypes about his 'lifestyle choices' are

---

107. Carter, *Margins*, p. 546.

reified by the offer of cheap wine. As a matter of process, then, the intended effect of crucifixion, that of dishonouring and delegitimizing the person and ideology of the accused, achieves maximum proficiency. In the end, Jesus the 'homeless one' dies alone, abandoned by his closest allies and also by God. The romanticization of Jesus' homelessness as a sublime object, then, is finally traversed as he meets a tortuous and fatal displacement.

While the resurrection provides divine vindication for the text's protagonist against the powers that condemned him, it does not necessarily re-establish the parameters of the fantasy. Jesus remains rejected by the social order that condemned him. The resurrection does, however, gesture toward a significant hole in the reigning ideological–political constellation. In this moment of restoration, Jesus is reconciled to his fictive kin, albeit temporarily, and exhorts them to keep the faith and extend their community to the wider world.

Conclusion

The primary purpose of this study has been to probe the ideological gap in the nexus between Jesus and homelessness, and additionally, to develop a more viable construction of a homeless Jesus within the Gospel of Matthew. It has not been the intention to produce a definitive new reading of the Matthean text (such a task is likely impossible). Rather, we ought to be raising more critical questions about our own assumptions and contexts for reading when we address issues and categories that clearly have some connection to the world in front of the text (and perhaps even more so when they appear to have no significance at all). The analysis undertaken has, of course, been limited by its own ideological parameters. A focus on the socio-economic and ideological–political function of homelessness has meant that an investigation into particular contextual nuances, such as gender or ethnicity, have given way to a broader, but still critical, construction of homelessness within a neoliberal context.

As was raised in Chapter 1, discussions about the causes of homelessness in contemporary society tend to swing between two entrenched positions: first, a dominant individualist understanding, which supposes that homelessness is caused primarily by the individual economic and moral failings of those affected; and second, a structuralist understanding, which contends that homelessness is the result of the structural failings of wider society. A radicalized embodiment of the structuralist explanation, however, posits that homelessness is an excess to the smooth, uninterrupted functioning of the ideological–political order. Homelessness emerges as an excremental remainder to the dominant arrangements of power and economic modes of production in society.

This book has argued that the connection between Jesus and homelessness is an exploitable parallax at which ideology comes into view. Although the interpretation of Jesus' homelessness is often filtered through neoliberal modes of thinking, it is at this very nexus that a peculiar contradiction emerges. Because Jesus is supposed to be the moral hero of the story, his homelessness gets sublimated; properties that typically accompany the experience of homelessness—desperation, destitution and offensiveness—are extracted. To speak of homelessness as a lifestyle choice adopted by Jesus, as has become an entrenched discourse in scholarship, is already to gentrify it.

Further, at the fantasmatic level, the underlying notion here is that a homeless Jesus, as a counter-cultural ideal, is still somehow subversive to the established order. In fact, because his homelessness is predominantly conceived of within a narrow framework of neoliberal ideology (i.e. Jesus 'chooses' his homelessness) and has its unsavoury 'bits' extracted, a homeless Jesus elevates the inherent self-negation of the capitalist process itself. In other words, a Jesus who chooses his homelessness merely functions to re-inscribe the dominant narrative that homelessness is a choice. A truly subversive Jesus is one whose homelessness is thrust upon him by external political, social and economic pressures, systems and institutions, such that the aforementioned institutions, or perhaps even the entire ideological–political order, is compelled to confront their/its abhorrent failure.

This study has advanced the discussion of Jesus' homelessness within six key Matthean texts (2.13-23; 4.12-25; 8.18-22; 13.53-58; 27.47-56, 38-50) and explored its residual meaning in several others (1.1-17; 3-4.11; 5–8; 6.25-34; 8.1-17; 10.1-42; 12.46-50). In doing so, I have detected how ideologies of homelessness in the world before the text shape and limit possibilities of meaning. But equally, I have uncovered texts that occasionally disrupt dominant ideological narratives. Such an investigation provides a solid basis from which the homelessness of Matthew's Jesus simulacrum can be seen to play out: it begins with the displacement of Jesus during the flight to Egypt in which the infant Jesus never returns to his original home place in Bethlehem but ends up in rural Nazareth. The marginal identity formed during his infancy is recapitulated at the beginning of his ministry, itself connected to the hostility surrounding John the Baptist's arrest. Jesus forms an alternative community of disciples, which functions as a surrogate home place. In responding to would-be followers, however, Jesus laments the desperation and destitution that accompany his homeless existence. This is illustrated especially when he returns to his hometown and is met with disdain and rejection. Through the Gospel narrative, Matthew's Jesus descends the socio-symbolic ladder to the expendable class. The production of a vulnerable, outsider identity is regarded as a contributing factor to his execution. The spectacle of crucifixion averts our gaze from the underlying ideological–political machinery that produces deviancy, and in this case, a homeless Messiah. The resurrection of Jesus three days later, however, opens a new space through which the dominant ideological constellation is paradoxically confronted.

What do we do after we have traversed the fantasy? While this study has drawn attention to an ideological blind spot in biblical interpretation, it leaves underexplored the next possible steps. The re-reading of texts has enabled the identification and re-narration of underlying antagonisms by reconfiguring fissures within the text's ideological texture. It has also drawn our attention yet again to the unstable division between the technical terms 'exegesis' and 'eisegesis' in the discipline of biblical studies. In wrestling with this false dichotomy, George Aichele supposes that

> [a] consequence of the post-structuralist shift is that any illusion of control from within the text over its own interpretation—whether through an author's intention or a set of deep values—evaporates. Instead responsibility is placed on the reader to acknowledge the ideological interests that 'guide' her reading. We still today sorely lack biblical scholarship that admits its own stakes in the texts, both ideologically and methodologically.[1]

Such a critique is well known in some quarters of biblical studies today but almost unheard of in others. It is not simply enough to lay out one's presuppositions as if that excuses one from engaging at a more theoretical level with how one's ideological context is shaping particular interpretive moves, and further, how it anchors one's *jouissance* to the fantasy that sustains dominant arrangements of power in society.

A major issue that has emerged within this study, which blurs the distinction between exegesis and eisegesis, is the philosophical problem of agency. How much agency does the character of Jesus really possess at various stages of the Matthean narrative? Social-scientific models that emphasize collectivistic over individual behaviour might be too constrictive in their application to the biblical text. They also overemphasize the capacity for freedom that Western subjects assume, thereby potentially re-inscribing a neoliberal emphasis on individual responsibility and self-sufficiency in the world before the text. Yet, without such models, high levels of independent and individual agency are often taken for granted and projected onto biblical characters during the interpretive process. Within a neoliberal context, in particular, the homeless subject is regularly ascribed a level of agency that does not correlate with his or her more complex socio-economic situation. This can also be said of the conventional depictions of Jesus and his itinerant mission. As has been demonstrated, however, Jesus' actions and potential for action are always mediated through an array of structural forces, as they are encoded within the world of the text. This complexity is something that social-scientific criticism, which relies primarily on limited models and generalizations, can potentially underrate, and so needs to be supplemented by an exploration of other textures of the text, not least its ideological texture.[2]

---

1. George Aichele, 'Against Exegesis', http://adrian.academia.edu/GAichele/Papers/1514661/Against_Exegesis.

2. It is curious that Jesus is often attributed with a level of agency and social mobility that seems at odds with his circumstances as they are constructed within the Matthean text. For example, the common assumption that Jesus is unemployed by choice; if he wanted to work as an artisan, he could have. Such a view is built upon

The realization that the homelessness of Matthew's Jesus has become romanticized also is reason to suggest that this ideological hermeneutic might be applied to other Jesus simulacra, or even literary and/or historical figures beyond the NT. Within the other canonical Gospels, for example, Luke's Jesus also laments the destitution of homelessness in Lk. 9.58 (cf. Mt. 8.20), and both the Markan and Lukan texts narrate the rejection of Jesus by his hometown (Mk 6.1-6//Lk. 4.16-30). However, John's Gospel contains neither of these episodes, and the crucial narrative event of the flight to Egypt appears only in Matthew (2.13-23).[3] Does this mean that the homelessness of Matthew's Jesus is more pronounced than that of Jesus simulacra from other Gospel texts? Furthermore, as was raised in the Introduction, the study of the historical Jesus has often made an explicit connection between Jesus and homelessness. With the subdiscipline's positivist focus on defining reliable criteria of authenticity, and public interest driving the appetite for particular reconstructions to serve theological and commercial markets, historical Jesus scholarship has often neglected to consider its own ideological implications. The biographical framing of historical Jesus research, no doubt linked to its theological underpinnings, does seem to nurture an uncritical idealization of Jesus' itinerancy and the related quest for a 'subversive' or 'counter-cultural' Jesus to imitate. To what extent are these studies complicit in the romanticization of homelessness?

Another avenue for potential research is Jesus simulacra in other religious and cultural contexts. Popular cultural afterlives of Jesus, for example, are commodities also linked to the market and so tend to reflect broader ideological trends about the construction and causes of homelessness. It is not uncommon to find depictions of Jesus in popular culture as a bum or vagabond. In what ways do these constructions interpret their biblical sources and how are such depictions complicit in framing our interpretation of the biblical text? Moreover, in the Qur'an, Jesus is frequently labelled the Messiah (Arabic: *al-masih*) (e.g. 3.45; 4.171-72). According to Amar Djuaballah, the title Messiah incorporates the activity of 'wandering' or 'traveling afar', 'for Jesus had an itinerant ministry and was in some ways a wanderer who had "nowhere to lay his head"'.[4] A religious figure outside the NT corpus that would be fruitful for future analysis is that of Saint Francis of Assisi—and his 'decision' to adopt a life of poverty. It is often

---

assumptions about individual entrepreneurship that are anachronistic within a collectivist society (and strangely enough do not even correspond to our neoliberal reality in which the ideal of full employment has given way to the goal of lowering inflation).

3. The key verb ἀναχωρέω is also a Matthean peculiarity and does not feature strongly in the other Gospels.

4. Amar Djaballah, 'Jesus in Islam', *SBJT* 8.1 (2004): 20; cf. James Robson, *Christ in Islam* (Dublin: Bardic, 2006).

overlooked that Francis, as the son of a wealthy cloth merchant, came from a privileged background, and so parallels to the Jesus simulacra are, as with the Cynics, already strained.[5] It would be interesting to explore these depictions of homelessness comparatively. In what ways does the interpretation of these and other figures help to sustain or disrupt the fantasmatic dimensions of our ideological predicament?

This, then, leads us to return once more to the claims with which this book began: first, the connection between Jesus and homelessness functions as a sublime object within biblical interpretation; and, second, its exploitation can potentially harness a new reading of homelessness within the Matthean text. The homelessness of Matthew's Jesus simulacrum is thrust upon him by external forces, involves desperation and chronic destitution, is offensive to others, and as a result traverses an idealization of homelessness in the text's ideological texture. To envisage the Matthean Jesus as an excess to the dominant arrangements of power and modes of production in society abruptly underscores this intriguing disconnect between the dominant interpretation of Jesus' homelessness and the construction of homelessness in the world before the text. With the ideological underpinnings of the nexus between Jesus and homelessness now exposed, a more careful approach to its interpretation and construction is now possible.

5. F.L. Cross and E.A. Livingstone (eds.), *The Oxford Dictionary of the Christian Church* (Oxford: Oxford University Press, 3rd edn, 1997), p. 632.

BIBLIOGRAPHY

Aarde, Andries G. van, 'The Evangelium Infantium, the Abandonment of Children, and the Infancy Narrative in Matthew 1 and 2 from a Social Scientific Perspective', *SBL 1992 Seminar Papers* (Atlanta, GA: Society of Biblical Literature, 1992), pp. 435-53).

Adam, A.K.M., *Faithful Interpretation: Reading the Bible in a Postmodern World* (Minneapolis, MN: Fortress Press, 2006).

— *What Is Postmodern Biblical Criticism?* (GBS; Minneapolis, MN: Fortress Press, 1995).

Ahern, Barnabas M., 'Staff or No Staff?', *CBQ* 5 (1943), pp. 332-37.

Aichele, George, 'Against Exegesis'. http://adrian.academia.edu/GAichele/Papers/1514661/Against_Exegesis.

— *Simulating Jesus: Reality Effects in the Gospels* (BibleWorld; London: Equinox, 2011).

Albright, William F., 'The Names "Nazareth" and "Nazorean"', *JBL* 65 (1946), pp. 397-401.

Aldrete, Gregory S., *Gestures and Acclamations in Ancient Rome* (Ancient Society and History; Baltimore, MD: Johns Hopkins University Press, 1999).

Allan, Graeme, 'He Shall Be Called—a Nazarite?', *ExpTim* 95.3 (1983), pp. 81-82.

Allison, Dale C., 'Anticipating the Passion: The Literary Reach of Matthew 26:47–27:56', *CBQ* 56 (1994), pp. 701-15.

— 'Jesus and Moses (Mt 5:1-2)', *ExpTim* 98.7 (1987), pp. 203-205.

— *The New Moses: A Matthean Typology* (Minneapolis, MN: Fortress Press, 1993).

Althusser, Louis, 'Ideology and Ideological State Apparatuses (Notes Towards an Investigation)', in *On Ideology* (London: Verso, 2008), pp. 1-60.

Amster, Randall, 'Patterns of Exclusion: Sanitizing Space, Criminalizing Homelessness', *Social Justice* 30.1 (2003), pp. 195-221.

Anderson, Janice Capel, 'Mary's Difference: Gender and Patriarchy in the Birth Narratives', *JR* 67.2 (1987), pp. 183-202.

— *Matthew's Narrative Web: Over, and Over, and Over Again* (JSNTSup, 91; Sheffield: Sheffield Academic Press, 1994).

— 'Matthew: Gender and Reading', in *A Feminist Companion to Matthew* (ed. Amy-Jill Levine; Sheffield: Sheffield Academic Press, 2001), pp. 25-51.

Anderson, Janice Capel, and Stephen D. Moore, 'Matthew and Masculinity', in *New Testament Masculinities* (ed. Stephen D. Moore and Janice Capel Anderson; Semeia Studies; Atlanta, GA: Society of Biblical Literature, 2003), pp. 67-91.

Ateek, Naim Stifan, *Justice and Only Justice: A Palestinian Theology of Liberation* (Maryknoll, NY: Orbis Books, 1989).

Avalos, Hector, *The End of Biblical Studies* (Amherst, NY: Prometheus, 2007).

— 'The Ideology of the Society of Biblical Literature and the Demise of an Academic Profession', *SBL Forum* (April 2006): http://sbl-site.org/Article.aspx?ArticleID=520.

Baarda, Tjitze, '"A Staff Only, Not a Stick": Disharmony of the Gospels and the Harmony of Tatian (Matthew 10,9f; Mark 6,8f; Luke 9,3 and 10,4)', in *The New Testament in Early Christianity* (ed. Jean-Marie Sevrin; Louvain: Leuven University Press, 1989), pp. 311-33.

Bammel, Ernst, 'The Baptist in Early Christian Tradition', *NTS* 18 (1971), pp. 95-128.

Barton, John, 'Historical-Critical Approaches', in *The Cambridge Companion to Biblical Interpretation* (ed. John Barton; Cambridge: Cambridge University Press, 1998), pp. 9-20.

— *The Nature of Biblical Criticism* (London: Westminster John Knox, 2007).

Barton, Stephen C., *Discipleship and Family Ties in Mark and Matthew* (SNTSMS, 80; Cambridge: Cambridge University Press, 1994).

Bauer, David R., *The Structure of Matthew's Gospel: A Study in Literary Design* (Bible and Literature Series; Sheffield: Sheffield Academic Press, 1988).

Beare, Francis Wright, *The Gospel according to Matthew* (Oxford: Basil Blackwell, 1981).

Beaton, Richard, *Isaiah's Christ in Matthew's Gospel* (SNTSMS, 123; Cambridge: Cambridge University Press, 2002).

Beck, Robert R., *Banished Messiah: Violence and Nonviolence in Matthew's Story of Jesus* (Eugene, OR: Wipf & Stock, 2010).

Betsworth, Sharon, 'What Child Is This? A Contextual Feminist Literary Analysis of the Child in Matthew 2', in *Matthew* (ed. Nicole Wilkinson Duran and James Grimshaw; Texts@Context; Minneapolis, MN: Fortress Press, 2013), pp. 49-63.

Betz, Otto, 'Was John the Baptist an Essene?' *BR* 6.6 (1990), pp. 18-25.

Bhabha, Homi, *The Location of Culture* (London: Routledge, 1994).

The Bible and Culture Collective, *The Postmodern Bible* (New Haven, CT: Yale University Press, 1995).

Binz, Stephen J., *The Passion and Resurrection Narratives of Jesus: A Commentary* (Collegeville, MN: Order of St. Benedict, 1989).

Blickenstaff, Marianne, *'While the Bridegroom Is with Them': Marriage, Family, Gender and Violence in the Gospel of Matthew* (JSNTSup, 292; London: T. & T. Clark, 2005).

Boer, Roland, *Marxist Criticism of the Bible* (London: T. & T. Clark, 2003).

— (ed.), *Secularism and Biblical Studies* (BibleWorld; London: Equinox, 2010).

— *Criticism of Theology: On Marxism and Theology III* (Historical Materialism, 27; Leiden: Brill, 2011).

— 'Twenty-Five Years of Marxist Biblical Criticism', *CBR* 5.3 (2007), pp. 298-321.

Bouma-Prediger, Steven, and Brian J. Walsh, *Beyond Homelessness: Christian Faith in a Culture of Displacement* (Grand Rapids, MI: Eerdmans, 2008).

Bourgois, Philippe, and Jeff Schonberg, *Righteous Dopefiend* (Berkeley, CA: University of California Press, 2009).

Brawley, Robert L., 'Homeless in Galilee', *HvTSt* 67.1 (2011): http://www.hts.org.za/index.php/HTS/article/view/863.

Brink, Laurie, '"Let the Dead Bury the Dead": Using Archaeology to Understand the Bible', *TBT* 49.5 (2011), pp. 291-96.

Brooke, G.J., 'The Wisdom of Matthew's Beatitudes (4Qbeat and Mt. 5:3-12)', *Scripture Bulletin* 19.2 (1989), pp. 35-41.

Brown, Raymond E., *The Birth of the Messiah: A Commentary on the Infancy Narratives in the Gospels of Matthew and Luke* (New York: Doubleday, 2nd edn, 1993).
— *The Death of the Messiah: A Commentary on the Passion Narratives in the Four Gospels*. Vol. 1 (New York: Doubleday, 1994).
— *The Death of the Messiah: A Commentary on the Passion Narratives in the Four Gospels*. Vol. 2 (New York: Doubleday, 1994).
Brueggemann, Walter, *The Prophetic Imagination* (Minneapolis, MN: Fortress Press, 2nd edn, 2001).
Bruner, Frederick Dale, *The Churchbook: Matthew 13–28*. Vol. 2 (Grand Rapids, MI: Eerdmans, 1990).
Buell, Denise Kimber, Jennifer A. Glancy, Marianne Bjelland Kartzow and Halvor Moxnes, 'Cultural Complexity and Intersectionality in the Study of the Jesus Movement', *BibInt* 18.4-5 (2010), pp. 309-12.
Burt, Martha R., 'Homelessness, Definitions and Estimates of', in *Encyclopedia of Homelessness* (ed. David Levinson; London: Sage, 2004), pp. 233-38.
Byrne, David. *Social Exclusion* (Maidenhead: Open University Press, 2nd edn, 2005).
Canaan, Joyce E., and Wesley Shumar (eds.), *Structure and Agency in the Neoliberal University* (New York: Routledge, 2008).
Caner, Daniel, *Wandering, Begging Monks: Spiritual Authority and the Promotion of Monasticism in Late Antiquity* (Berkeley, CA: University of California Press, 2002).
Carey, Holly J., *Jesus' Cry from the Cross: Towards a First-Century Understanding of the Intertextual Relationship between Psalm 22 and the Narrative of Mark's Gospel* (LNTS, 398; London: T. & T. Clark, 2009).
Carter, Warren, 'The Gospel of Matthew', in *A Postcolonial Commentary on the New Testament Writings* (ed. Fernando F. Segovia and R.S. Sugirtharajah; London: T. & T. Clark, 2007), pp. 69-104.
— 'Matthew 1–2 and Roman Political Power', in *New Perspectives on the Nativity* (ed. Jeremy Corley; London: T. & T. Clark, 2009), pp. 77-90.
— 'Matthew 4:18-22 and Matthean Discipleship: An Audience-Oriented Perspective', *CBQ* 59 (1997), pp. 58-75.
— *Matthew and Empire: Initial Explorations* (Harrisburg, PA: Trinity Press International, 2001).
— *Matthew and the Margins: A Sociopolitical and Religious Reading* (Maryknoll, NY: Orbis Books, 2000).
— *The Roman Empire and the New Testament: An Essential Guide* (Nashville, TN: Abingdon Press, 2006).
Casey, Maurice, *The Solution to the 'Son of Man' Problem* (LNTS, 343; London: T. & T. Clark, 2007).
Chamberlain, Chris, and David Mackenzie, 'Understanding Contemporary Homelessness: Issues of Definition and Meaning', *Australian Journal of Social Issues* 27.4 (1992), pp. 274-97.
Chancey, Mark A., *Greco-Roman Culture and the Galilee of Jesus* (SNTSMS, 134; Cambridge: Cambridge University Press, 2005).
Claussen, Carsten, 'Meeting, Community, Synagogue: Different Frameworks of Ancient Jewish Congregations in the Diaspora', in *The Ancient Synagogue: From its Origins until 200 CE* (ed. Birger Olsson and Magnus Zetterholm; Stockholm: Almqvist & Wiksell International, 2003), pp. 144-67.

Collins, Adela Yarbro, 'Finding Meaning in the Death of Jesus', *JR* 78.2 (1998), pp. 175-96.

Cornwall, Susannah, and David Nixon, 'Readings from the Road: Contextual Bible Study with a Group of Homeless and Vulnerably-Housed People', *ExpTim* 123.1 (2011), pp. 12-19.

Cousland, J.R.C., *The Crowds in the Gospel of Matthew* (NovTSup 102; Leiden: Brill, 2002).

Cromhout, Markus, 'J D Crossan's Construct of Jesus' "Jewishness": A Critical Assessment', *Acta patristica et byzantina* 17 (2006), pp. 155-78.

Crook, Zeba A., 'On the Treatment of Miracles in New Testament Scholarship', *Studies in Religion* 40 (2011), pp. 461-78.

— 'Structure versus Agency in Studies of the Biblical Social World: Engaging with Louise Lawrence', *JSNT* 29 (2007), pp. 251-75.

Crosby, Michael H., *House of Disciples: Church, Economics, and Justice in Matthew* (Eugene, OR: Wipf & Stock, 1988).

Cross, F.L., and E.A. Livingstone (eds.), *The Oxford Dictionary of the Christian Church* (Oxford: Oxford University Press, 3rd edn, 1997).

Crossan, John Dominic, *The Historical Jesus: The Life of a Mediterranean Jewish Peasant* (San Francisco, CA: HarperSanFrancisco, 1991).

Crossley, James G., *Jesus in an Age of Neoliberalism: Quests, Scholarship and Ideology* (BibleWorld; Sheffield: Equinox, 2012).

— *Jesus in an Age of Terror: Scholarly Projects for a New American Century* (BibleWorld; London: Equinox, 2008).

— 'The Semitic Background to Repentance in the Teaching of John the Baptist and Jesus', *JSHJ* 2.2 (2004), pp. 138-57.

— *Why Christianity Happened: A Sociohistorical Account of Christian Origins (26–50 CE)* (Louisville, KY: Westminster John Knox, 2006).

Daly, Robert J., 'The Eucharist and Redemption: The Last Supper and Jesus' Understanding of his Death', *BTB* 11 (1981), pp. 21-27.

Davies, W.D., *The Setting of the Sermon on the Mount* (Cambridge: Cambridge University Press, 1964).

Davies, W.D., and Dale C. Allison, *The Gospel according to Saint Matthew 1–7*. Vol. 1 (ICC; Edinburgh: T. & T. Clark, 1988).

— *The Gospel according to Saint Matthew 8–18*. Vol. 2 (ICC; Edinburgh: T. & T. Clark, 1991).

— *The Gospel according to Saint Matthew 19–28*. Vol. 3 (ICC; Edinburgh: T. & T. Clark, 1997).

Desjardins, Michel, *Peace, Violence and the New Testament* (Biblical Seminar, 46; Sheffield: Sheffield Academic Press, 1997).

Deutsch, Celia M., *Lady Wisdom, Jesus, and the Sages: Metaphor and Social Context in Matthew's Gospel* (Harrisburg, PA: Trinity Press International, 1996).

Diehl, Judy, 'Anti-Imperial Rhetoric in the New Testament', *CBR* 10.1 (2011), pp. 9-52.

Dixon, Suzanne, *The Roman Family* (London: Johns Hopkins University Press, 1992).

Djaballah, Amar, 'Jesus in Islam', *SBJT* 8.1 (2004), pp. 14-30.

Dodson, Derek S., *Reading Dreams: An Audience-Critical Approach to the Dreams in the Gospel of Matthew* (LNTS, 397; London: T. & T. Clark, 2009).

Donaldson, Terence L., 'The Mockers and the Son of God (Matthew 27.37-44): Two Characters in Matthew's Story of Jesus', *JSNT* 41 (1991), pp. 3-18.

Downing, F. Gerald, *Cynics and Christian Origins* (Edinburgh: T. & T. Clark, 1992).

— 'Deeper Reflections on the Jewish Cynic Jesus', *JBL* 117 (1998), pp. 97-104.

Duling, Dennis C., 'Empire: Theories, Methods, Models', in *The Gospel of Matthew in its Roman Imperial Context* (ed. John Riches and David C. Sim; London: T. & T. Clark, 2005), pp. 49-74.

— *A Marginal Scribe: Studies in the Gospel of Matthew in a Social-Scientific Perspective* (Eugene, OR: Cascade, 2011).

Dupuis, Ann, and David Thorns, 'Home, Home Ownership and the Search for Ontological Security', *Sociological Review* 46.1 (1998), pp. 24-47.

Dyck, Jonathan E., 'A Map of Ideology for Biblical Critics', in *Rethinking Contexts, Rereading Texts: Contributions from the Social Sciences to Biblical Interpretation* (ed. M. Daniel Carroll R.; Sheffield: Sheffield Academic Press, 2000), pp. 108-28.

Eagleton, Terry, *Holy Terror* (Oxford: Oxford University Press, 2005).

— *Ideology: An Introduction* (London: Verso, 1991).

— *The Illusions of Postmodernism* (Malden, MA: Blackwell, 1996).

— *Literary Theory: An Introduction* (Minneapolis, MN: University of Minnesota Press, anniversary edn, 2008).

Echica, Ramon D., 'The Political Context of the Infancy Narratives and the Apolitical Devotion to the Santo Niño', *Hapag* 7.1 (2010), pp. 37-51.

Edwards, Richard Alan, *The Sign of Jonah in the Theology of the Evangelists and Q* (London: SCM, 1971).

Elliott, John H., *A Home for the Homeless* (Eugene, OR: Wipf & Stock, 1990).

Eloff, Mervyn, 'Exile, Restoration and Matthew's Genealogy of Jesus Ὁ ΧΡΙΣΤΟΣ', *Neot* 38.1 (2004), pp. 75-87.

Engels, Friedrich, 'The Housing Question', in *Volksstaat* (reprinted by the Co-operative Publishing Society of Foreign Workers, 1872), online at http://www.marxists. org/archive/marx/works/1872/housing-question/index.htm.

Erickson, Richard J., 'Divine Injustice?: Matthew's Narrative Strategy and the Slaughter of the Innocents (Matthew 2:13-23)', *JSNT* 64 (1996), pp. 5-27.

Evans, Craig A., *Ancient Texts for New Testament Studies: A Guide to the Background Literature* (Peabody, MA: Hendrickson Publishers, 2005).

— 'Aspects of Exile and Restoration in the Proclomation of Jesus and the Gospels', in *Exile: Old Testament, Jewish, and Christian Conceptions* (ed. James M. Scott; Leiden: Brill, 1997), pp. 299-328.

— *Matthew* (NCBC; Cambridge: Cambridge University Press, 2012).

Fanon, Frantz, *The Wretched of the Earth* (trans. Constance Farrington; London: Penguin, 1963).

Fenton, J.C., *Saint Matthew* (Middlesex: Penguin, 1963).

Filson, Floyd V., *A Commentary on the Gospel according to St Matthew* (London: Adam & Charles Black, 1960).

Forbes, Greg, 'Darkness over All the Land: Theological Imagery in the Crucifixion Scene', *RTR* 66.2 (2007), pp. 83-96.

Foscarinis, Maria, 'Downward Spiral: Homelessness and its Criminalization', *Yale Law and Policy Review* 14.1 (1996), pp. 1-64.

Foscarinis, Maria, Kelly Cunningham-Bowers, and Kristen E. Brown, 'Out of Sight— Out of Mind?: The Continuing Trend toward the Criminalization of Homelessness', *Georgetown Journal on Poverty Law and Policy* 6.2 (1999), pp. 145-64.

Foster, George M., 'Peasant Society and the Image of Limited Good', *American Anthropologist* 67.2 (1965), pp. 293-315.

Foster, Robert, 'Why on Earth Use "Kingdom of Heaven"? Matthew's Terminology Revisited', *NTS* 48 (2002), pp. 487-99.

France, R.T., *The Gospel according to Matthew: An Introduction and Commentary* (Leicester: InterVarsity, 1985).

— *The Gospel of Matthew* (NICNT; Grand Rapids, MI: Eerdmans, 2007).

— 'Herod and the Children of Bethlehem', *NovT* 21.2 (1979), pp. 98-120.

Fredriksen, Paula, 'Why Was Jesus Crucified, but His Followers Were Not?' *JSNT* 29 (2007), pp. 415-19.

Freyne, Sean, *Galilee: From Alexander the Great to Hadrian* (Wilmington, DE: Michael Glazier, 1980).

Gadamer, Hans-Georg, *Truth and Method* (trans. Joel Weinsheimer and Donald G. Marshall; London: Continuum, 2nd edn, 2004).

Gaertner, Jan Felix, 'The Discourse of Displacement in Greco-Roman Antiquity', in *Writing Exile: The Discourse of Displacement in Greco-Roman Antiquity and Beyond* (ed. Jan Felix Gaertner; Leiden: Brill, 2007), pp. 1-20.

Gale, Aaron, *Redefining Ancient Borders: The Jewish Scribal Framework of Matthew's Gospel* (New York: T. & T. Clark, 2005).

Galvin, John P., 'Jesus' Approach to Death: An Examination of Some Recent Studies', *TS* 41.4 (1980), pp. 713-44.

Geisterfer, Priscilla, 'Full Turns and Half Turns: Engaging the Dialogue/Dance between Elisabeth Schüssler Fiorenza and Vernon Robbins', in *Her Master's Tools? Feminist and Postcolonial Engagements of Historical-Critical Discourse* (ed. Caroline Vander Stichele and Todd Penner; Atlanta, GA: Society of Biblical Literature, 2005), pp. 129-44.

Good, Deirdre, 'The Verb Ἀναχωρέω in Matthew's Gospel', *NovT* 32.1 (1990), pp. 1-12.

Goodman, Martin, *State and Society in Roman Galilee, A.D. 132–212* (Totowa, NJ: Rowan & Allanheld, 1983).

Graves, Thomas H., 'A Story Ignored: An Exegesis of Matthew 2:13-23', *Faith and Mission* 5.1 (1987), pp. 66-76.

Gray, John, *False Dawn: The Delusions of Global Capitalism* (London: Granta, 1998).

Green, Joel B., Scot McKnight, and I. Howard Marshall (eds.), *Dictionary of Jesus and the Gospels* (Downers Grove, IL: InterVarsity, 1992).

Griffiths, J.G., 'Wisdom about Tomorrow', *HvTSt* 53 (1960), pp. 219-21.

Grimshaw, James P., *The Matthean Community and the World: An Analysis of Matthew's Food Exchange* (New York: Peter Lang, 2008).

Groot, Shiloh, and Darrin Hodgetts, 'Homemaking on the Streets and Beyond', *Community, Work and Family* 15.3 (2012), pp. 255-71.

Guijarro, Santiago, 'The Family in First-Century Galilee', in *Constructing Early Christian Families* (ed. Halvor Moxnes; London, New York: Routledge, 1997), pp. 42-65.

Gurtner, Daniel M., *The Torn Veil: Matthew's Exposition of the Death of Jesus* (SNTSMS, 139; Cambridge: Cambridge University Press, 2007).

Habel, Norman C., 'Introducing Ecological Hermeneutics', in *Exploring Ecological Hermeneutics* (ed. Norman C. Habel and Peter Trudinger; Atlanta, GA: Society of Biblical Literature, 2008), pp. 1-8.

Hagner, Donald A., *Matthew 1–13*. Vol. 1 (WBC; Nashville, TN: Thomas Nelson, 1993).

Hales, Shelley, *The Roman House and Social Identity* (Cambridge: Cambridge University Press, 2003).

Hall, Joanne, 'Marginalization Revisited: Critical, Postmodern, and Liberation Perspectives', *Advances in Nursing Studies* 22.2 (1999), pp. 88-102.

Hall, Joanne M., Patricia E. Stevens, and Afaf Ibrahim Meleis, 'Marginalization: A Guiding Concept for Valuing Diversity in Nursing Knowledge Development', *Advances in Nursing Studies* 16.4 (1994), pp. 23-41.

Hanson, K.C., 'The Galilean Fishing Economy and the Jesus Tradition', *BTB* 27 (1997), pp. 99-111.

Hare, Douglas R.A., 'How Jewish Is the Gospel of Matthew?' *CBQ* 62 (2000), pp. 264-77.

— *Matthew* (Louisville, KY: Westminster John Knox, 2009).

Harrington, Daniel J., *The Gospel of Matthew* (Sacra Pagina; Collegeville, MN: Liturgical Press, 2007).

Harris, William V., 'The Theoretical Possibility of Extensive Infanticide in the Graeco-Roman World', *Classical Quarterly* 32.1 (1982), pp. 114-16.

Harvey, David, *A Brief History of Neoliberalism* (Oxford: Oxford University Press, 2005).

— 'Social Justice, Postmodernism and the City', *International Journal of Urban and Regional Research* 16 (1992), pp. 588-601.

Hatina, Thomas R., 'From History to Myth and Back Again: The Historicizing Function of Scripture in Matthew 2', in *Biblical Interpretation in the Early Christian Gospels: The Gospel of Matthew* (ed. Thomas R. Hatina; London: T. & T. Clark, 2008), pp. 98-118.

Heidegger, Martin, 'Building Dwelling Thinking', in *Poetry, Language, Thought* (New York: Harper & Row, 1971), pp. 143-61.

Hengel, Martin, *The Charismatic Leader and his Followers* (trans. James C.G. Greig; Edinburgh: T. & T. Clark, 1981).

— *Crucifixion in the Ancient World and the Folly of the Message of the Cross* (Philadelphia, PA: Fortress Press, 1977).

Henten, Jan W. van, 'Matthew 2:16 and Josephus' Portrayal of Herod', in *Jesus, Paul, and Early Christianity: Studies in Honour of Henk Jan de Jonge* (ed. Rieuwerd Buitenwerf, Harm W Hollander, H.J. de Jonge and Johannes Tromp; Leiden: Brill, 2008), pp. pp. 101-22.

Hertig, Paul, 'Geographical Marginality in the Matthean Journeys of Jesus', *SBL 1999 Seminar Papers* (Atlanta, GA: Society of Biblical Literature, 1999), pp. 472-89.

Hester, James D., 'Socio-Rheotorical Criticism and the Parable of the Tenants', *JSNT* 14 (1992), pp. 27-56.

Higgins, Paul, and Mitch Mackinem, *Thinking about Deviance: A Realistic Perspective* (Lanham, MD: Rowman & Littlefield, 2nd edn, 2008).

Hobbs, T.R., 'Soldiers in the Gospels: A Neglected Agent', in *Social Scientific Models for Interpreting the Bible* (ed. John J. Pilch; Leiden: Brill, 2001), pp. 328-49.

Hood, Jason B., *The Messiah, his Brothers, and the Nations: Matthew 1.1-17* (LNTS, 441; London: T. & T. Clark, 2011).

Hooker, Morna D., 'Is the Son of Man Problem Really Insoluble?' In *Text and Interpretation* (ed. E. Best and R. McL. Wilson; Cambridge: Cambridge University Press, 1979), pp. 155-68.

Horsley, Richard A., *The Liberation of Christmas: The Infancy Narratives in Social Context* (New York: Crossroad, 1989).

— *Sociology and the Jesus Movement* (New York: Crossroad, 1989).

— 'Synagogues in Galilee and the Gospels', in *Evolution of the Synagogue: Problems and Progress* (ed. Howard Clark Kee and Lynn H. Cohick; Harrisburg, PA: Trinity Press International, 1999), pp. 46-69.

Horsley, Richard A., and John S. Hanson, *Bandits, Prophets, and Messiahs: Popular Movements in the Time of Jesus* (Minneapolis, MN: Winston, 1985).

Huizenga, Leroy Andrew, 'Matt 1:1: "Son of Abraham" as a Christological Category', *HBT* 30.2 (2008), pp. 103-13.

— 'Obedience unto Death: The Matthean Gethsemane and Arrest Sequence and the Aqudah', *CBQ* 71 (2009), pp. 507-26.

Hurtado, Larry, and Paul Owen (eds.), *Who Is This Son of Man? The Latest Scholarship on a Puzzling Expression of the Historical Jesus* (London: Continuum, 2011).

Jacobson, Arland D., *The First Gospel: An Introduction to Q* (Sonoma, CA: Polebridge Press, 1992).

Jameson, Fredric, *The Political Unconscious: Narrative as a Socially Symbolic Act* (London: Routledge, 1983).

— *Postmodernism, or, the Cultural Logic of Late Capitalism* (London: Verso, 1991).

Jennings, Theodore W., and Tat-Siong Benny Liew, 'Mistaken Identities but Model Faith: Rereading the Centurion, the Chap, and the Christ in Matthew 8:5-13', *JBL* 123 (2004), pp. 467-94.

Jensen, Morten Hørning, 'Rural Galilee and Rapid Changes: An Investigation of the Socio-Economic Dynamics and Developments in Roman Galilee', *Biblica* 93 (2012), pp. 43-67.

Jobling, David, and Tina Pippin (eds.), *Ideological Criticism of Biblical Texts* (Semeia, 59; Atlanta, GA: Scholars Press, 1992).

Johnson, Marshall D., *The Purpose of the Biblical Genealogies with Special Reference to the Setting of the Genealogies of Jesus* (SNTSMS, 8; Cambridge: Cambridge University Press, 1969).

Kawash, Samira, 'The Homeless Body', *Public Culture* 10.2 (1997), pp. 319-39.

Kee, Howard Clark, 'Defining the First-Century CE Synagogue: Problems and Progress', *NTS* 41 (1995), pp. 481-500.

Keener, Craig S., *The Gospel of Matthew: A Socio-Rhetorical Commentary* (Grand Rapids, MI: Eerdmans, 2009).

Kelhoffer, James A., *The Diet of John the Baptist: 'Locusts and Wild Honey' in Synoptic and Patristic Interpretation* (Tübingen: Mohr Siebeck, 2005).

Kennard, J. Spencer, 'Nazorean and Nazareth', *JBL* 66 (1947), pp. 79-81.

— 'Was Capernaum the Home of Jesus?', *JBL* 65 (1946), pp. 131-41.

Kilpatrick, G.D., *The Origins of the Gospel according to St Matthew* (Oxford: Oxford University Press, 1946).

Kingsbury, Jack Dean, *Matthew as Story* (Philadelphia, PA: Fortress Press, 2nd edn, 1988).

— *Matthew: Structure, Christology, Kingdom* (Minneapolis, MN: Fortress Press, 1975).

— 'On Following Jesus: The "Eager" Scribe and the "Reluctant" Disciple (Matthew 8:18-22)', *NTS* 34 (1988), pp. 45-59.

— 'The Verb *Akolouthein* ("to Follow") as an Index of Matthew's View of his Community', *JBL* 97 (1978), pp. 56-73.

Klassen, William, *Judas: Betrayer or Friend of Jesus?* (Minneapolis, MN: Fortress Press, 2004).

Koegel, Paul, 'Causes of Homelessness: Overview', in *Encyclopedia of Homelessness* (ed. David Levinson; London: Sage, 2004), pp. 50-58.

Kohler, Kaufmann, *The Origins of the Synagogue and the Church* (New York: Macmillan, 1929).

Lacan, Jacques, *The Ethics of Psychoanalysis, 1959–1960* (trans. Dennis Porter; London: Tavistock, 1992).

LaCocque, André, 'Le grand dri de Jésus dans Matthieu 27/50', *ETR* 75.2 (2000), pp. 161-87.

Landes, G.M., 'Matthew 12.40 as an Interpretation of "the Sign of Jonah" against its Biblical Background', in *The Word of the Lord Shall Go Forth* (ed. C.L. Meyers and M. O'Connor; Winona Lake, IN: Eisenbrauns, 1983), pp. 665-84.

LaVerdiere, Eugene, 'The Passion Story as Prophecy', *Emmanuel* 93 (1987), pp. 85-90.

Lawrence, Louise Joy, *An Ethnography of the Gospel of Matthew* (WUNT, 2; Tübingen: Mohr Siebeck, 2003).

Lee, Jung Young, *Marginality: The Key to Multicultural Theology* (Minneapolis, MN: Augsburg Fortress Press, 1995).

Lefebvre, Henri, *The Production of Space* (trans. Donald Nicholson-Smith; Oxford: Blackwell, 1991).

Lenski, Gerhard E., *Power and Privilege: A Theory of Social Stratification*; New York: McGraw-Hill, 1966).

Levine, Amy-Jill, *The Social and Ethnic Dimensions of Matthean Salvation History* (Lewiston, NY: Edwin Mellen, 1988).

Levine, Lee I., *The Ancient Synagogue: The First Thousand Years* (New Haven, CT: Yale University Press, 2000).

Loubser, Johannes A., 'Invoking the Ancestors: Some Socio-Rhetorical Aspects of the Genealogies in the Gospels of Matthew and Luke', *Neot* 39.1 (2005), pp. 127-40.

Love, Stuart L., 'The Household: A Major Social Component for Gender Analysis in the Gospel of Matthew', *BTB* 23 (1993), pp. 21-31.

— *Jesus and Marginal Women: The Gospel of Matthew in Social-Scientific Perspective* (Eugene, OR: Cascade, 2009).

Lukács, Georg, *History and Class Consciousness: Studies in Marxist Dialectics* (trans. Rodney Livingston; London: Merlin, 1971).

Lundbom, Jack R., *Jeremiah 21–36* (Anchor Bible; New York: Doubleday, 2004).

Luz, Ulrich, *Matthew 1–7* (trans. James E. Crouch; Hermeneia; Minneapolis, MN: Fortress Press, 2007).

— *Matthew 8–20* (trans. James E. Crouch; Hermeneia; Minneapolis, MN: Fortress Press, 2001).

— *Matthew 21–28* (trans. James E. Crouch; Hermeneia; Minneapolis, MN: Fortress Press, 2005).

— *Matthew in History: Interpretation, Influence, and Effects* (Minneapolis, MN: Fortress Press, 1994).

— *Studies in Matthew* (trans. Rosemary Selle; Grand Rapids, MI: Eerdmans, 2005).

MacAdam, Henry I., 'Domus Domini: Where Jesus Lived (Capernaum and Bethany in the Gospels', *TR* 25.1 (2004), pp. 46-76.

MacDonald, Margaret Y., 'Kinship and Family in the New Testament World', in *Understanding the Social World of the New Testament* (ed. Dietmar Neufeld and Richard E. DeMaris; London: Routledge, 2010), pp. 29-43.

Mack, Burton L., *The Lost Gospel: The Book of Q and Christian Origins* (San Francisco, CA: HarperSanFrancisco, 1994).

Mack, Burton L., and Vernon K. Robbins, *Patterns of Persuasion in the Gospels* (Sonoma, CA: Polebridge Press, 1989).

Malina, Bruce J., 'Collectivism in Mediterranean Culture', in *Understanding the Social World of the New Testament* (ed. Dietmar Neufeld and Richard E. DeMaris; London: Routledge, 2010), pp. 17-28.

Malina, Bruce J., and Jerome H. Neyrey, *Calling Jesus Names: The Social Value of Labels in Matthew* (Sonoma, CA: Polebridge Press, 1988).

Mallett, Shelley, 'Understanding Home: A Critical Review of the Literature', *Sociological Review* 51.1 (2004), pp. 62-89.

Marcus, Joel, 'Meggitt on the Madness and Kingship of Jesus', *JSNT* 29 (2007), pp. 421-24.

Marohl, Matthew J., *Joseph's Dilemma: 'Honor Killing' in the Birth Narrative of Matthew* (Eugene, OR: Cascade, 2008).

Marshall, Anthony J., 'Symbols and Showmanship in Roman Public Life: The Fasces', *Phoenix* 38.2 (1984), pp. 120-41.

Martinez, Aquiles Ernesto, 'Jesus, the Immigrant Child: A Diasporic Reading of Matthew 2:1-23', *Apuntes* 26.3 (2006), pp. 84-114.

Marx, Karl, *Capital: A Critique of Political Economy*. Vol. 1 (Moscow: Progress Publishers, 1887).

Marx, Karl, and Friedrich Engels, 'Letters from London', in *Collected Works* (London: Lawrence & Wishart, 1975), pp. 379-91.

— *Selected Works*. Vol. 1 (Moscow: Progress Publishers, 1969).

McAlpine, Thomas H., *Sleep, Divine and Human, in the Old Testament* (JSOTSup, 38; Sheffield: Sheffield Academic Press, 1987).

McCane, Byron R., '"Let the Dead Bury their Own Dead": Secondary Burial and Matt 8:21-22', *HTR* 83 (1990), pp. 31-43.

— 'Simply Irresistible: Augustus, Herod, and the Empire', *JBL* 127 (2008), pp. 725-35.

McNeile, A.H., 'Τότε in St. Matthew', *JTS* 12 (1911), pp. 127-28.

Meanwell, Emily, 'Experiencing Homelessness: A Review of Recent Literature', *Sociology Compass* 6.1 (2012), pp. 72-85.

Meggitt, Justin J., 'The Madness of King Jesus: Why Was Jesus Put to Death, but his Followers Were Not?' *JSNT* 29 (2007), pp. 379-413.

Meier, John P., 'Antioch', in *Antioch and Rome: New Testament Cradles of Catholic Christianity* (ed. Raymond E. Brown and John P. Meier; Mahwah, NJ: Paulist Press, 1983), pp. 12-86.

— 'John the Baptist in Matthew's Gospel', *JBL* 99 (1980), pp. 383-405.

— *A Marginal Jew: Rethinking the Historical Jesus*. Vol. 1 (New York: Doubleday, 1991).

— *Matthew* (Collegeville, MN: Liturgical Press, 1980).

Menken, Martinus J., '"Out of Egypt I Have Called my Son": Some Observations on the Quotation from Hosea 11.1 in Matthew 2.15', in *The Wisdom of Egypt* (ed. Anthony Hilhorst and George H. van Kooten; Leiden: Brill, 2005), pp. 143-52.

Montiglio, Silvia, *Wandering in Ancient Greek Culture* (Chicago: University of Chicago Press, 2005).

Moore, Stephen D., 'The "Turn to Empire" in Biblical Studies', *Search* 35 (2012), pp. 19-27.

Moore, Stephen D., and Yvonne Sherwood, *The Invention of the Biblical Scholar: A Critical Manifesto* (Minneapolis, MN: Fortress Press, 2011).

Moxnes, Halvor, 'Landscape and Spatiality: Placing Jesus', in *Understanding the Social World of the New Testament* (ed. Dietmar Neufeld and Richard E. DeMaris; New York: Routledge, 2010), pp. 90-106.

— *Putting Jesus in his Place: A Radical Vision of Household and Kingdom* (Louisville, KY: Westminster John Knox, 2003).

Murphy-O'Connor, Jerome, 'Fishers of Fish, Fishers of Men', *BR* 15.3 (1999), pp. 22-49.

— *Keys to Jerusalem: Collected Essays* (Oxford: Oxford University Press, 2012).

Myles, Robert J., 'Echoes of Displacement in Matthew's Genealogy of Jesus', *Colloquium* 45 (2013), pp. 31-41.

— 'Probing the Homelessness of Jesus with Žižek's Sublime Object', *Bible and Critical Theory* 9.1 (2013), pp. 15-26.

Myles, Robert J., and James G. Crossley, 'Biblical Scholarship, Jews and Israel: On Bruce Malina, Conspiracy Theories and Ideological Contradictions', *Bible and Interpretation* (2012), http://www.bibleinterp.com/opeds/myl368013.shtml.

Neirynck, F., 'Απο Τοτε Ηρξατο and the Structure of Matthew', *ETL* 64 (1988), pp. 21-59.

Neufeld, Dietmar, and Richard E. DeMaris (eds.), *Understanding the Social World of the New Testament* (New York: Routledge, 2010).

Neyrey, Jerome H., *Honor and Shame in the Gospel of Matthew* (Louisville, KY: Westminster John Knox, 1998).

— 'Jesus, Gender, and the Gospel of Matthew', in *New Testament Masculinities* (ed. Stephen D. Moore and Janice Capel Anderson; Semeia Studies; Atlanta, GA: Society of Biblical Literature, 2003), pp. 43-66.

Nguyen, Thanh Van, 'In Solidarity with the Strangers: The Flight into Egypt', *TBT* 45.4 (2007), pp. 219-24.

Nineham, Dennis E., 'The Genealogy in St. Matthew's Gospel and its Significance for the Study of the Gospels', *BJRL* 58 (1976), pp. 451-68.

Nolland, John, *The Gospel of Matthew: A Commentary on the Greek Text* (Grand Rapids, MI: Eerdmans, 2005).

Notley, R. Steven, 'The Sea of Galilee: Development of an Early Christian Toponym', *JBL* 128 (2009), pp. 183-88.

O'Kane, Martin, 'The Flight into Egypt: Icon of Refuge for the H(a)unted', in *Borders, Boundaries and the Bible* (ed. Martin O'Kane; Sheffield: Sheffield Academic Press, 2002), pp. 15-60.

O'Neill, J.C., 'The Charge of Blasphemy at Jesus' Trial before the Sanhedrin', in *The Trial of Jesus* (ed. Ernst Bammel; London: SCM, 1970), pp. 72-77.

Oakman, Douglas E., *Jesus and the Economic Questions of his Day* (Lewiston, NY: Edwin Mellen, 1986).

— 'The Shape of Power and Political-Economy in Herodian Galilee', in *Liberating Biblical Study* (ed. Laurel Dykstra and Ched Myers; Eugene, OR: Wipf & Stock, 2011), pp. 147-61.

Oden, Amy G. (ed.), *And You Welcomed Me: A Sourcebook on Hospitality in Early Christianity* (Nashville, TN: Abingdon Press, 2001).

Orton, David E., *The Understanding Scribe: Matthew and the Apocalyptic Ideal* (JSNTSup, 25; Sheffield: Sheffield Academic Press, 1989).

Osiek, Carolyn, 'The Women at the Tomb: What Are They Doing There?' *HvTSt* 53.1-2 (1997), pp. 103-18.

Overman, J. Andrew, *Matthew's Gospel and Formative Judaism: The Social World of the Matthean Community* (Minneapolis, MN: Fortress Press, 1990).

Patterson, Stephen J., *Beyond the Passion: Rethinking the Death and Life of Jesus* (Minneapolis, MN: Fortress Press, 2004).

Pennington, Jonathan T., *Heaven and Earth in the Gospel of Matthew* (NovTSup, 126; Leiden: Brill, 2007).

Pesch, Rudolf, '"He Will Be Called a Nazorean": Messianic Exegesis in Matthew 1–2', in *The Gospels and the Scriptures of Israel* (ed. Craig A. Evans and W. Richard Stegner; Sheffield: Sheffield Academic Press, 1994), pp. 129-78.

Pippin, Tina, 'Ideology, Ideological Criticism, and the Bible', *CRBS* 4 (1996), pp. 51-78.

Pleace, Nicholas, 'Single Homelessness as Social Exclusion: The Unique and the Extreme', *Social Policy and Administration* 32 (1998), pp. 46-59.

Plummer, Alfred, *An Exegetical Commentary on the Gospel according to St Matthew* (London: Robert Scott, 1909).

Powell, Mark Allan, 'Literary Approaches and the Gospel of Matthew', in *Methods for Matthew* (ed. Mark Allan Powell; Cambridge: Cambridge University Press, 2009), pp. 44-82.

— *What Is Narrative Criticism?* (GBS; Minneapolis, MN: Augsburg Fortress Press, 1990).

Power, Edmond, 'The Staff of the Apostles: A Problem in Gospel Harmony', *Biblica* 4 (1923), pp. 241-66.

Pryor, John W., 'John 4:44 and the Patris of Jesus', *CBQ* 49 (1987), pp. 254-63.

Przybylski, Benno, *Righteousness in Matthew and his World of Thought* (Cambridge: Cambridge University Press, 1980).

Raheb, Mitri, *I Am a Palestinian Christian* (trans. Ruth C.L. Gritsch; Minneapolis, MN: Fortress Press, 1995).

Reed, David A., '"Saving Judas"—a Social Scientific Approach to Judas's Suicide in Matthew 27:3-10', *BTB* 35 (2005), pp. 51-59.

Reed, Randall William, 'The Problem of Ideology in Biblical Studies', *BSR* 40.4 (2011), pp. 17-23.

'Refugee', in *Merriam–Webster's Dictionary of Law* (Springfield, MA: Merriam-Webster, 1996), p. 414.

Repschinski, Boris, *The Controversy Stories in the Gospel of Matthew: Their Redaction, Form and Relevance for the Relationship between the Matthean Community and Formative Judaism* (Göttingen: Vandenhoeck & Ruprecht, 2000).

Resseguie, James L., *Narrative Criticism of the New Testament: An Introduction* (Grand Rapids, MI: Baker Academic, 2005).

Richardson, Peter, *Herod: King of the Jews and Friend of the Romans* (Columbia, SC: University of South Carolina Press, 1996).

Riches, John, 'Contextual Bible Study: Some Reflections', *ExpTim* 117.1 (2005), pp. 23-26.

Rivkin, Ellis, 'Locating John the Baptizer in Palestinian Judaism: The Political Dimension', *SBL 1983 Seminar Papers* (Atlanta, GA: Society of Biblical Literature, 1983), pp. 79-85.

Robbins, Vernon K., *Exploring the Texture of Texts: A Guide to Socio-Rhetorical Interpretation* (Valley Forge, PA: Trinity Press International, 1996).

— *The Invention of Christian Discourse*. Vol. 1 (Blandform Forum: Deo, 2009).

— *Jesus the Teacher: A Socio-Rhetorical Interpretation of Mark* (Minneapolis, MN: Fortress Press, 1984).

— 'Rhetography: A New Way of Seeing the Familiar Text', in *Words Well Spoken: George Kennedy's Rhetoric of the New Testament* (ed. C. Clifton Black and Duane F. Watson; Waco, TX: Baylor University Press, 2008), pp. 81-106.

— 'The Rhetorical Full-Turn in Biblical Interpretation and its Relevance for Feminist Hermeneutics', in *Her Master's Tools? Feminist and Postcolonial Engagements of Historical-Critical Discourse* (ed. Caroline Vander Stichele and Todd Penner; Atlanta, GA: Society of Biblical Literature, 2005), pp. 109-28.

— *The Tapestry of Early Christian Discourse: Rhetoric, Society and Ideology* (London: Routledge, 1996).

Robson, James, *Christ in Islam* (Dublin: Bardic, 2006).

Robson, John, John Reid and Agnes Marwick, 'The Homelessness of Christ', *ExpTim* 8.5 (1897), pp. 221-26.

Rogerson, J.W., and John Vincent, *The City in Biblical Perspective* (BCCW; London: Equinox, 2009).

Ruddick, Susan, 'Heterotopias of the Homeless: Strategies and Tactics of Placemaking in Los Angeles', *Journal of Theory, Culture, and Politics* 3.3 (1990), pp. 184-201.

— *Young and Homeless in Hollywood: Mapping Social Identities* (New York: Routledge, 1996).

Rykwert, Joseph, 'House and Home', *Social Research* 58.1 (1991), pp. 51-62.

Saddington, D.B., 'The Centurion in Matthew 8:5-13: Consideration of the Proposal of Theodore W. Jennings, Jr., and Tat-Siong Benny Liew', *JBL* 125 (2006), pp. 140-42.

Saldarini, Anthony J., *Matthew's Christian-Jewish Community* (Chicago: University of Chicago Press, 1994).

— *Pharisees, Scribes and Sadducees in Palestinian Society* (Grand Rapids, MI: Eerdmans, 2nd edn, 2001).

Schaberg, Jane, *The Illegitmacy of Jesus: A Feminist Theological Interpretation of the Infancy Narratives* (Sheffield: Sheffield Phoenix, anniversary edn, 2006).

Schnackenburg, Rudolf, *The Gospel of Matthew* (trans. Robert R. Barr; Grand Rapids, MI: Eerdmans, 2002).

Schüssler Fiorenza, Elisabeth, *The Power of the Word: Scripture and the Rhetoric of Empire* (Minneapolis, MN: Fortress Press, 2007).

— 'Reading Scripture in the Context of Empire', in *The Bible in the Public Square: Reading the Signs of the Times* (ed. Cynthia Briggs Kittredge, Ellen Bradshaw Aitken and Jonathan A. Draper; Minneapolis, MN: Fortress Press, 2008), pp. 157-71.

— *Rhetoric and Ethic: The Politics of Biblical Studies* (Minneapolis, MN: Fortress Press, 1999).

Schweizer, Eduard, *The Good News according to Matthew* (trans. David E. Green; London: SPCK, 1975).

Scrimshaw, Susan C.M., 'Infanticide in Human Populations: Societal and Individual Concerns', in *Infanticide: Comparative and Evolutionary Perspectives* (ed. Glenn Hausfater and Sarah Blaffer Hrdy; New York: Aldine, 2008), pp. 439-62.

Segovia, Fernando F., 'Cultural Studies and Contemporary Biblical Criticism: Ideological Criticism as Mode of Discourse', in *Reading from This Place: Social Location and Biblical Interpretation in Global Perspective* (ed. Fernando F. Segovia and Mary Ann Tolbert; Minneapolis, MN: Augsburg Fortress Press, 1995), pp. 1-17.

— 'Postcolonial Criticism and the Gospel of Matthew', in *Methods for Matthew* (ed. Mark Allan Powell; Cambridge: Cambridge University Press, 2009), pp. 194-237.

Senior, Donald, *Matthew* (Nashville, TN: Abingdon Press, 1998).

— *The Passion of Jesus in the Gospel of Matthew* (Wilmington, DE: Michael Glazier, 1985).

— *What Are They Saying About Matthew?* (Mahwah, NJ: Paulist Press, 1996).

Siedlecki, Armin, 'The Bible, David Jobling and Ideological Criticism', in *Voyages in Uncharted Waters: Essays on the Theory and Practice of Biblical Interpretation in Honor of David Jobling* (ed. Bergen Wesley J. and Armin Siedlecki; Sheffield: Sheffield Phoenix, 2006), pp. 80-86.

Siker, Judy Yates, 'Matthew 26:47-56', *Interpretation* 58 (2004), pp. 386-89.

Sim, David C., *Apocalyptic Eschatology in the Gospel of Matthew* (SNTSMS, 88; Cambridge: Cambridge University Press, 1996).

— 'The Pacifist Jesus and the Violent Jesus in the Gospel of Matthew', *HvTSt* 67.1 (2011), http://www.hts.org.za/index.php/HTS/article/view/860.

Slee, Michelle, *The Church in Antioch in the First Century: Communion and Conflict* (JSNTSup, 244; London: T. & T. Clark, 2003).

Smit, Peter-Ben, 'Something about Mary? Remarks about the Five Women in the Matthean Genealogy', *NTS* 56 (2010), pp. 191-207.

Snodgrass, Klyne, *The Parable of the Wicked Tenants* (Tübingen: Mohr, 1983).

Soares Prabhu, George M., *The Formula Quotations in the Infancy Narrative of Matthew* (Rome: Biblical Institute Press, 1976).

Soja, Edward W., *Thirdspace: Journeys to Los Angeles and Other Real-and-Imagined Places* (Malden, MA: Blackwell, 1996).

Spivak, Gayatri Chakravorty, 'Can the Subaltern Speak?' In *Marxism and the Interpretation of Culture* (ed. Cary Nelson and Lawrence Grossberg; Urbana, IL: University of Illinois Press, 1988), pp. 271-314.

Ste Croix, G.E.M. de, *The Class Struggle in the Ancient Greek World* (Ithaca, NY: Cornell University Press, 1981).

Stegemann, Ekkehard W., and Wolfgang Stegemann, *The Jesus Movement: A Social History of its First Century* (trans. O.C. Dean Jr; Edinburgh: T. & T. Clark, 1999).

Stegemann, Wolfgang, 'Vagabond Radicalism in Early Christianity?: A Historical and Theological Discussion of a Thesis Proposed by Gerd Theissen', in *God of the Lowly: Socio-Historical Interpretations of the Bible* (ed. Willy Schottroff and Wolfgang Stegemann; Maryknoll, NY: Orbis Books, 1984), pp. 148-68.

Stivers, Laura, *Disrupting Homelessness: Alternative Christian Approaches* (Minneapolis, MN: Fortress Press, 2011).

Stoutenburg, Dennis C., '"Out of my Sight!", "Get behind Me!", or "Follow after Me!": There Is No Choice in God's Kingdom', *JETS* 36.1 (1993), pp. 173-78.

Strange, James F., and Hershel Shanks, 'Has the House Where Jesus Stayed in Capernaum Been Found?' *BAR* 8.6 (1982), pp. 26-37.

Stratton, Beverly J., 'Ideology', in *Handbook of Postmodern Biblical Interpretation* (ed. A.K.M. Adam; St Louis, MO: Chalice, 2000), pp. 120-27.

Sturch, Richard L., 'The Πατρίς of Jesus', *JTS* 28 (1977), pp. 94-96.

Suggit, John, 'Comrade Judas: Matthew 26:50', *JTSA* 63 (1988), pp. 56-58.

Talbert, Charles H., *Matthew* (Grand Rapids, MI: Baker, 2010).

— *Reading the Sermon on the Mount: Character Formation and Decision Making in Matthew 5–7* (Grand Rapids, MI: Baker, 2004).

Talbot, Chris, 'Social Exclusion and Homelessness: Everyone's Responsibility' (Adelaide: Uniting Care, Wesley, 2003).

Taylor, Joan E., *The Immerser: John the Baptist within Second Temple Judaism* (Grand Rapids, MI: Eerdmans, 1997).

Theissen, Gerd, *Der Schatten des Galiläers: Historische Jesusforschung in erzählender Form* (Munich: Christian Kaiser Verlag, 1986).

— *Sociology of Early Palestinian Christianity* (Philadelphia, PA: Fortress Press, 1978).

Thiselton, Anthony C., *New Horizons in Hermeneutics* (Grand Rapids, MI: Zondervan, 1992).

Thoburn, Nicholas, 'Difference in Marx: The Lumpenproletariat and the Proletarian Unnamable', *Economy and Society* 31 (2002), pp. 434-60.

Trainor, Michael F., *The Quest for Home: The Household in Mark's Community* (Collegeville, MN: Michael Glazier, 2001).

Veltmeyer, Henry, *The Canadian Class Structure* (Toronto: Garamond, 1986).

Vermes, Geza, *Jesus the Jew: A Historian's Reading of the Gospels* (London: SCM, 1983).

— *The Nativity: History and Legend* (London: Penguin, 2006).

— *The Religion of Jesus the Jew* (London: SCM, 1993).

Verseput, Donald J., 'The Faith of the Reader and the Narrative of Matthew 13.53–16.20', *JSNT* 46 (1992), pp. 3-24.

Viljoen, F.P., 'Power and Authority in Matthew's Gospel', *Acta theologica* 31 (2011), pp. 329-45.

Viljoen, Francois P., 'The Significance of Dreams and the Star in Matthew's Infancy Narrative', *HvTSt* 64.2 (2008), pp. 845-60.

Waetjen, Herman C., 'The Genealogy as the Key to the Gospel according to Matthew', *JBL* 95 (1976), pp. 205-30.

Wainwright, Elaine M., 'Feminist Criticism and the Gospel of Matthew', in *Methods for Matthew* (ed. Mark Allan Powell; Cambridge: Cambridge University Press, 2009), pp. 83-117.

— *Shall We Look for Another? A Feminist Rereading of the Matthean Jesus* (Maryknoll, NY: Orbis Books, 1998).

— *Towards a Feminist Critical Reading of the Gospel according to Matthew* (BZNW, 60; Berlin: de Gruyter, 1991).

— *Women Healing/Healing Women: The Genderization of Healing in Early Christianity* (BibleWorld; London: Equinox, 2006).

Watson, Duane F., 'Why We Need Socio-Rhetorical Commentary and What It Might Look Like', in *Rhetorical Criticism and the Bible* (ed. Stanley E. Porter and Dennis L. Stamps; London: Sheffield Academic Press, 2002), pp. 129-57.

Weaver, Dorothy Jean, *Matthew's Missionary Discourse: A Literary Critical Analysis* (JSNTSup, 38; Sheffield: Sheffield Academic Press, 1990).

West, Gerald O., *The Academy of the Poor: Towards a Dialogical Reading of the Bible* (Interventions, 2; Sheffield: Sheffield Academic Press, 1999).

— (ed.), *Reading Other-Wise: Socially Engaged Biblical Scholars Reading with their Local Communities* (Atlanta, GA: Society of Biblical Literature, 2007).

Wetter, Anne-Mareike, 'Balancing the Scales: The Construction of the Exile as Countertradition in the Bible', in *From Babylon to Eternity: The Exile Remembered and Constructed in Text and Tradition* (ed. Bob Becking, Alex Cannegieter, Wilfred van de Poll and Anne-Mareike Wetter' BibleWorld; London: Equinox, 2009), pp. 34-56.

White, R.E.O., 'That "Cry of Dereliction" . . . ?', *ExpTim* 113.6 (2002), pp. 188-89.

Wilde, Oscar, *The Soul of the Man under Socialism* (New York: Max N. Maisel, 1915).

Wilkins, Michael J., *The Concept of Disciple in Matthew's Gospel* (NovTSup, 59; Leiden: Brill, 1988).

Willitts, Joel, *Matthew's Messianic Shepherd-King: In Search of 'the Lost Sheep of the House of Israel'* (BZNW, 147; Berlin: de Gruyter, 2007).

Wink, Walter, *John the Baptist in the Gospel Tradition* (SNTSMS, 7; Cambridge: Cambridge University Press, 2006)).

Witherington III, Ben, *The Jesus Quest: The Third Search for the Jew of Nazareth* (Downers Grove, IL: InterVarsity Press, 1995).

Wright, N.T., *The New Testament and the People of God* (Minneapolis, MN: Fortress Press, 1992).

Wright, N.T., and Marcus J. Borg, *The Meaning of Jesus: Two Visions* (New York: HarperCollins, 1999).

Wuellner, Wilhelm H., *The Meaning of 'Fishers of Men'* (Philadelphia, PA: Westminster, 1967).

Yamasaki, Gary, *John the Baptist in Life and Death: Audience-Oriented Criticism of Matthew's Narrative* (JSNTSup, 167; Sheffield: Sheffield Academic Press, 1998).

Yeivin, Z., 'Ancient Chorazin Comes Back to Life', *BAR* 13.5 (1987), pp. 22-36.

Zilonka, Paul, 'The Pain of Migration', *TBT* 26.6 (1991), pp. 351-56.

Žižek, Slavoj, *First as Tragedy, Then as Farce* (London: Verso, 2009).

— *In Defense of Lost Causes* (London: Verso, 2008).

— *Less Than Nothing: Hegel and the Shadow of Dialectical Materialism* (London: Verso, 2012).

— *Living in the End Times* (London: Verso, 2010).

— *The Parallax View* (Short Circuits; Cambridge: MIT Press, 2006).

— *The Plague of Fantasies* (London: Verso, 1997).

— *The Sublime Object of Ideology* (London: Verso, 1989).

— *Violence* (Big Ideas; London: Profile Books, 2008).

— *The Year of Dreaming Dangerously* (London: Verso, 2012).

INDEX OF REFERENCES

INDEX OF AUTHORS

CPSIA information can be obtained at www.ICGtesting.com
Printed in the USA
LVOW04*0259100715

445676LV00004B/20/P